PRETTY DEADLY

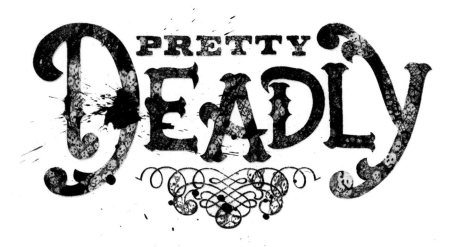

VOLUME ONE
THE SHRIKE

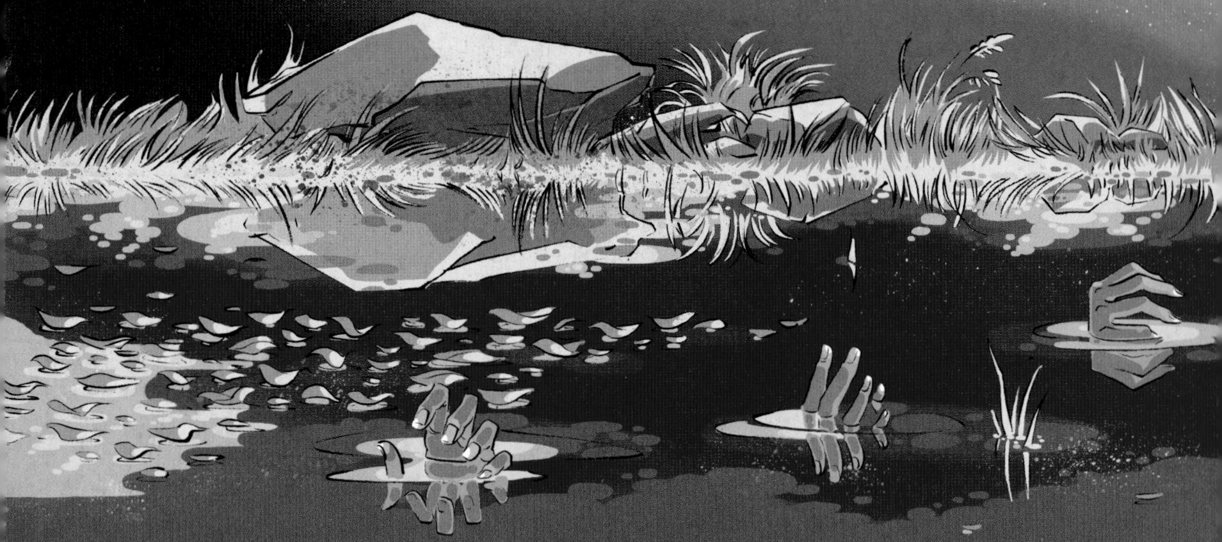

KELLY SUE DECONNICK
script

EMMA RIOS
art & cover

JORDIE BELLAIRE
colors

SIGRID ELLIS
edits

CLAYTON COWLES
letters

ON TWITTER

@kellysue @emmartian @whoajordie @claytoncowles @sigridellis

ROBERT KIRKMAN - chief operating officer ERIK LARSEN - chief financial officer TODD MCFARLANE - president MARC SILVESTRI - chief executive officer
JIM VALENTINO - vice-president ERIC STEPHENSON - publisher RON RICHARDS - director of business development JENNIFER DE GUZMAN - director of trade book sales
KAT SALAZAR - director of pr & marketing JEREMY SULLIVAN - director of digital sales EMILIO BAUTISTA - sales assistant BRANWYN BIGGLESTONE - senior accounts manager
EMILY MILLER - accounts manager JESSICA AMBRIZ - administrative assistant TYLER SHAINLINE - events coordinator DAVID BROTHERS - content manager
JONATHAN CHAN - production manager DREW GILL - art director MEREDITH WALLACE - print manager MONICA GARCIA - senior production artist
JENNA SAVAGE - production artist ADDISON DUKE - production artist TRICIA RAMOS - production assistant

PRETTY DEADLY, VOLUME ONE: THE SHRIKE. First printing. April 2014. ISBN: 978-1-60706-962-1. Published by Image Comics, Inc. Office of publication: 2001 Center Street, 6th Floor, Berkeley, CA 94704.

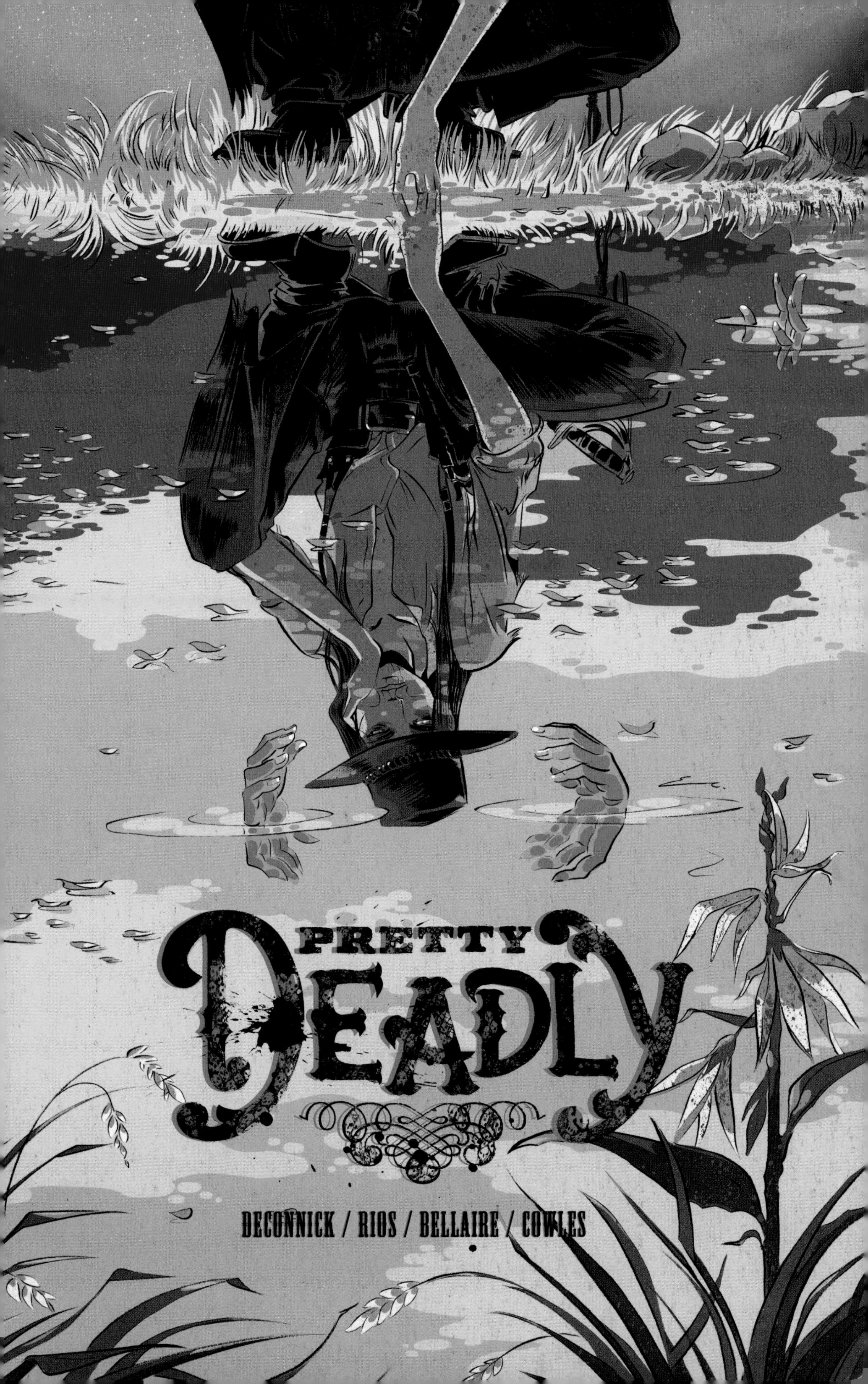
PRETTY
DEADLY
DECONNICK / RIOS / BELLAIRE / COWLES

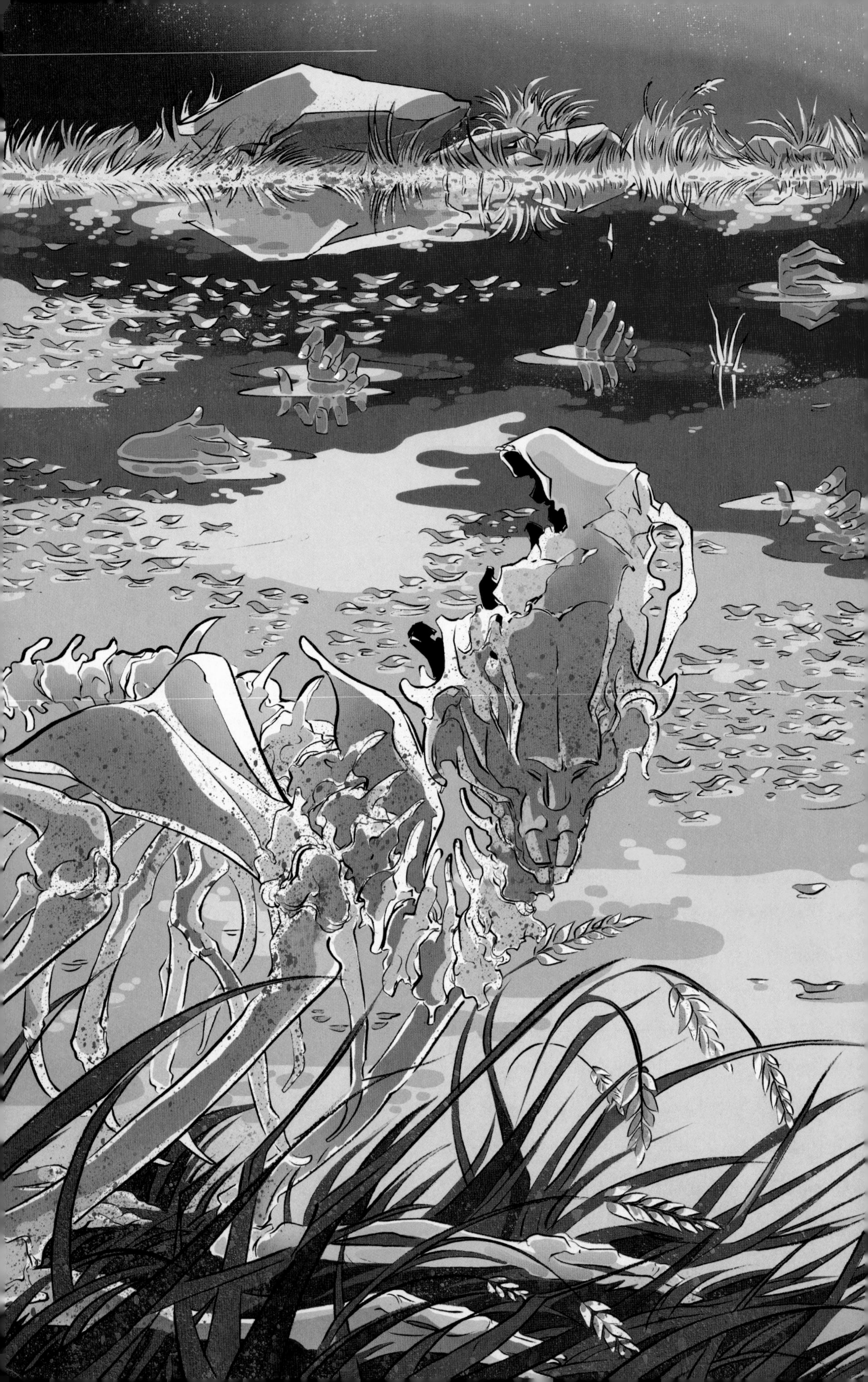

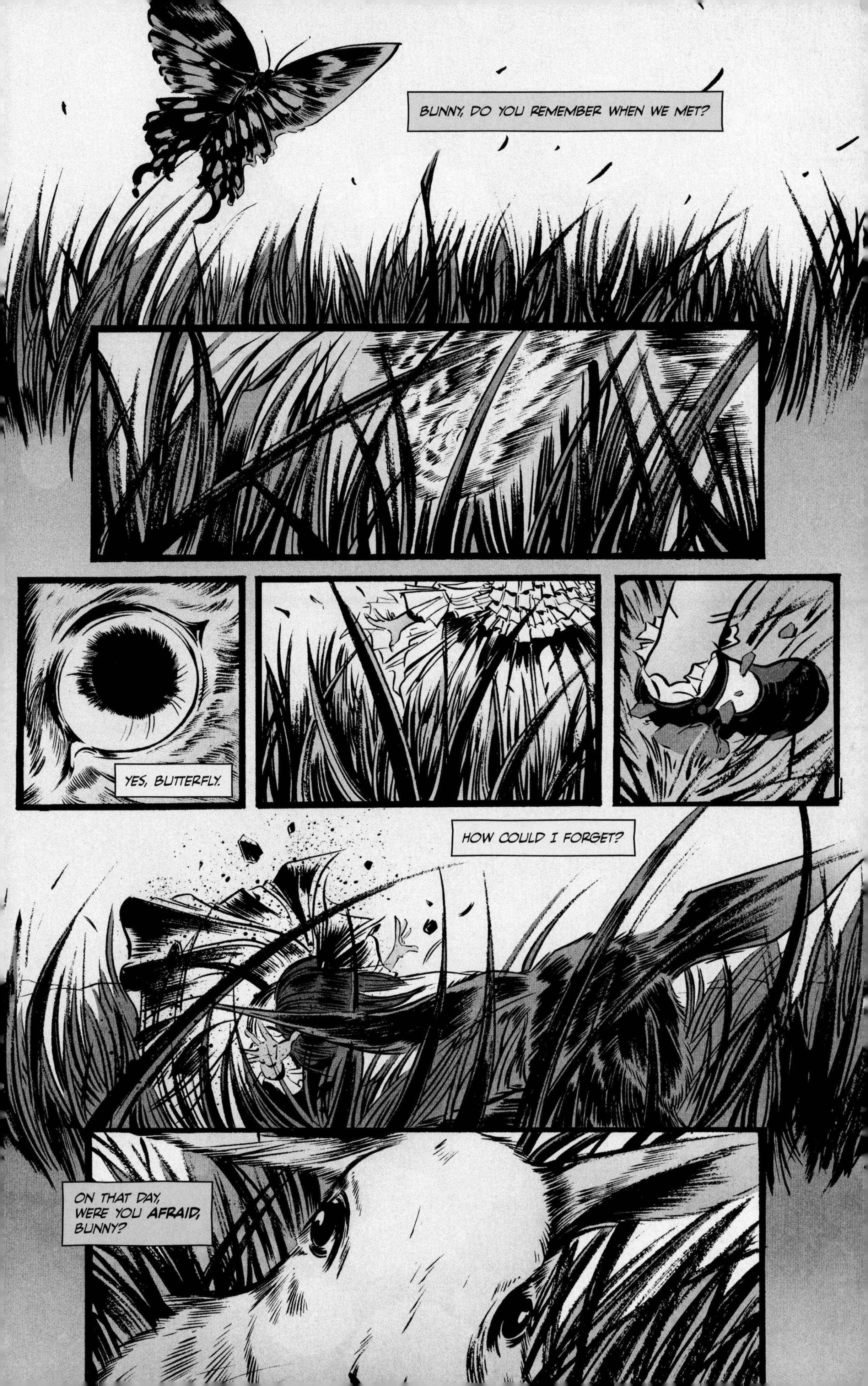
BUNNY, DO YOU REMEMBER WHEN WE MET?
YES, BUTTERFLY.
HOW COULD I FORGET?
ON THAT DAY, WERE YOU **AFRAID**, BUNNY?

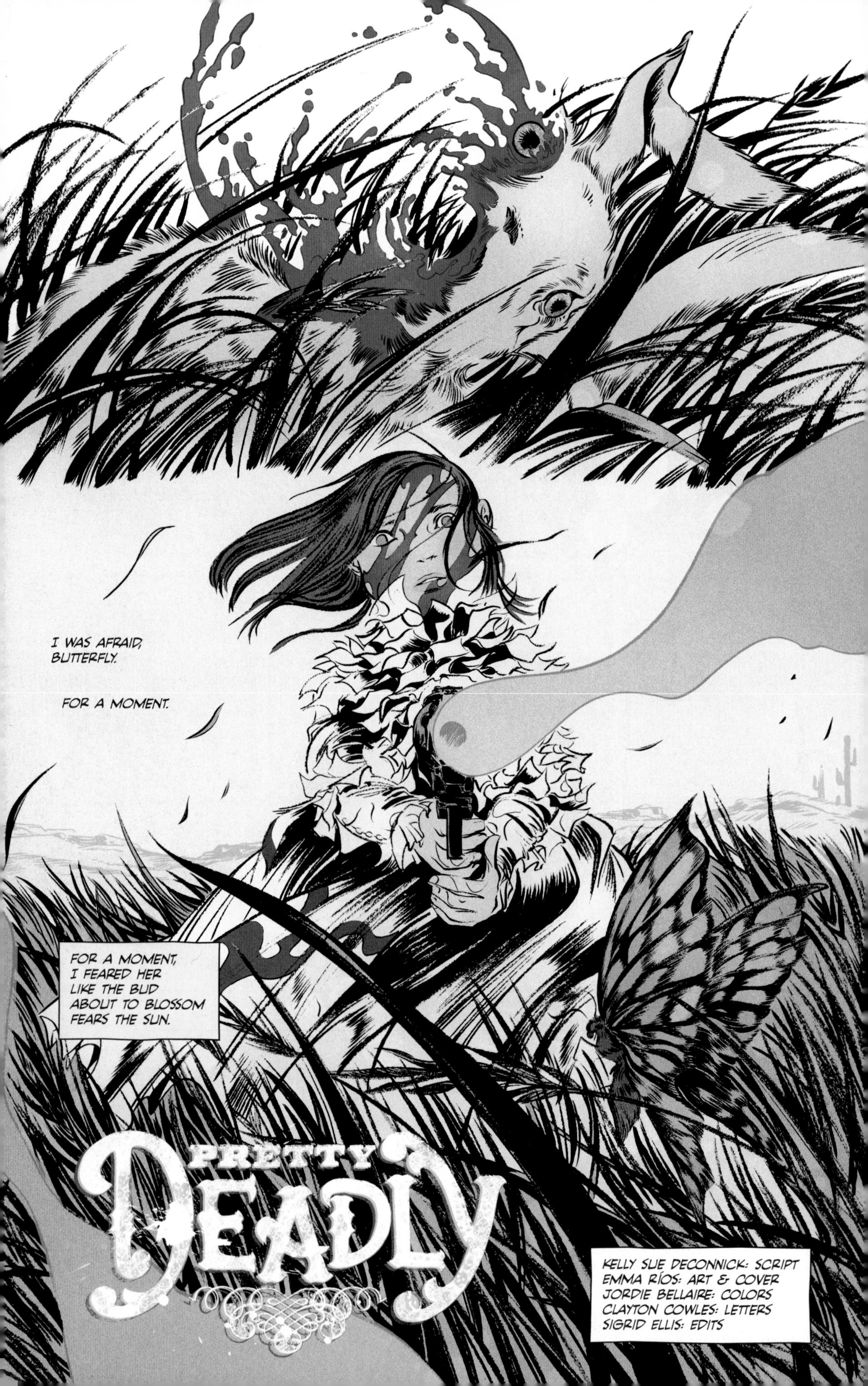
I WAS AFRAID, BUTTERFLY.
FOR A MOMENT.
FOR A MOMENT, I FEARED HER LIKE THE BUD ABOUT TO BLOSSOM FEARS THE SUN.
PRETTY DEADLY
KELLY SUE DECONNICK: SCRIPT
EMMA RÍOS: ART & COVER
JORDIE BELLAIRE: COLORS
CLAYTON COWLES: LETTERS
SIGRID ELLIS: EDITS

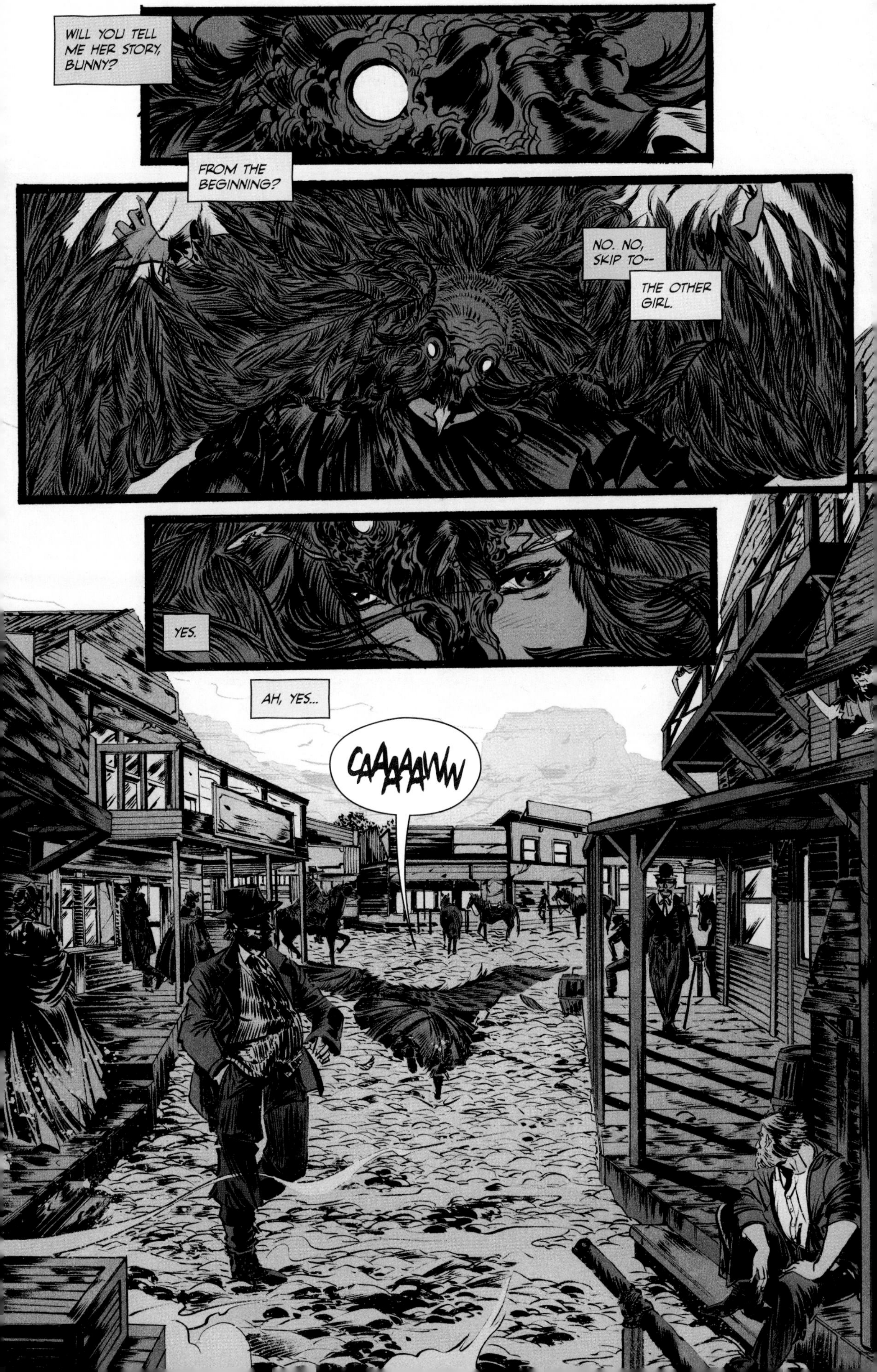
WILL YOU TELL ME HER STORY, BUNNY?
FROM THE BEGINNING?
NO. NO, SKIP TO--
THE OTHER GIRL.
YES.
AH, YES...
CAAAAAAWW

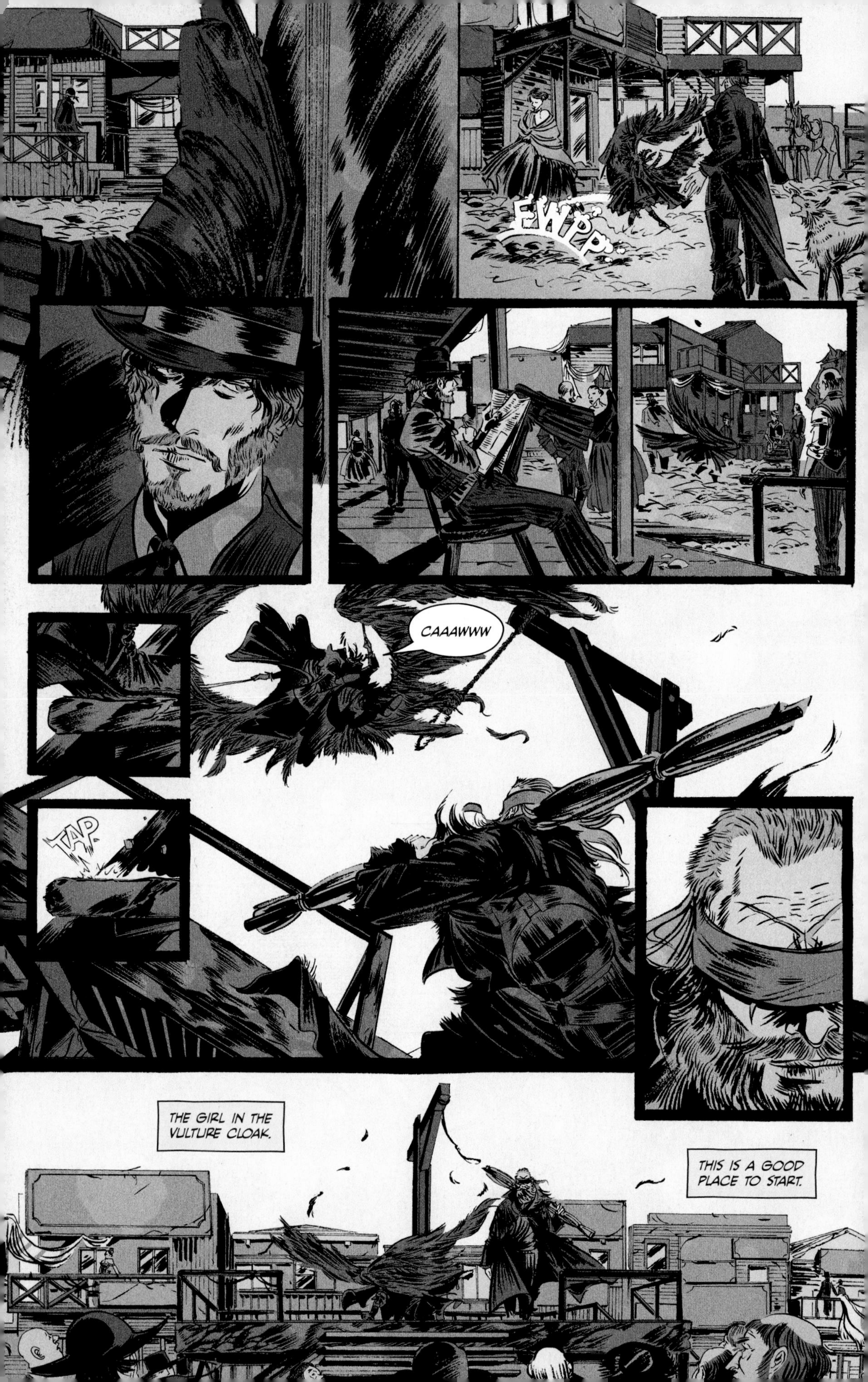
EWPP
CAAAWWW
TAP
THE GIRL IN THE VULTURE CLOAK.
THIS IS A GOOD PLACE TO START.

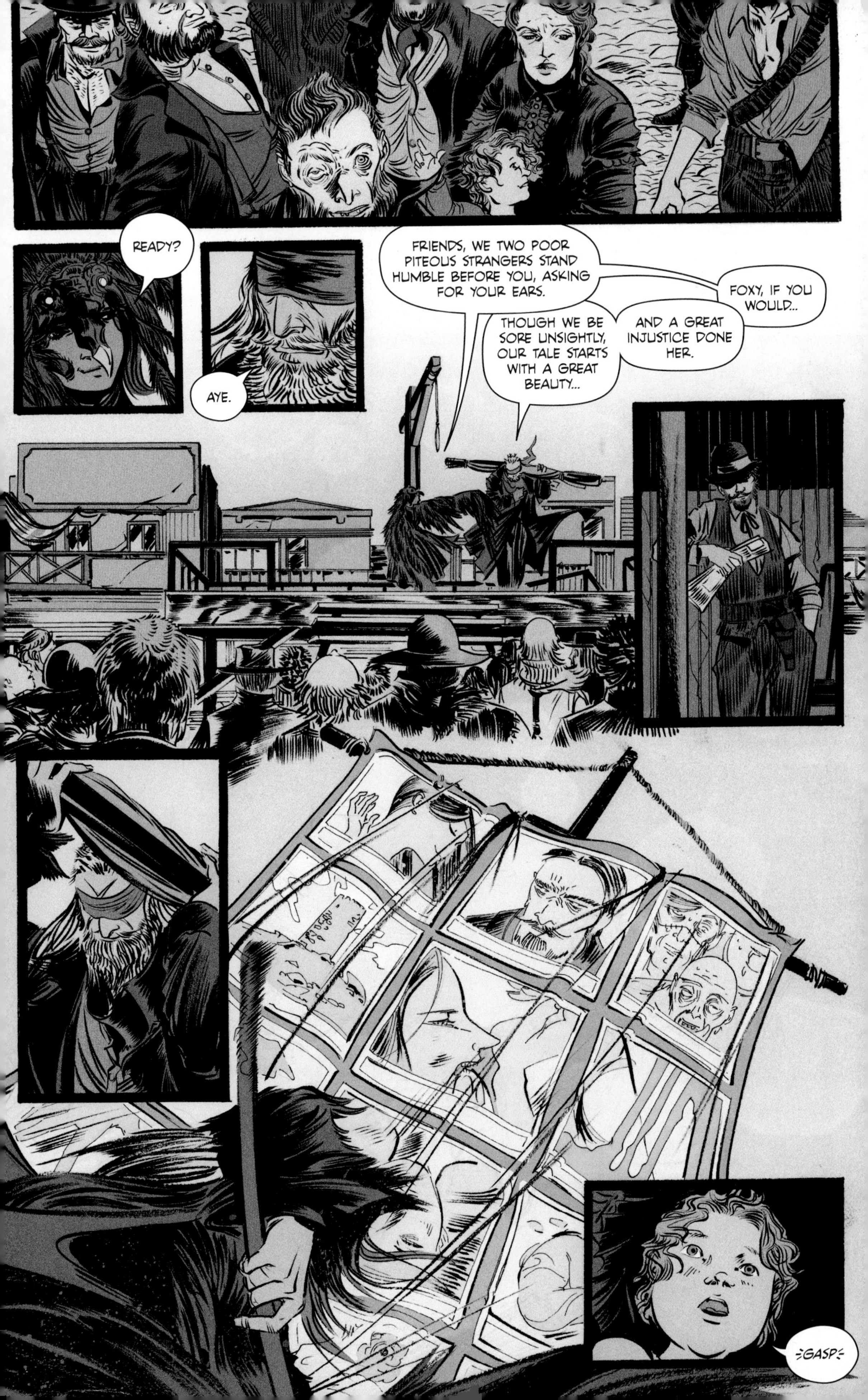

READY?
AYE.
FRIENDS, WE TWO POOR PITEOUS STRANGERS STAND HUMBLE BEFORE YOU, ASKING FOR YOUR EARS.
THOUGH WE BE SORE UNSIGHTLY, OUR TALE STARTS WITH A GREAT BEAUTY...
AND A GREAT INJUSTICE DONE HER.
FOXY, IF YOU WOULD...
GASP

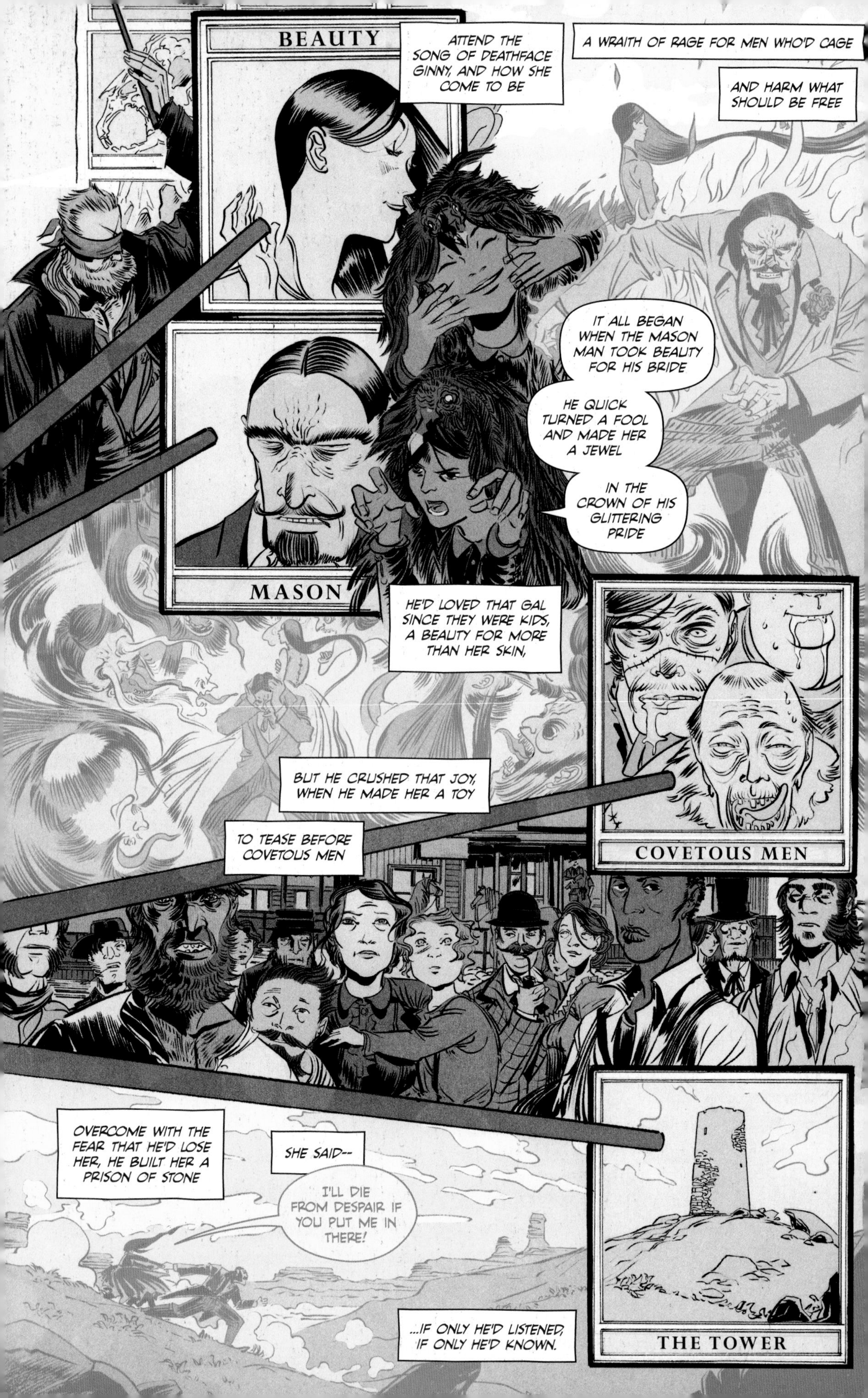
BEAUTY
ATTEND THE SONG OF DEATHFACE GINNY, AND HOW SHE COME TO BE
A WRAITH OF RAGE FOR MEN WHO'D CAGE
AND HARM WHAT SHOULD BE FREE
IT ALL BEGAN WHEN THE MASON MAN TOOK BEAUTY FOR HIS BRIDE
HE QUICK TURNED A FOOL AND MADE HER A JEWEL
IN THE CROWN OF HIS GLITTERING PRIDE
MASON
HE'D LOVED THAT GAL SINCE THEY WERE KIDS, A BEAUTY FOR MORE THAN HER SKIN,
BUT HE CRUSHED THAT JOY, WHEN HE MADE HER A TOY
TO TEASE BEFORE COVETOUS MEN
COVETOUS MEN
OVERCOME WITH THE FEAR THAT HE'D LOSE HER, HE BUILT HER A PRISON OF STONE
SHE SAID--
I'LL DIE FROM DESPAIR IF YOU PUT ME IN THERE!
...IF ONLY HE'D LISTENED, IF ONLY HE'D KNOWN.
THE TOWER

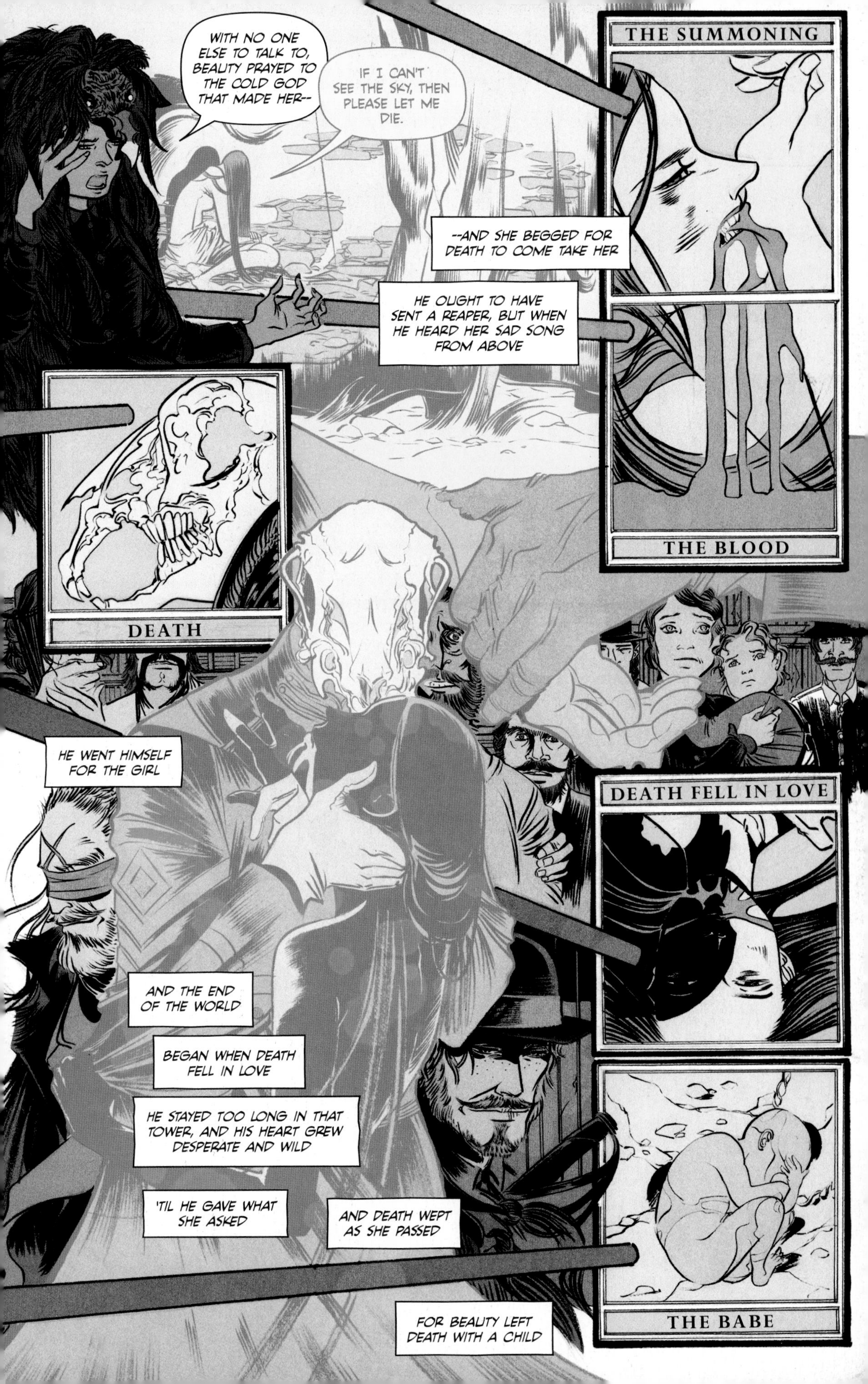

WITH NO ONE ELSE TO TALK TO, BEAUTY PRAYED TO THE COLD GOD THAT MADE HER--
IF I CAN'T SEE THE SKY, THEN PLEASE LET ME DIE.
THE SUMMONING
--AND SHE BEGGED FOR DEATH TO COME TAKE HER
HE OUGHT TO HAVE SENT A REAPER, BUT WHEN HE HEARD HER SAD SONG FROM ABOVE
THE BLOOD
DEATH
HE WENT HIMSELF FOR THE GIRL
DEATH FELL IN LOVE
AND THE END OF THE WORLD
BEGAN WHEN DEATH FELL IN LOVE
HE STAYED TOO LONG IN THAT TOWER, AND HIS HEART GREW DESPERATE AND WILD
'TIL HE GAVE WHAT SHE ASKED
AND DEATH WEPT AS SHE PASSED
FOR BEAUTY LEFT DEATH WITH A CHILD
THE BABE

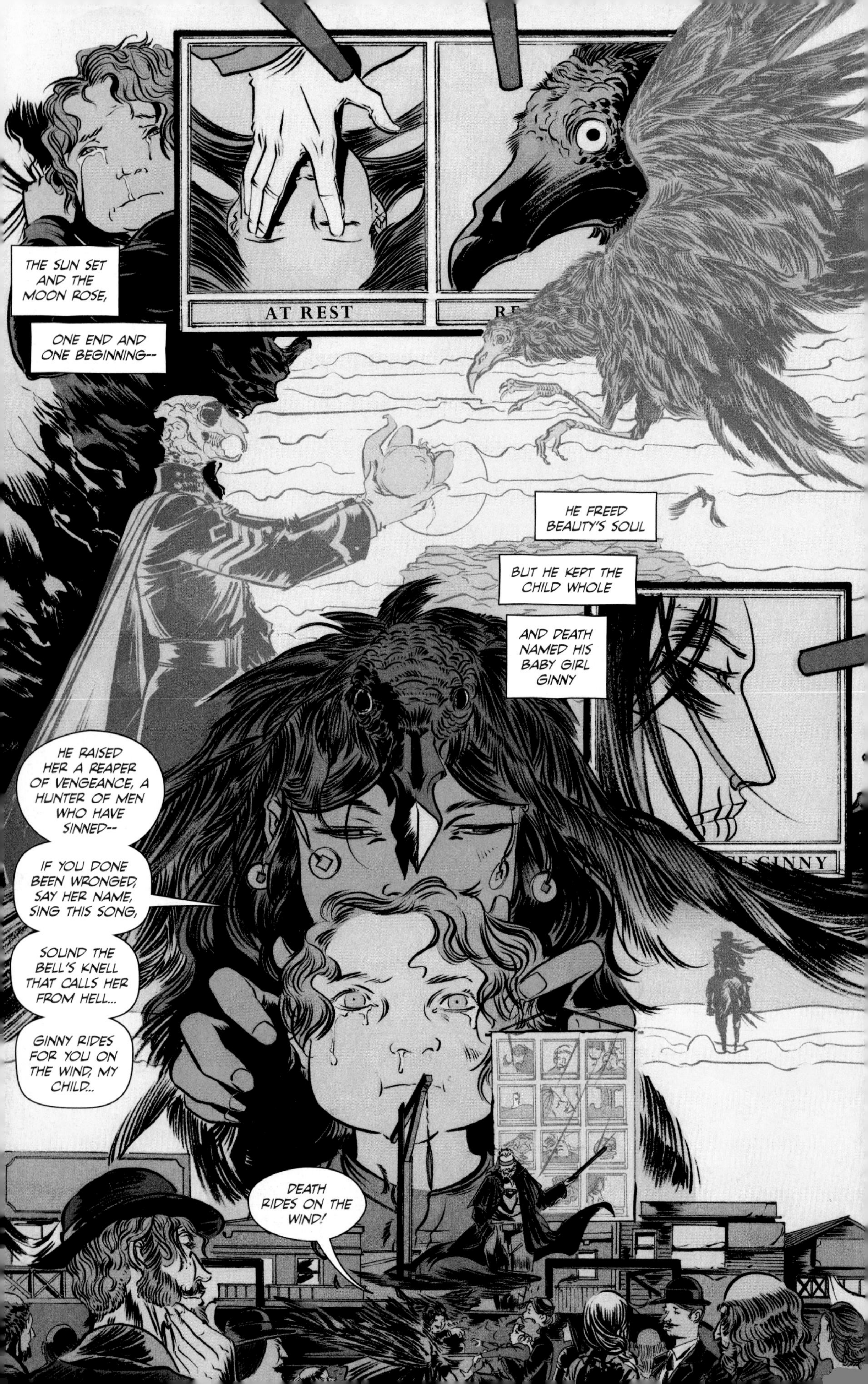
AT REST
THE SUN SET AND THE MOON ROSE,
ONE END AND ONE BEGINNING--
HE FREED BEAUTY'S SOUL
BUT HE KEPT THE CHILD WHOLE
AND DEATH NAMED HIS BABY GIRL GINNY
HE RAISED HER A REAPER OF VENGEANCE, A HUNTER OF MEN WHO HAVE SINNED--
IF YOU DONE BEEN WRONGED, SAY HER NAME, SING THIS SONG,
SOUND THE BELL'S KNELL THAT CALLS HER FROM HELL...
GINNY RIDES FOR YOU ON THE WIND, MY CHILD...
DEATH RIDES ON THE WIND!

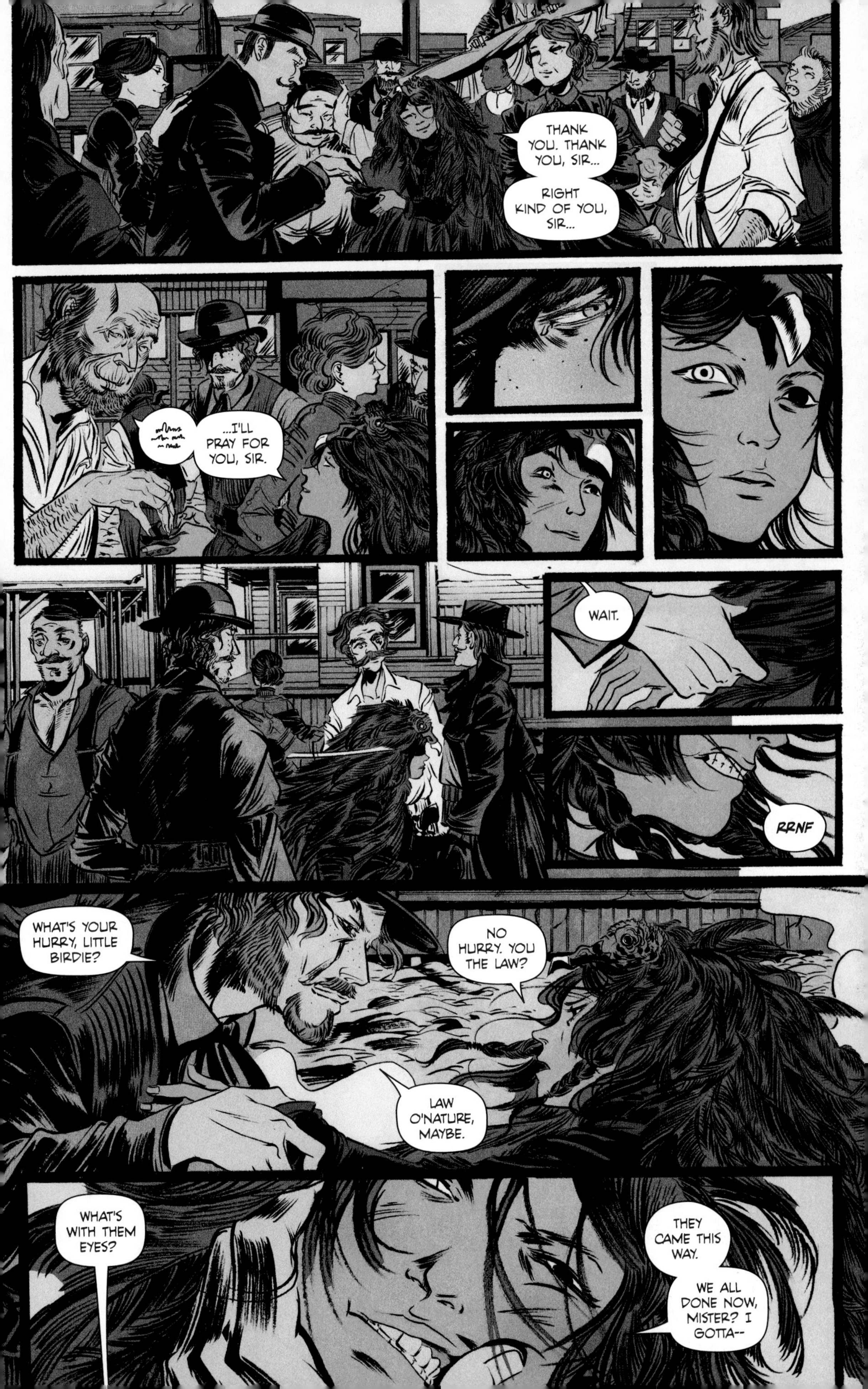
THANK YOU. THANK YOU, SIR...
RIGHT KIND OF YOU, SIR...
...I'LL PRAY FOR YOU, SIR.
WAIT.
RRNF
WHAT'S YOUR HURRY, LITTLE BIRDIE?
NO HURRY. YOU THE LAW?
LAW O'NATURE, MAYBE.
WHAT'S WITH THEM EYES?
THEY CAME THIS WAY.
WE ALL DONE NOW, MISTER? I GOTTA--

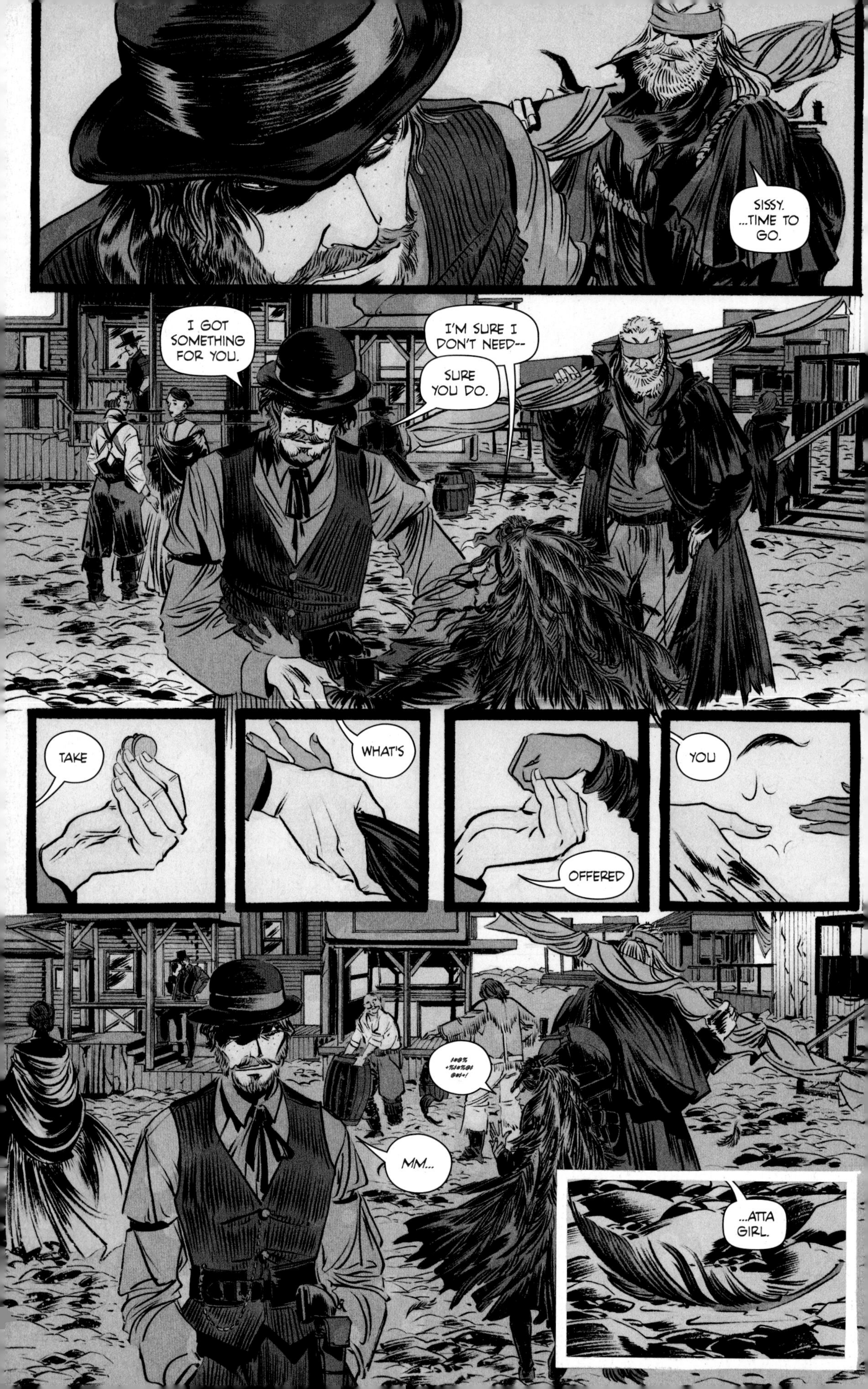
SISSY. ...TIME TO GO.
I GOT SOMETHING FOR YOU.
I'M SURE I DON'T NEED--
SURE YOU DO.
TAKE
WHAT'S
OFFERED
YOU
MM...
...ATTA GIRL.

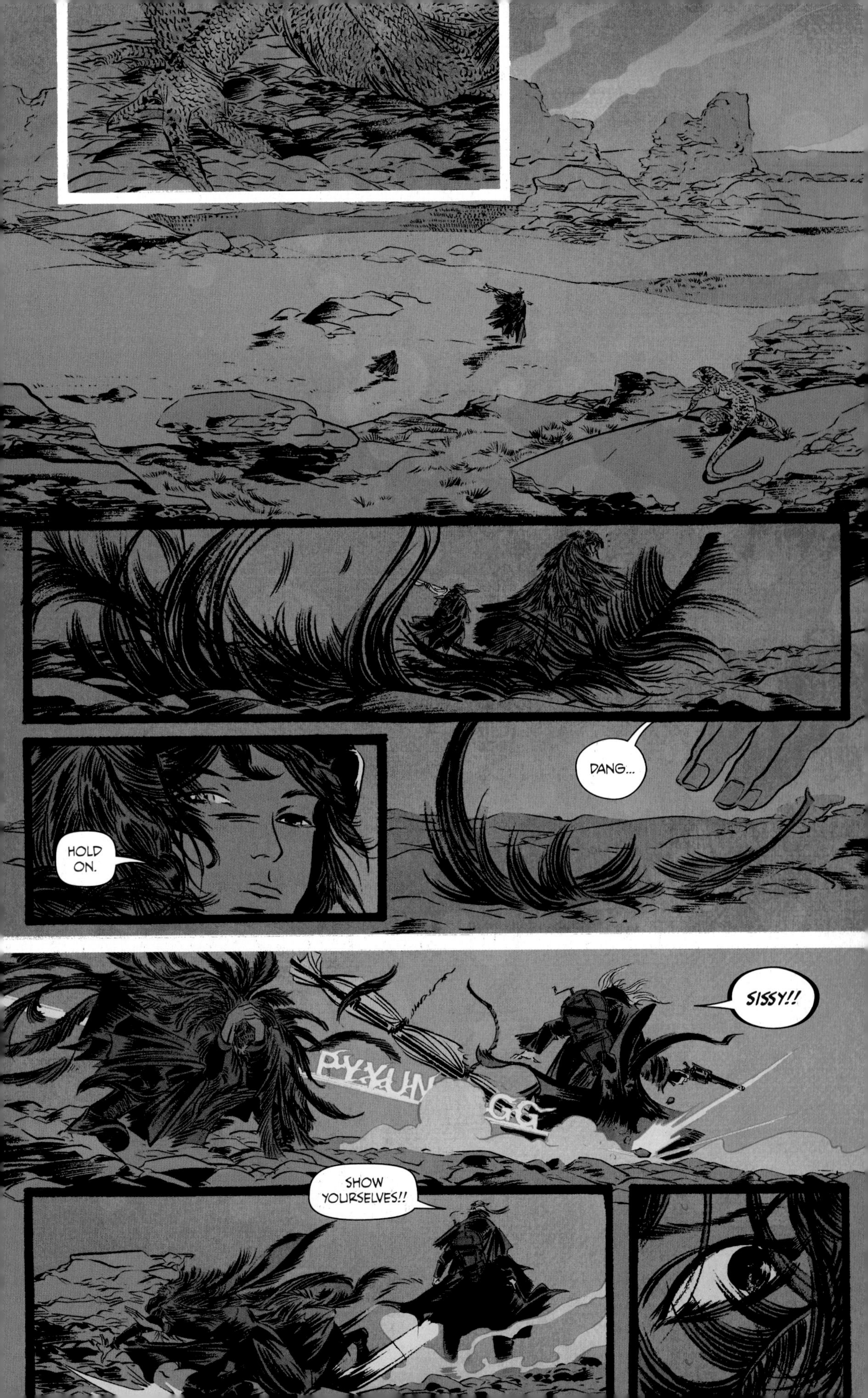
DANG...
HOLD ON.
SISSY!!
PYYXUN GG
SHOW YOURSELVES!!

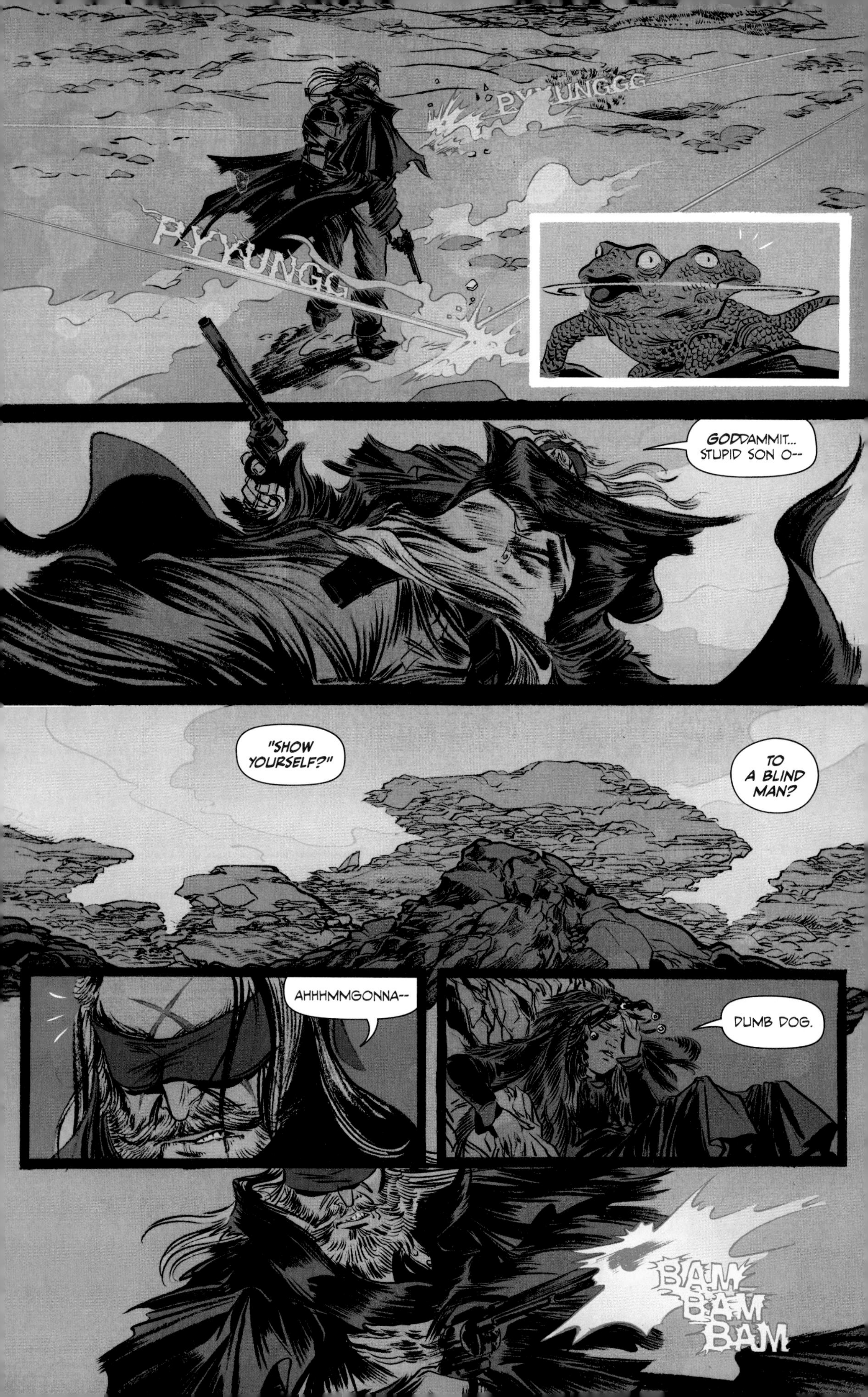
PYYUNGGG
PYYUNGG
GODDAMMIT... STUPID SON O--
"SHOW YOURSELF?"
TO A BLIND MAN?
AHHHMMGONNA--
DUMB DOG.
BAM BAM BAM

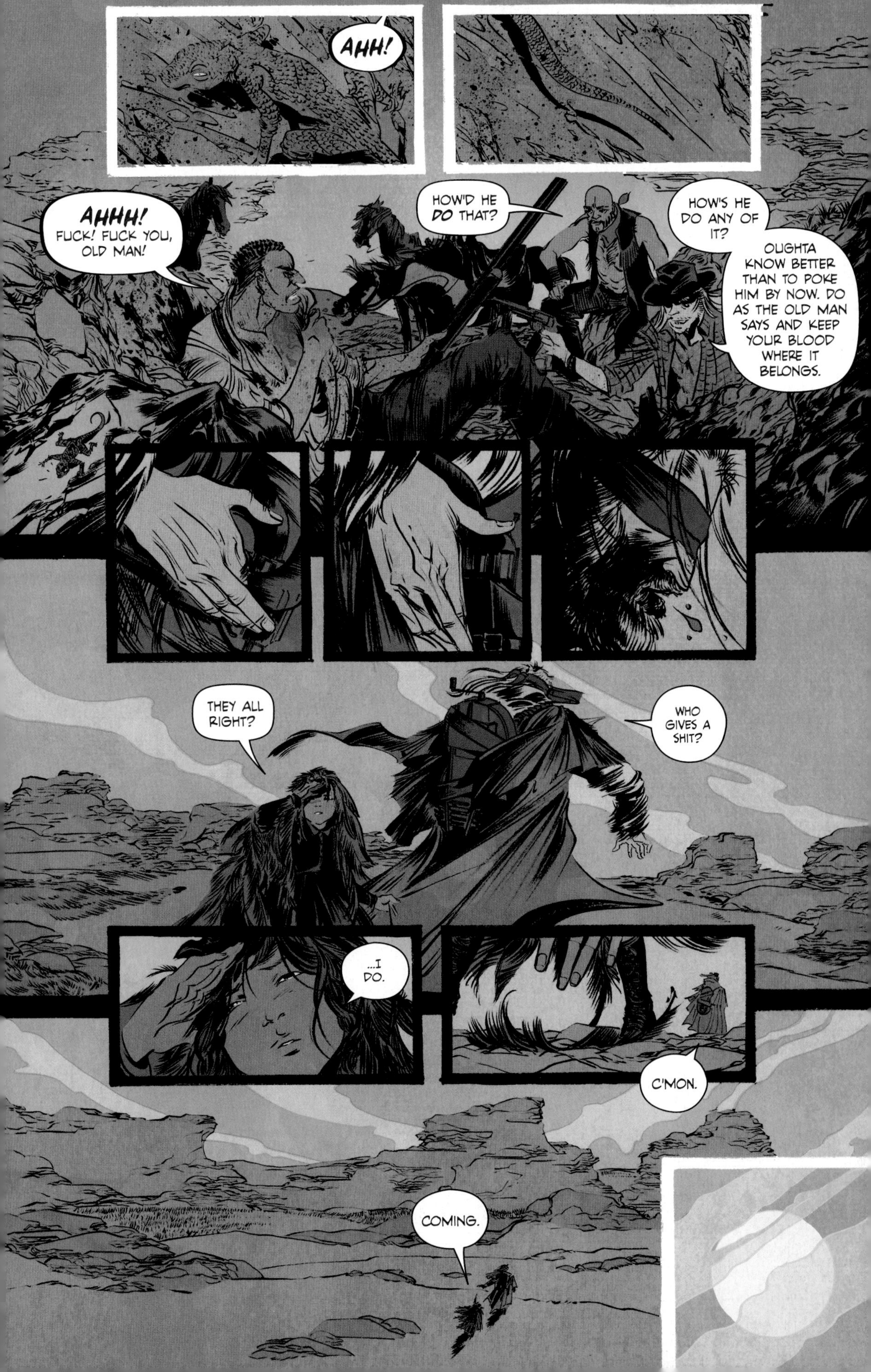
AHH!
AHHH! FUCK! FUCK YOU, OLD MAN!
HOW'D HE DO THAT?
HOW'S HE DO ANY OF IT?
OUGHTA KNOW BETTER THAN TO POKE HIM BY NOW. DO AS THE OLD MAN SAYS AND KEEP YOUR BLOOD WHERE IT BELONGS.
THEY ALL RIGHT?
WHO GIVES A SHIT?
...I DO.
C'MON.
COMING.

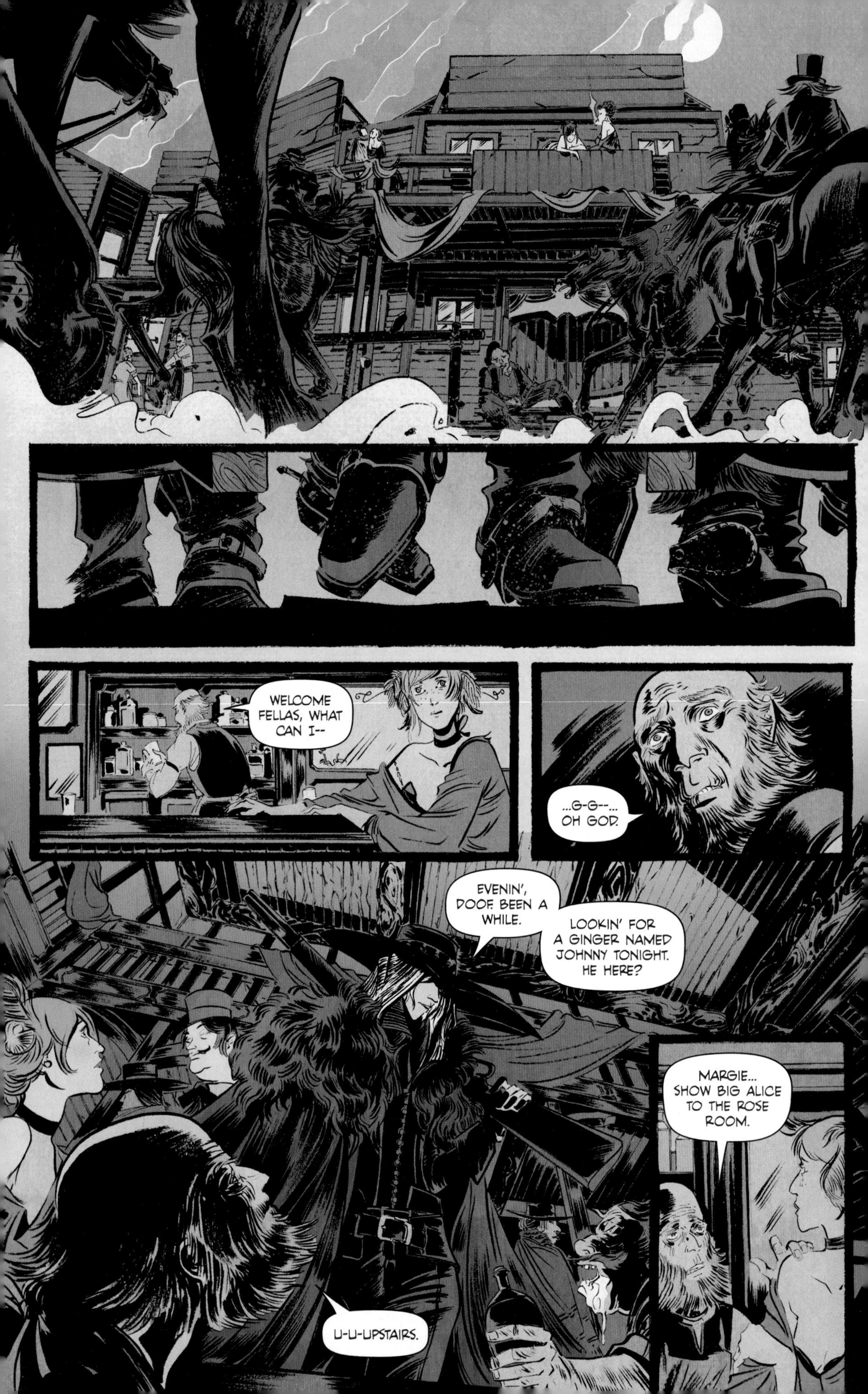
WELCOME FELLAS, WHAT CAN I--
...G-G--... OH GOD.
EVENIN', DOOF. BEEN A WHILE.
LOOKIN' FOR A GINGER NAMED JOHNNY TONIGHT. HE HERE?
U-U-UPSTAIRS.
MARGIE... SHOW BIG ALICE TO THE ROSE ROOM.

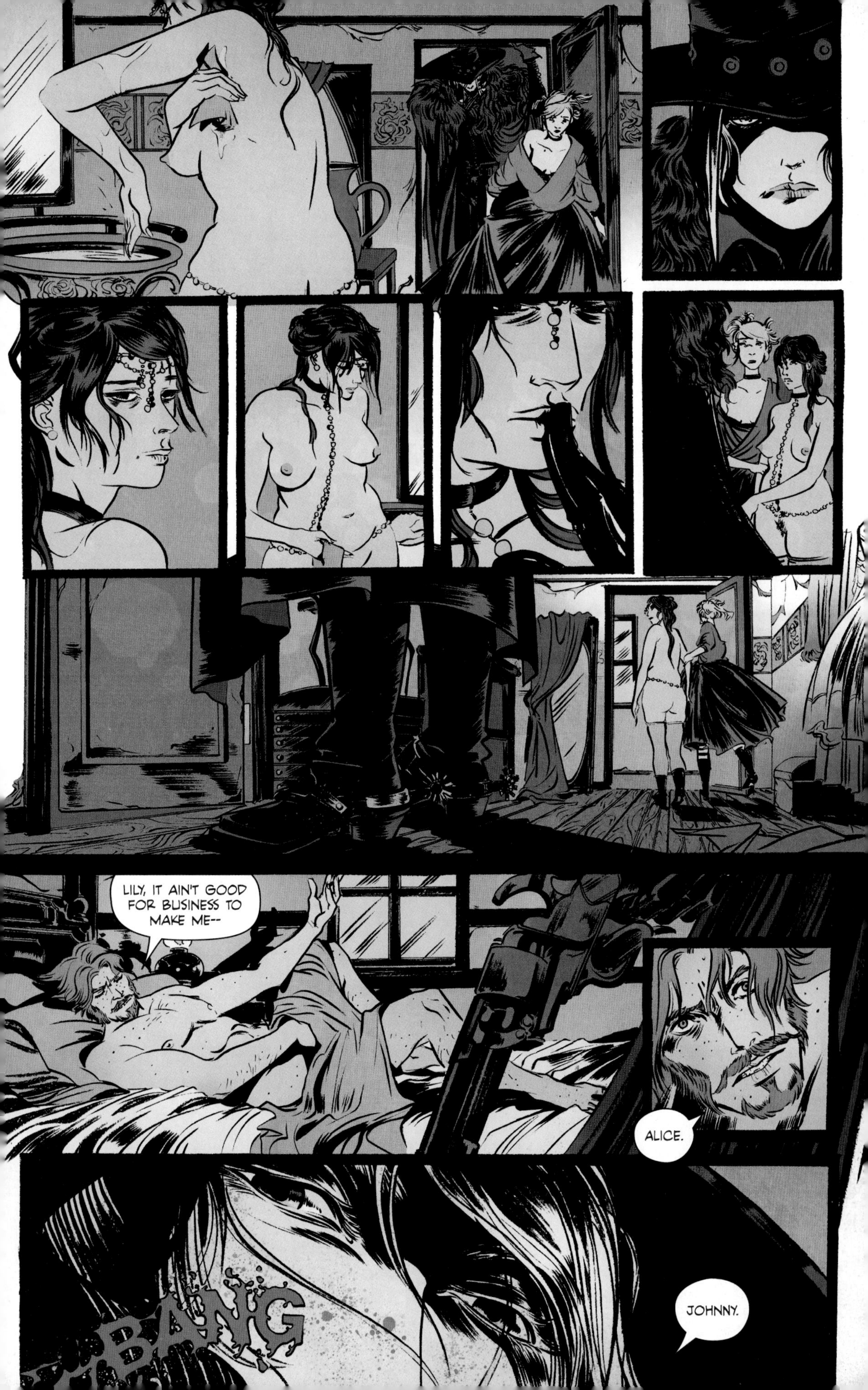
LILY, IT AIN'T GOOD FOR BUSINESS TO MAKE ME--
ALICE.
BANG
JOHNNY.

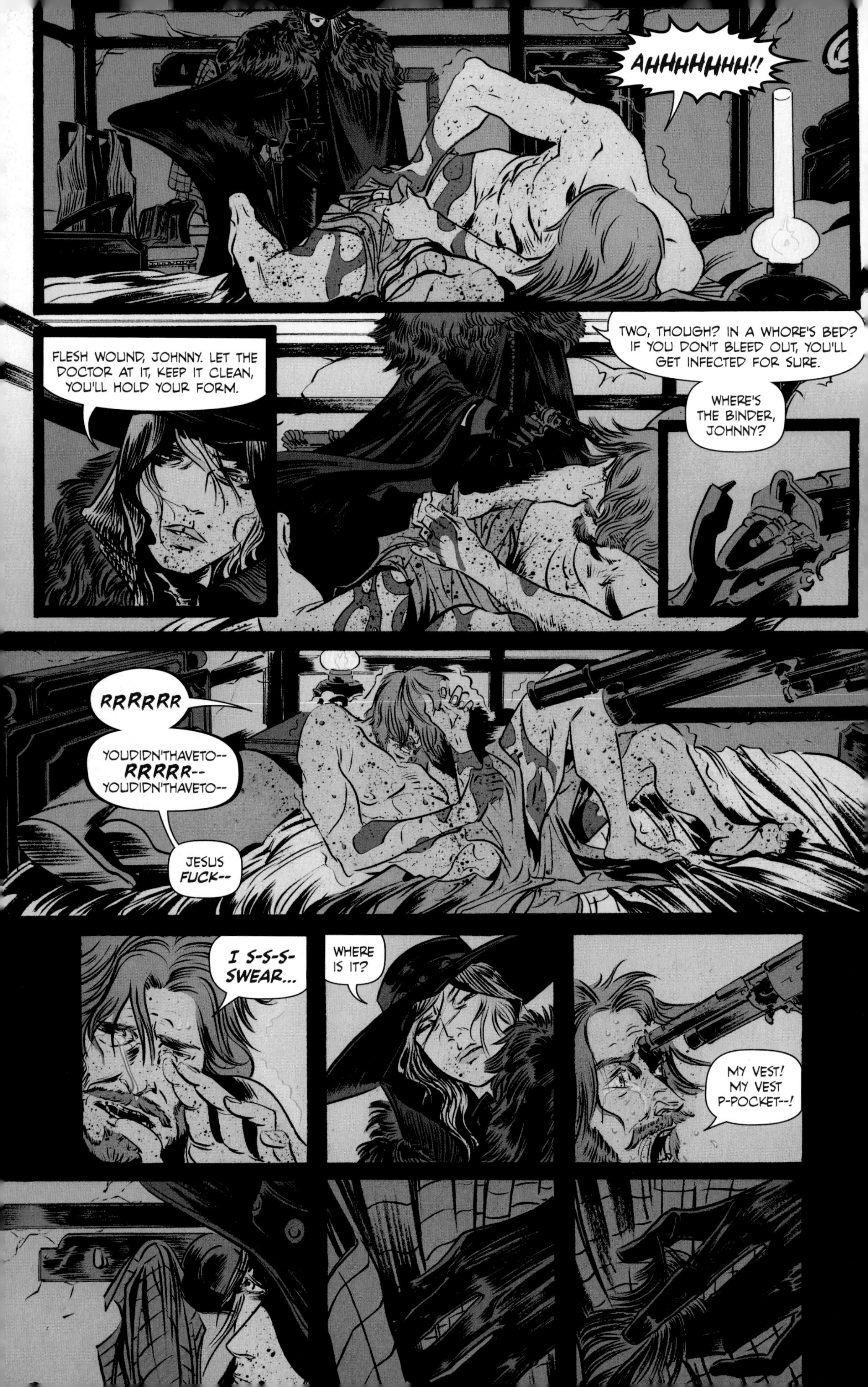
AHHHHHHH!!
FLESH WOUND, JOHNNY. LET THE DOCTOR AT IT, KEEP IT CLEAN, YOU'LL HOLD YOUR FORM.
TWO, THOUGH? IN A WHORE'S BED? IF YOU DON'T BLEED OUT, YOU'LL GET INFECTED FOR SURE.
WHERE'S THE BINDER, JOHNNY?
RRRRRR
YOUDIDN'THAVETO-- RRRRR-- YOUDIDN'THAVETO--
JESUS FUCK--
I S-S-S-SWEAR...
WHERE IS IT?
MY VEST! MY VEST P-POCKET--!

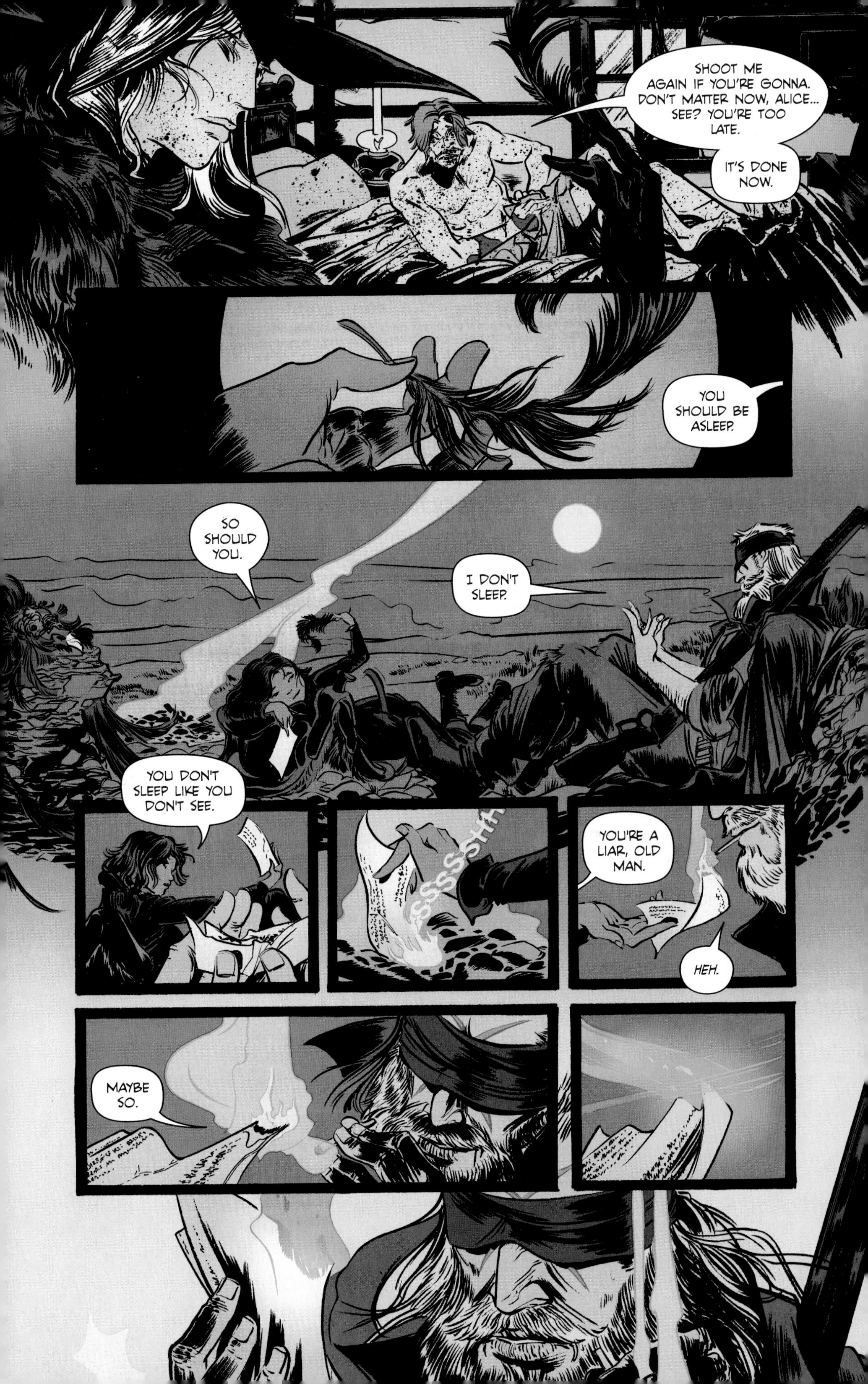
SHOOT ME AGAIN IF YOU'RE GONNA. DON'T MATTER NOW, ALICE... SEE? YOU'RE TOO LATE.
IT'S DONE NOW.
YOU SHOULD BE ASLEEP.
SO SHOULD YOU.
I DON'T SLEEP.
YOU DON'T SLEEP LIKE YOU DON'T SEE.
SSSSSHH
YOU'RE A LIAR, OLD MAN.
HEH.
MAYBE SO.

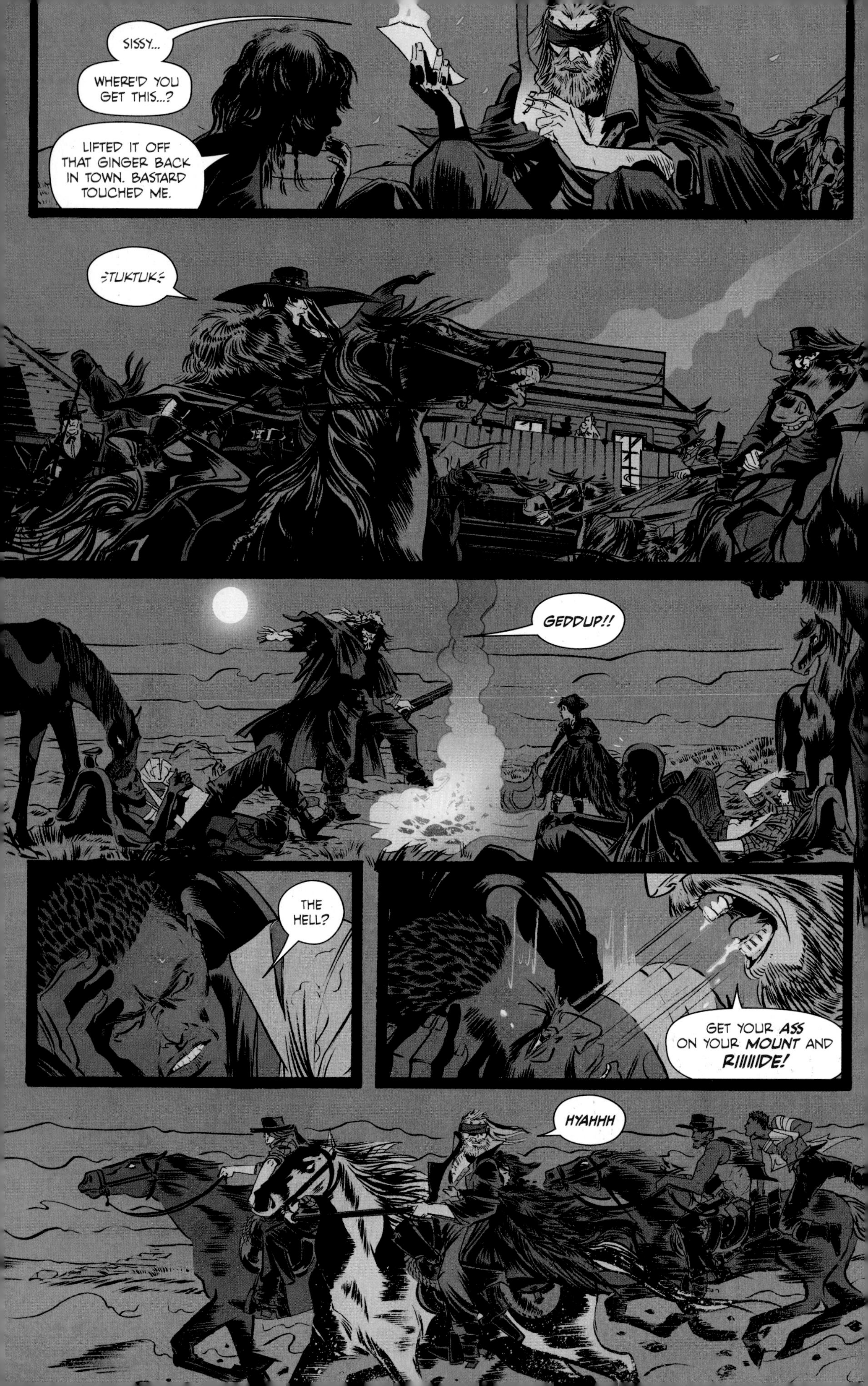
SISSY...
WHERE'D YOU GET THIS...?
LIFTED IT OFF THAT GINGER BACK IN TOWN. BASTARD TOUCHED ME.
TUKTUK
GEDDUP!!
THE HELL?
GET YOUR ASS ON YOUR MOUNT AND RIIIIIDE!
HYAHHH

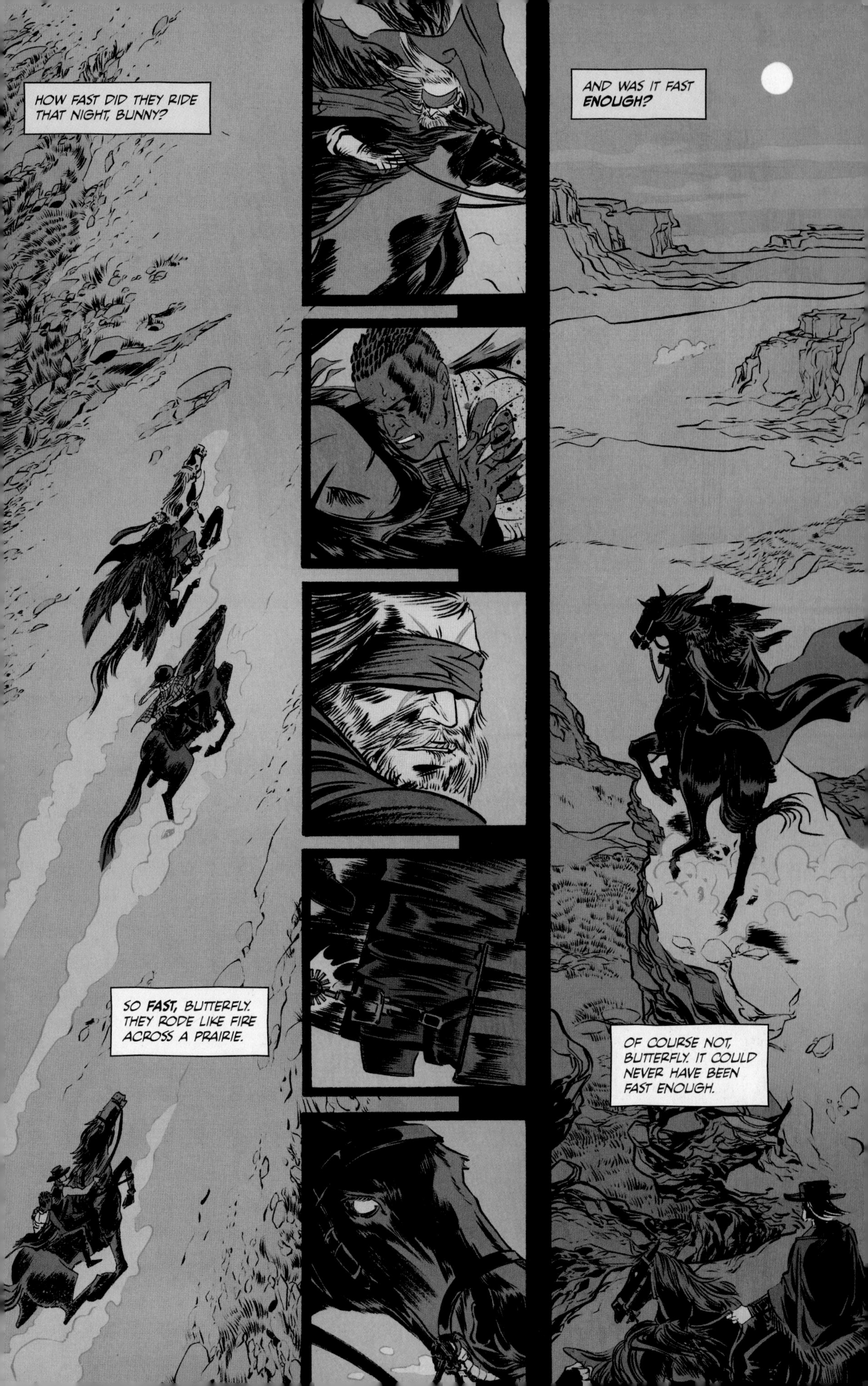
HOW FAST DID THEY RIDE THAT NIGHT, BUNNY?
SO FAST, BUTTERFLY. THEY RODE LIKE FIRE ACROSS A PRAIRIE.
AND WAS IT FAST ENOUGH?
OF COURSE NOT, BUTTERFLY. IT COULD NEVER HAVE BEEN FAST ENOUGH.

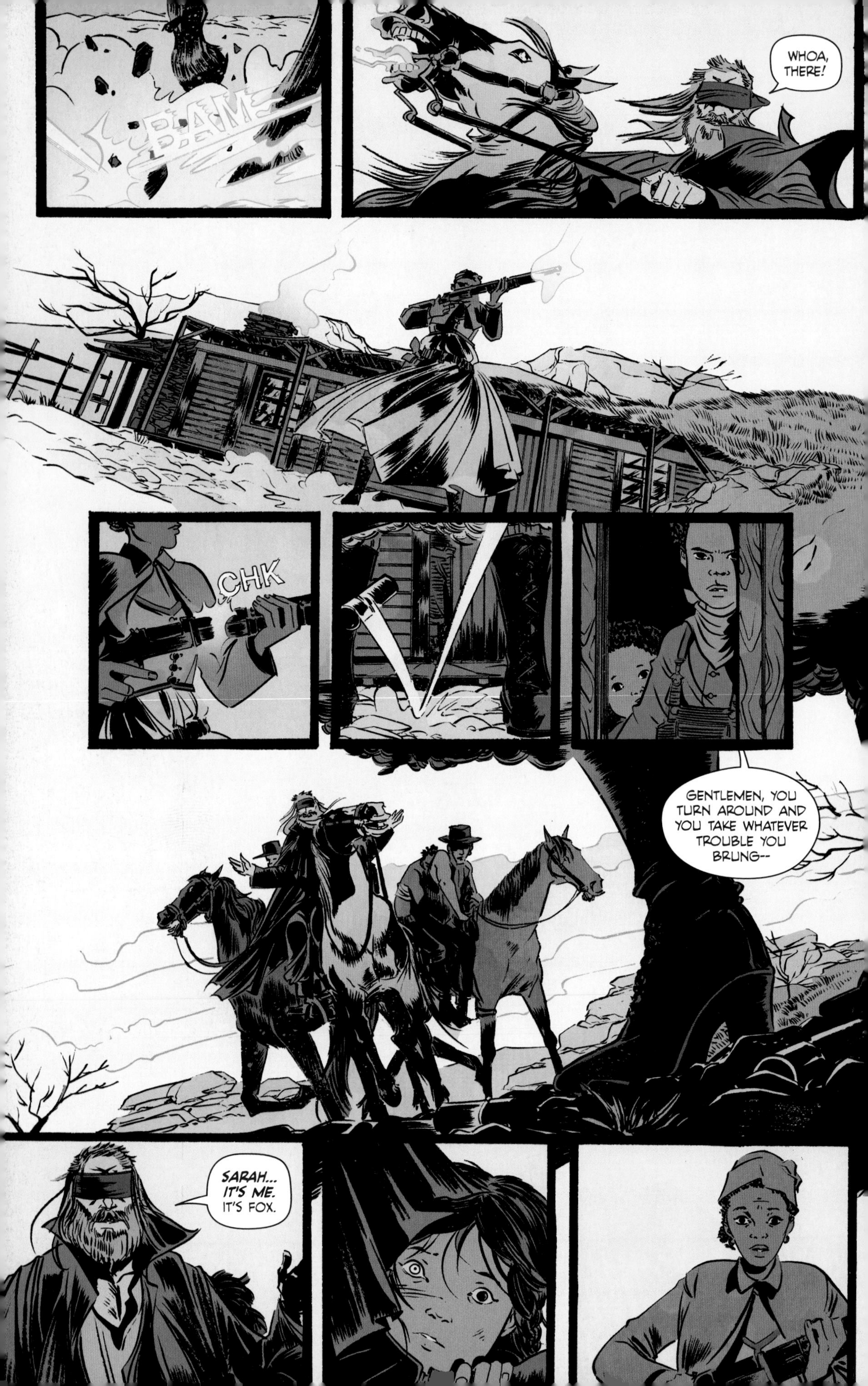
BAM
WHOA, THERE!
CHK
GENTLEMEN, YOU TURN AROUND AND YOU TAKE WHATEVER TROUBLE YOU BRUNG--
SARAH... IT'S ME. IT'S FOX.

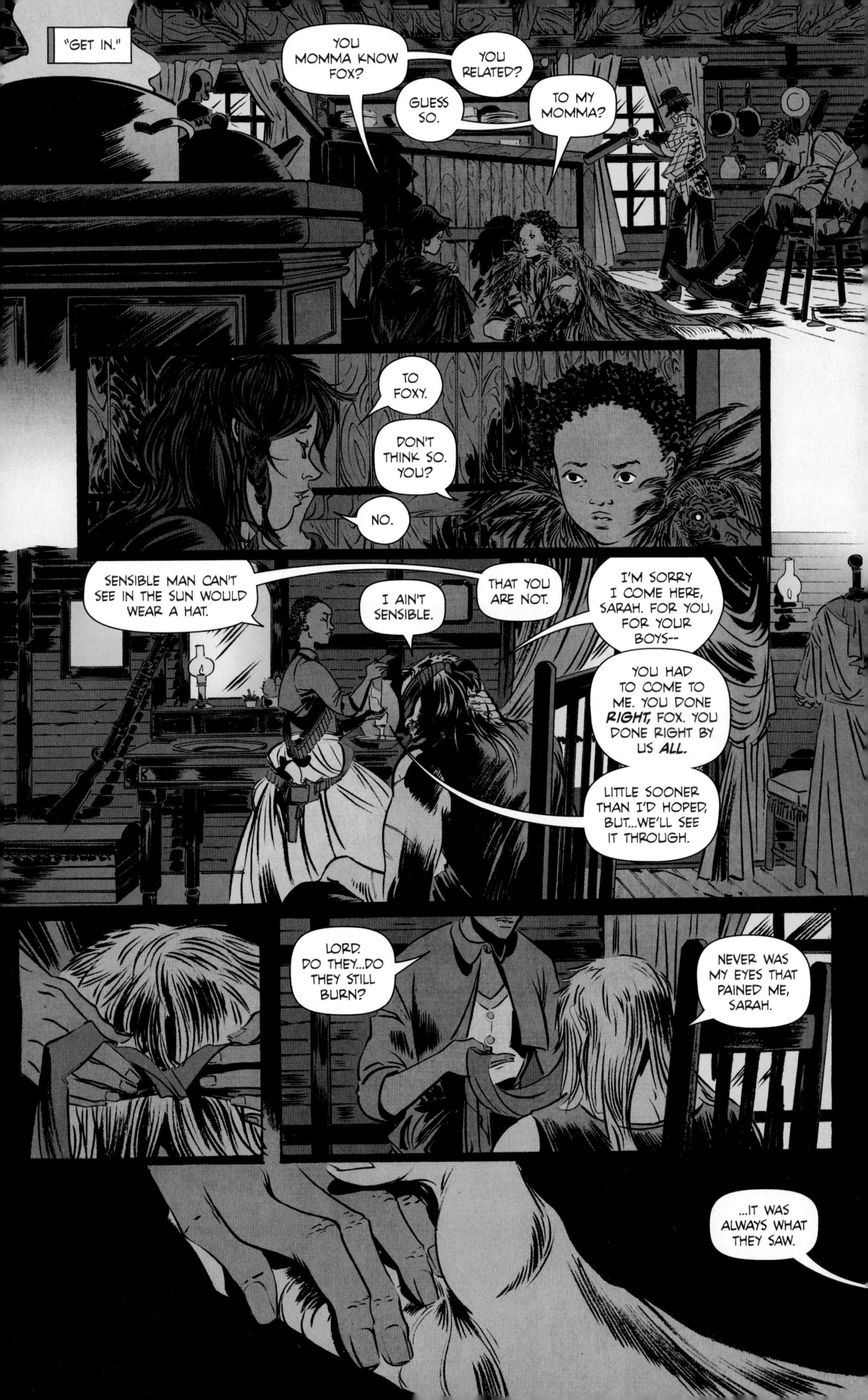
"GET IN."
YOU MOMMA KNOW FOX?
YOU RELATED?
GUESS SO.
TO MY MOMMA?
TO FOXY.
DON'T THINK SO. YOU?
NO.
SENSIBLE MAN CAN'T SEE IN THE SUN WOULD WEAR A HAT.
I AIN'T SENSIBLE.
THAT YOU ARE NOT.
I'M SORRY I COME HERE, SARAH. FOR YOU, FOR YOUR BOYS--
YOU HAD TO COME TO ME. YOU DONE RIGHT, FOX. YOU DONE RIGHT BY US ALL.
LITTLE SOONER THAN I'D HOPED, BUT...WE'LL SEE IT THROUGH.
LORD. DO THEY...DO THEY STILL BURN?
NEVER WAS MY EYES THAT PAINED ME, SARAH.
...IT WAS ALWAYS WHAT THEY SAW.

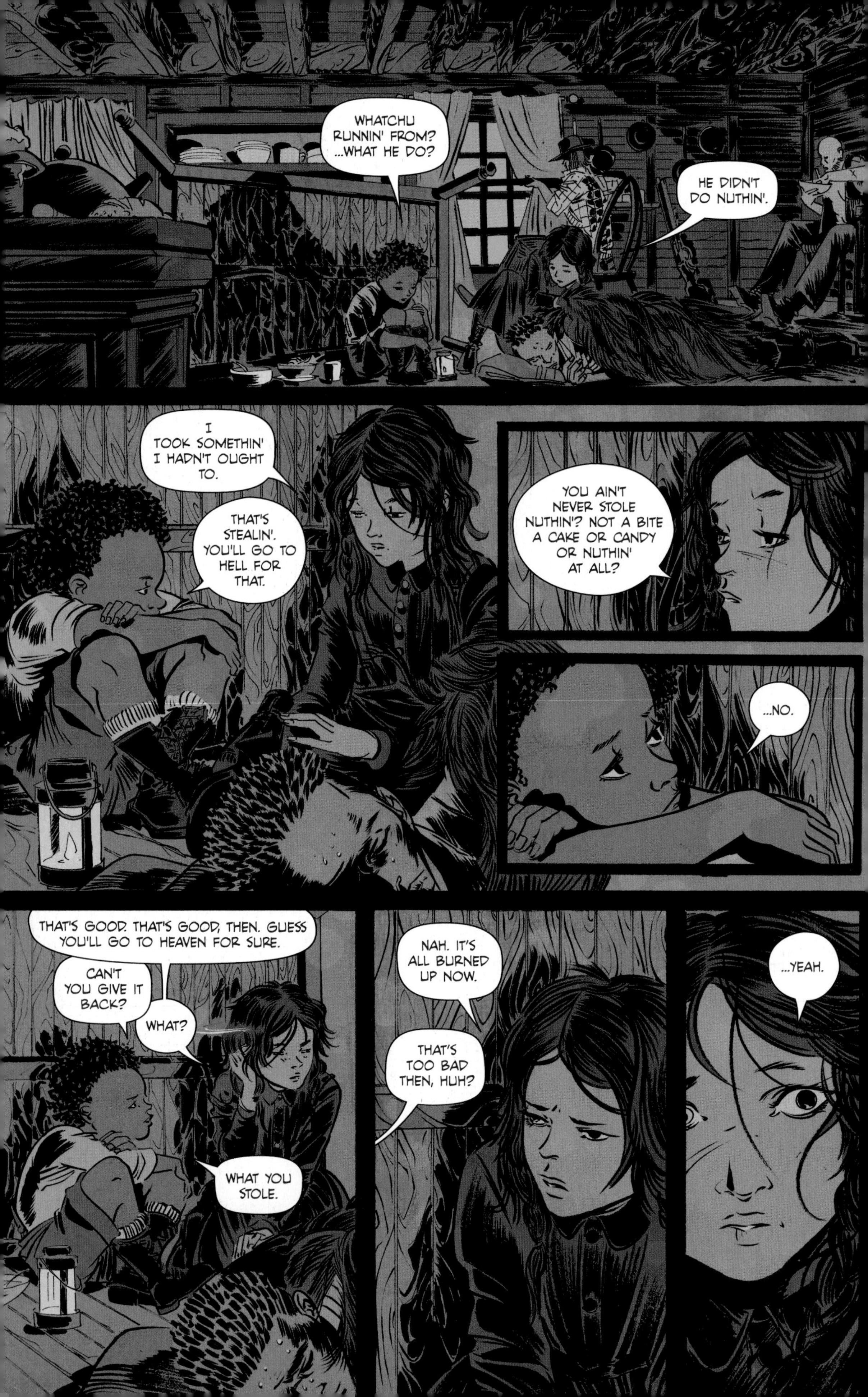
WHATCHU RUNNIN' FROM? ...WHAT HE DO?
HE DIDN'T DO NUTHIN'.
I TOOK SOMETHIN' I HADN'T OUGHT TO.
THAT'S STEALIN'. YOU'LL GO TO HELL FOR THAT.
YOU AIN'T NEVER STOLE NUTHIN'? NOT A BITE A CAKE OR CANDY OR NUTHIN' AT ALL?
...NO.
THAT'S GOOD. THAT'S GOOD, THEN. GUESS YOU'LL GO TO HEAVEN FOR SURE.
CAN'T YOU GIVE IT BACK?
WHAT?
WHAT YOU STOLE.
NAH. IT'S ALL BURNED UP NOW.
THAT'S TOO BAD THEN, HUH?
...YEAH.

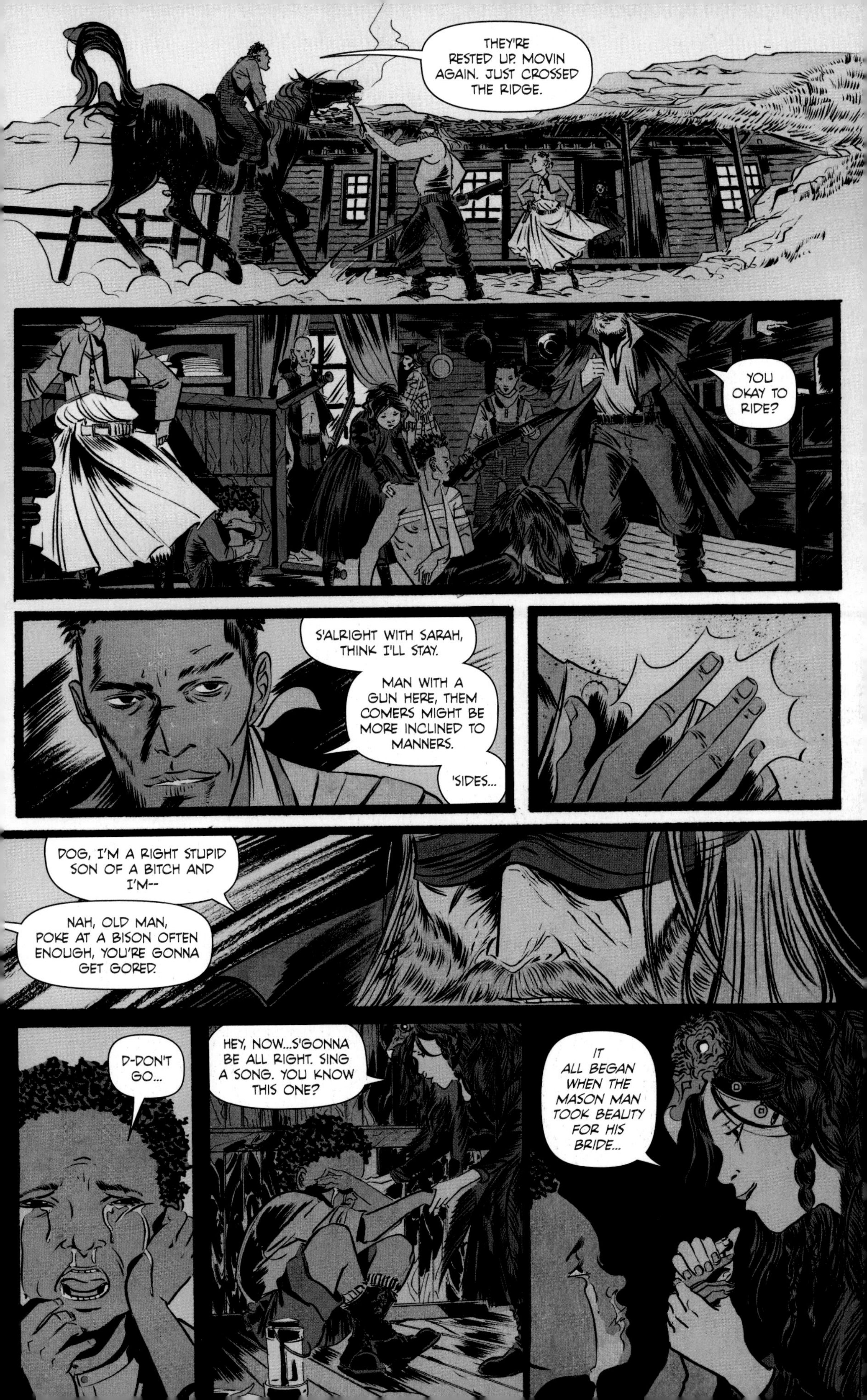
THEY'RE RESTED UP. MOVIN AGAIN. JUST CROSSED THE RIDGE.
YOU OKAY TO RIDE?
S'ALRIGHT WITH SARAH, THINK I'LL STAY.
MAN WITH A GUN HERE, THEM COMERS MIGHT BE MORE INCLINED TO MANNERS.
'SIDES...
DOG, I'M A RIGHT STUPID SON OF A BITCH AND I'M--
NAH, OLD MAN, POKE AT A BISON OFTEN ENOUGH, YOU'RE GONNA GET GORED.
D-DON'T GO...
HEY, NOW...S'GONNA BE ALL RIGHT. SING A SONG. YOU KNOW THIS ONE?
IT ALL BEGAN WHEN THE MASON MAN TOOK BEAUTY FOR HIS BRIDE...

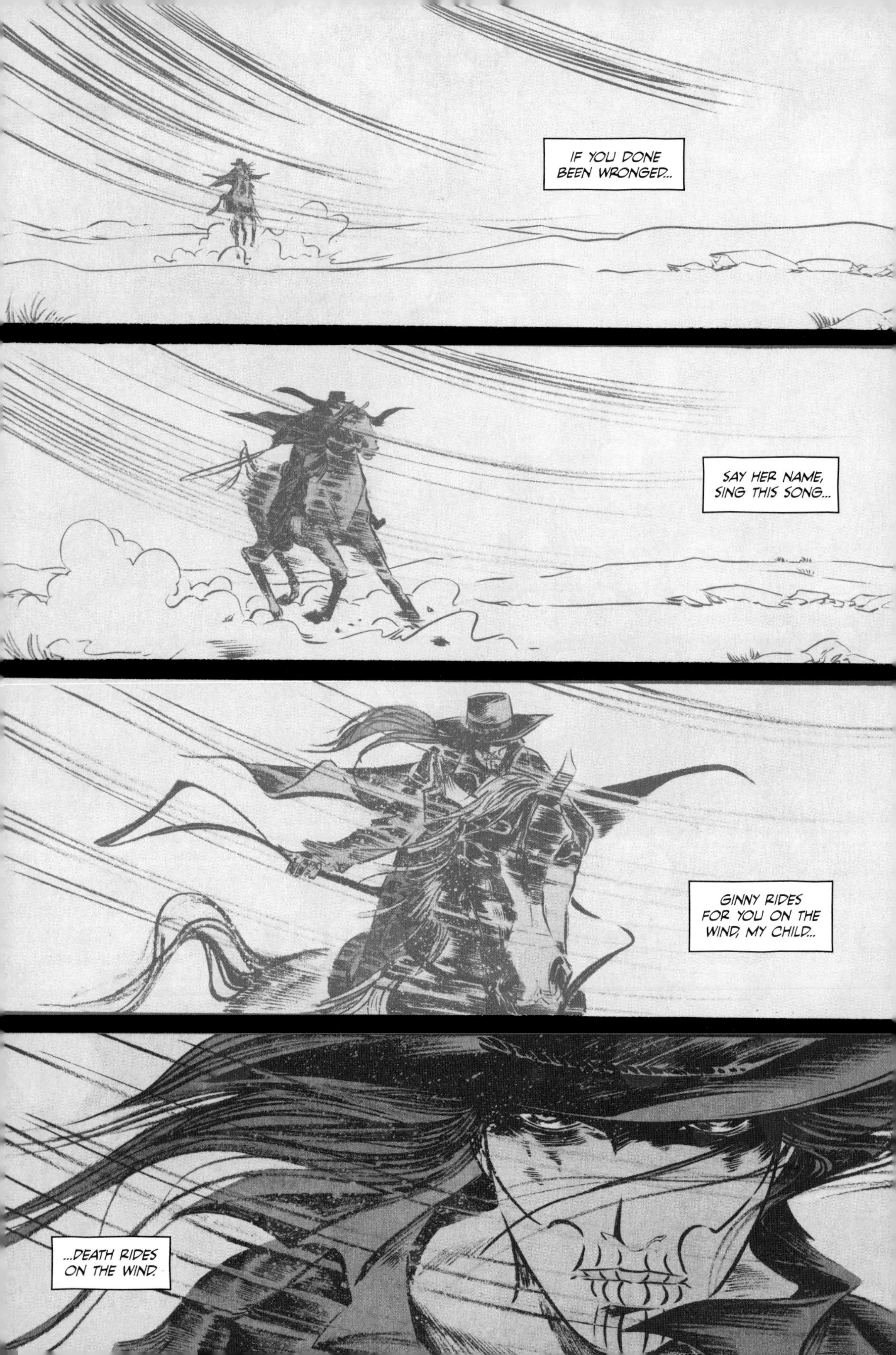
IF YOU DONE BEEN WRONGED...
SAY HER NAME, SING THIS SONG...
GINNY RIDES FOR YOU ON THE WIND, MY CHILD...
...DEATH RIDES ON THE WIND.

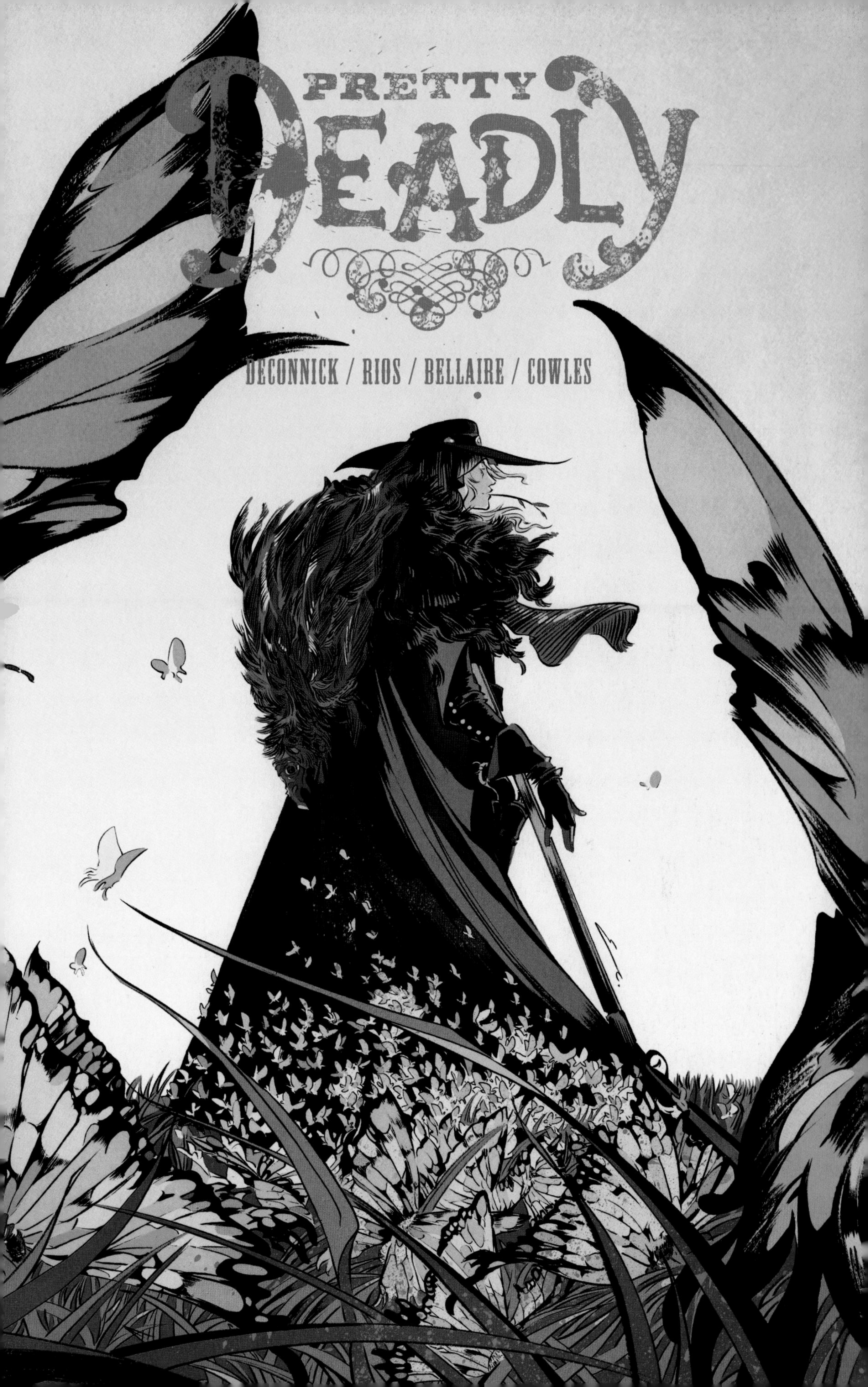
PRETTY DEADLY
DECONNICK / RIOS / BELLAIRE / COWLES

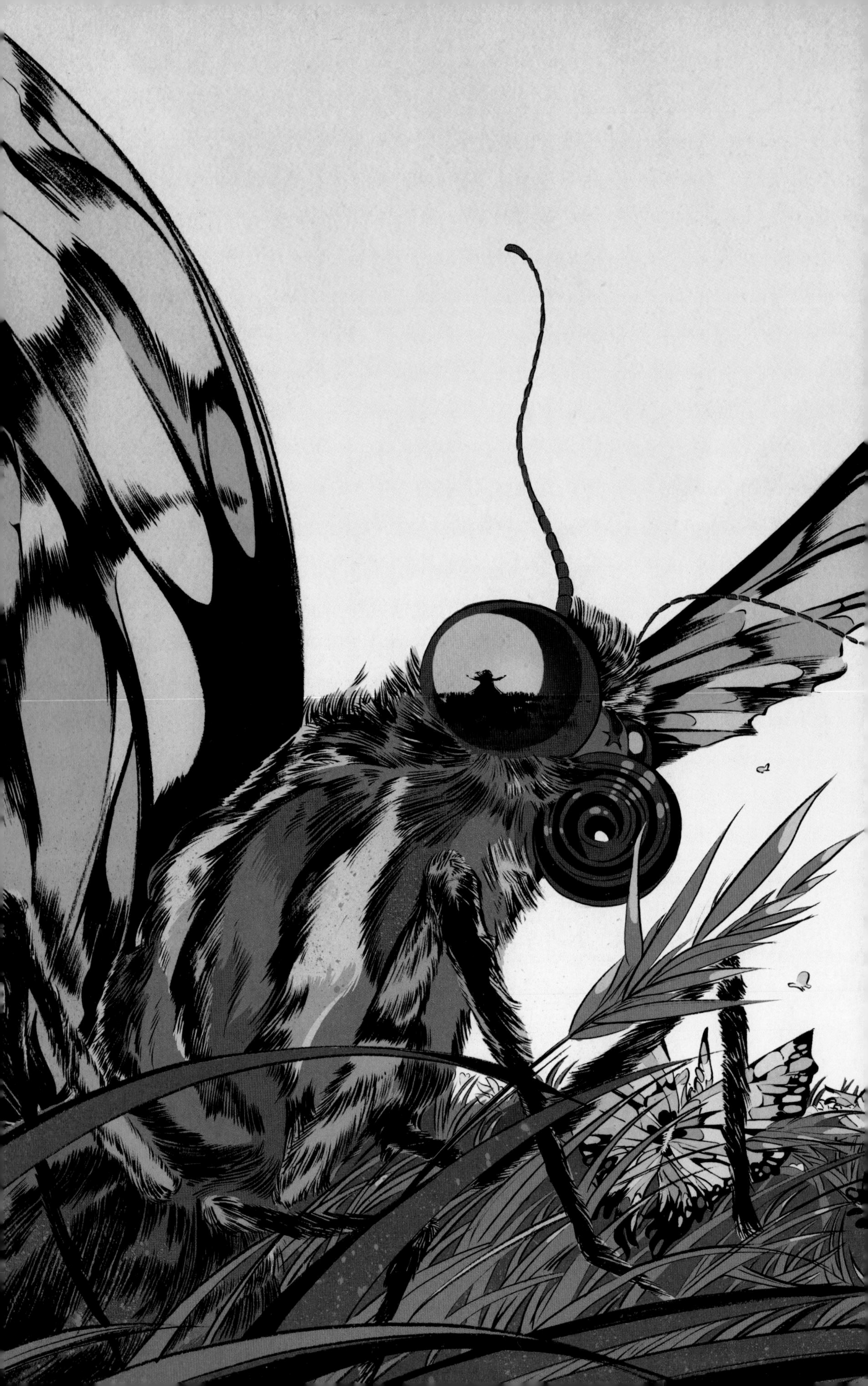

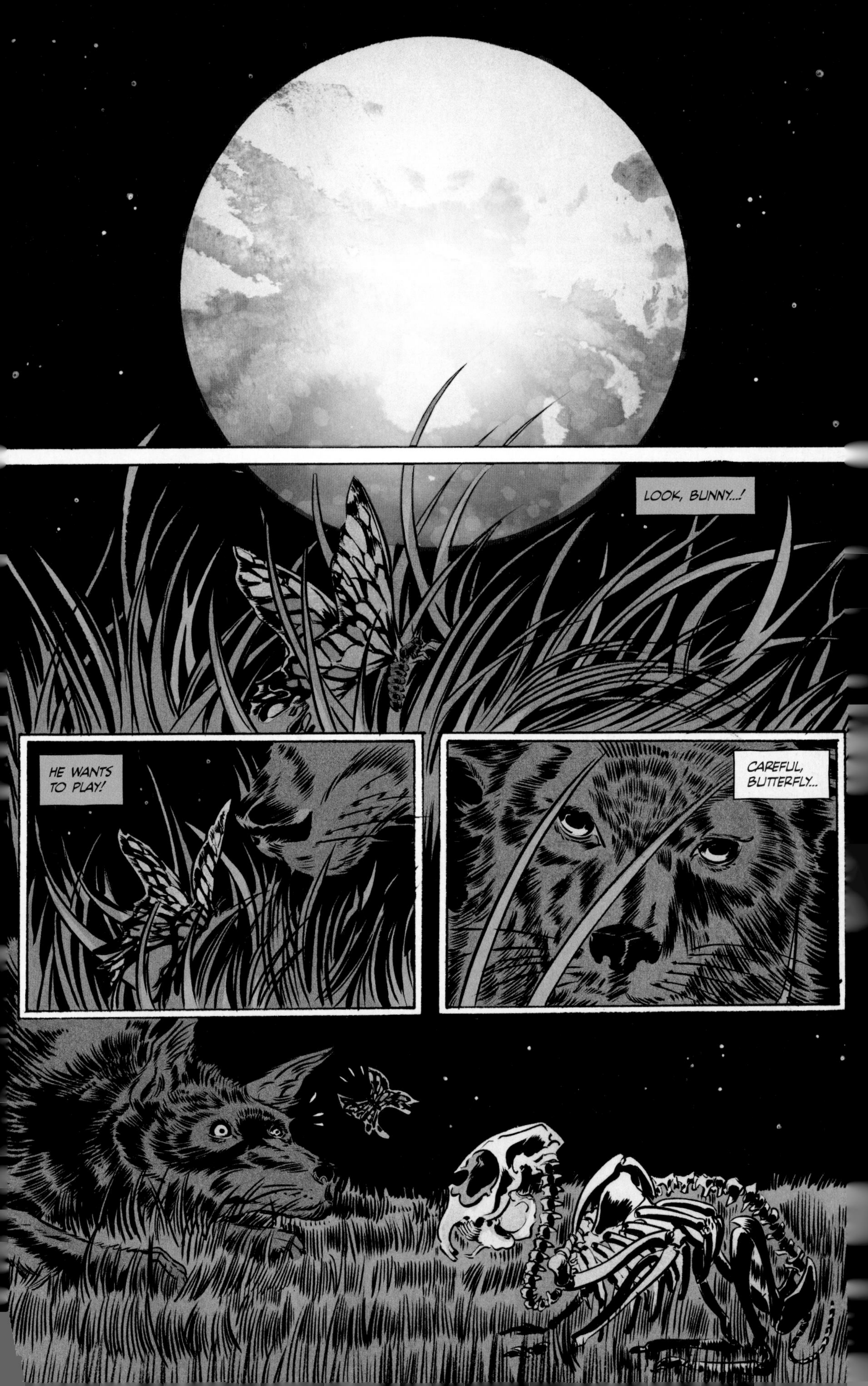
LOOK, BUNNY...!
HE WANTS TO PLAY!
CAREFUL, BUTTERFLY...

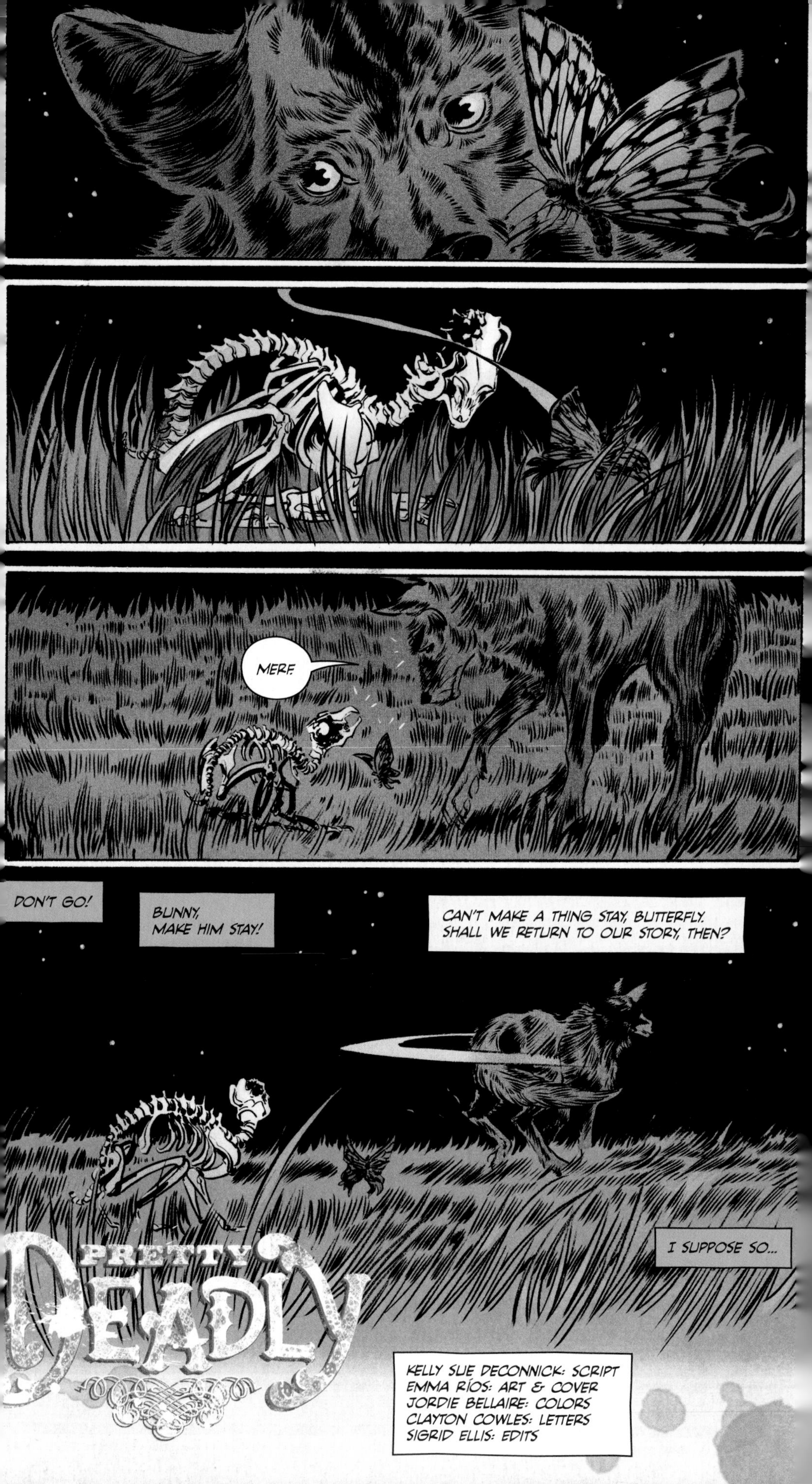
MERF.
DON'T GO!
BUNNY, MAKE HIM STAY!
CAN'T MAKE A THING STAY, BUTTERFLY. SHALL WE RETURN TO OUR STORY, THEN?
I SUPPOSE SO...
PRETTY DEADLY
KELLY SUE DECONNICK: SCRIPT
EMMA RÍOS: ART & COVER
JORDIE BELLAIRE: COLORS
CLAYTON COWLES: LETTERS
SIGRID ELLIS: EDITS

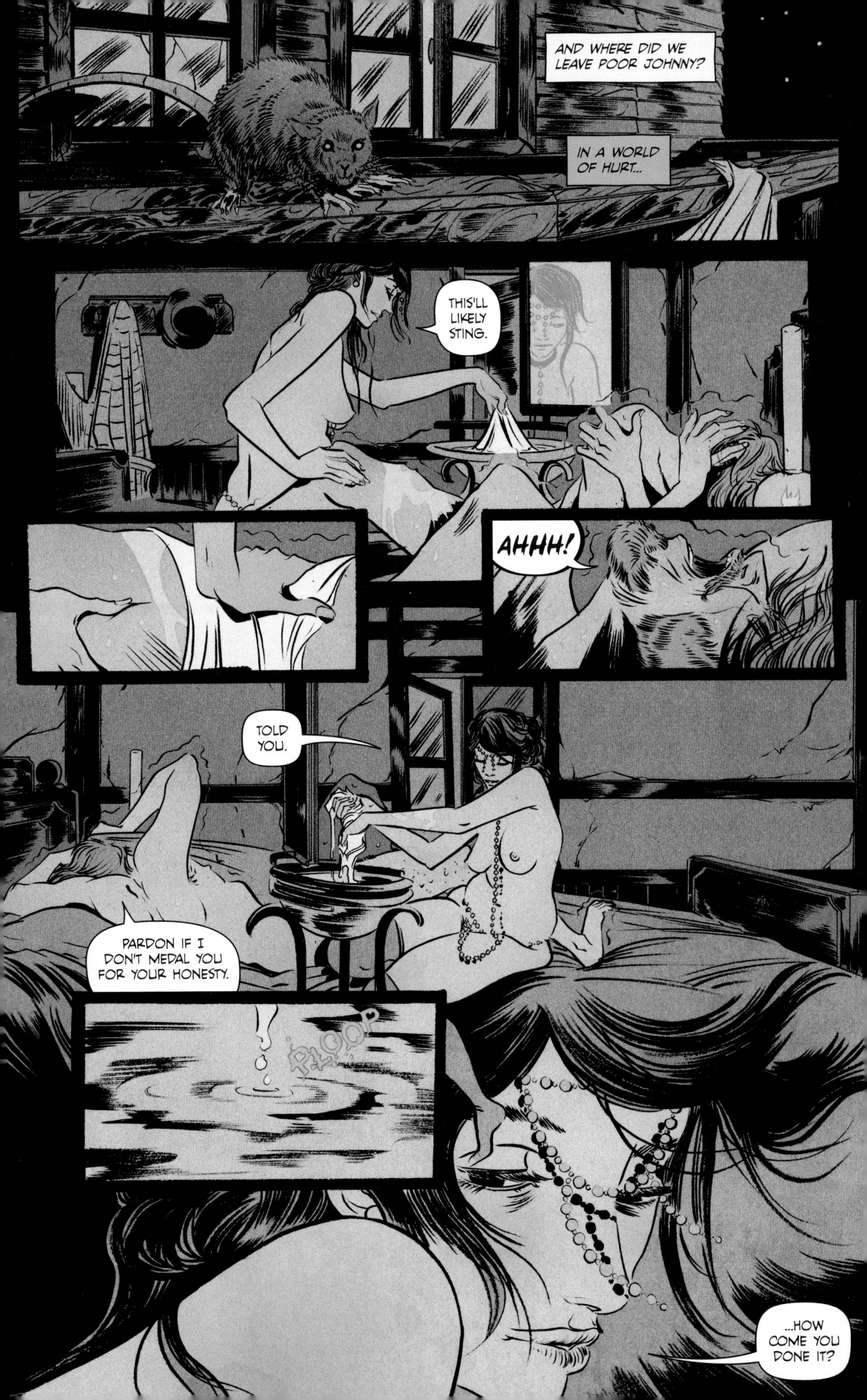
AND WHERE DID WE LEAVE POOR JOHNNY?
IN A WORLD OF HURT...
THIS'LL LIKELY STING.
AHHH!
TOLD YOU.
PARDON IF I DON'T MEDAL YOU FOR YOUR HONESTY.
...HOW COME YOU DONE IT?

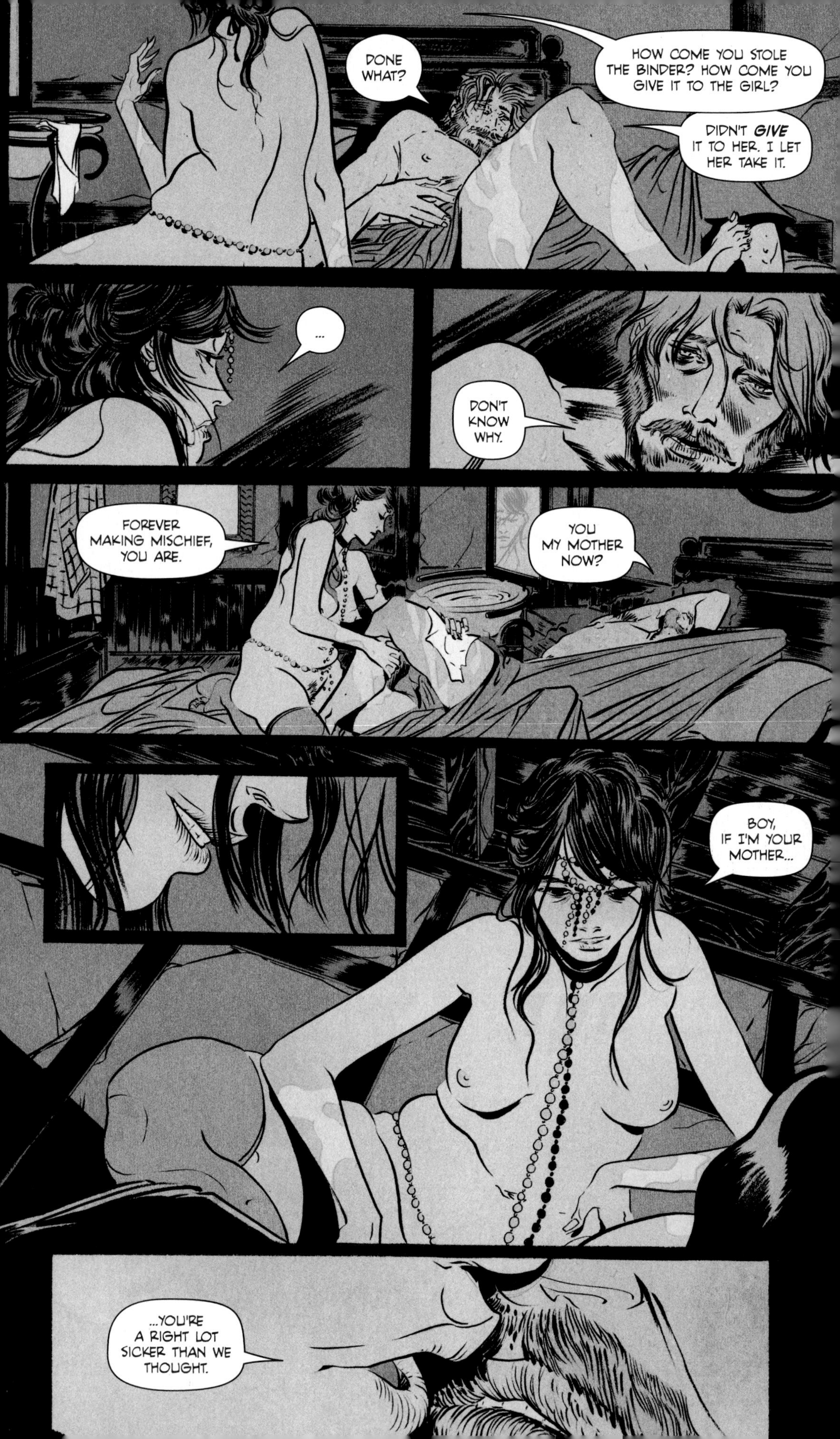
DONE WHAT?
HOW COME YOU STOLE THE BINDER? HOW COME YOU GIVE IT TO THE GIRL?
DIDN'T GIVE IT TO HER. I LET HER TAKE IT.
...
DON'T KNOW WHY.
FOREVER MAKING MISCHIEF, YOU ARE.
YOU MY MOTHER NOW?
BOY, IF I'M YOUR MOTHER...
...YOU'RE A RIGHT LOT SICKER THAN WE THOUGHT.

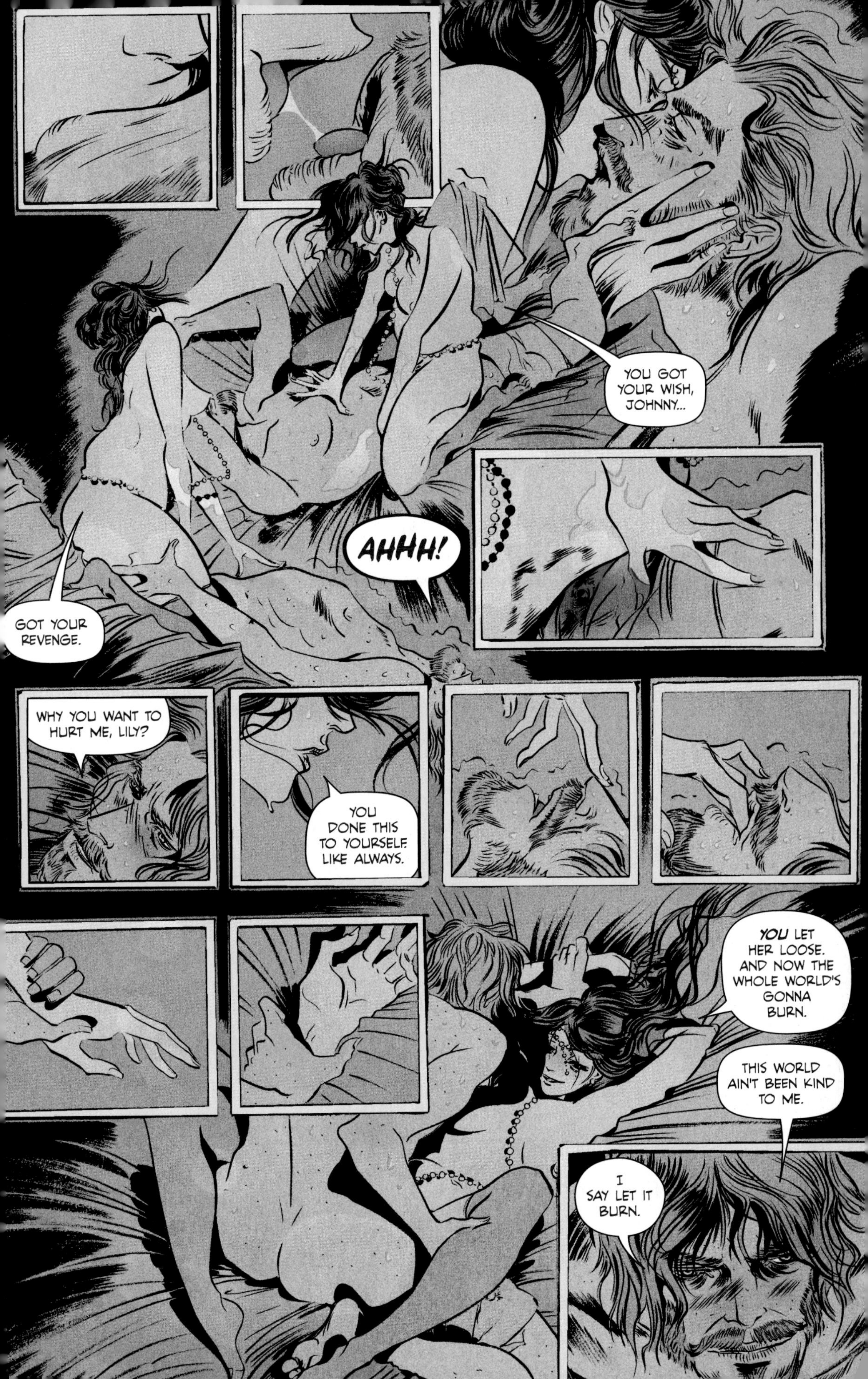
YOU GOT YOUR WISH, JOHNNY...
GOT YOUR REVENGE.
AHHH!
WHY YOU WANT TO HURT ME, LILY?
YOU DONE THIS TO YOURSELF. LIKE ALWAYS.
YOU LET HER LOOSE. AND NOW THE WHOLE WORLD'S GONNA BURN.
THIS WORLD AIN'T BEEN KIND TO ME.
I SAY LET IT BURN.

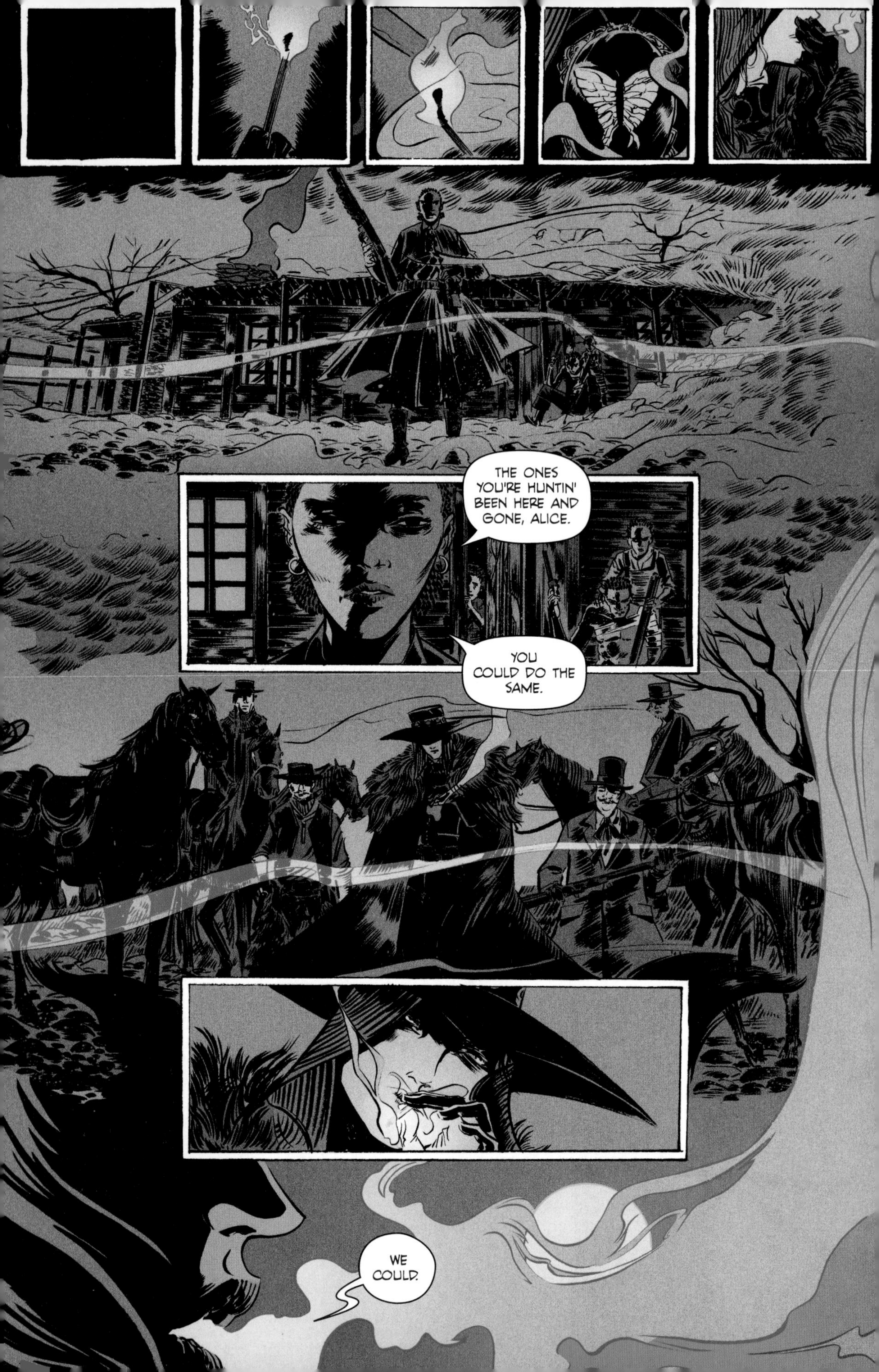
THE ONES YOU'RE HUNTIN' BEEN HERE AND GONE, ALICE.
YOU COULD DO THE SAME.
WE COULD.

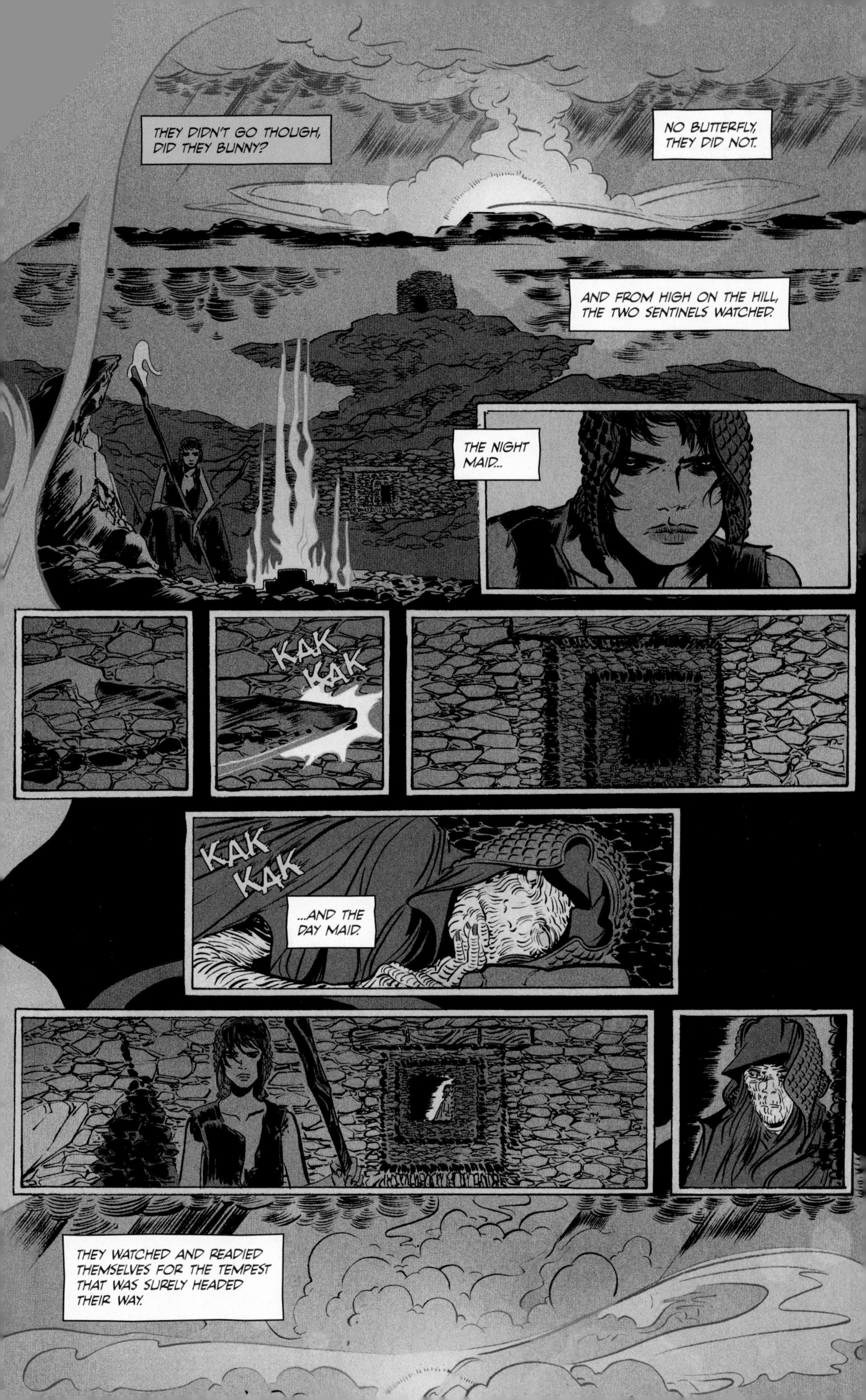
THEY DIDN'T GO THOUGH, DID THEY BUNNY?
NO BUTTERFLY, THEY DID NOT.
AND FROM HIGH ON THE HILL, THE TWO SENTINELS WATCHED.
THE NIGHT MAID...
KAK KAK
KAK KAK
...AND THE DAY MAID.
THEY WATCHED AND READIED THEMSELVES FOR THE TEMPEST THAT WAS SURELY HEADED THEIR WAY.

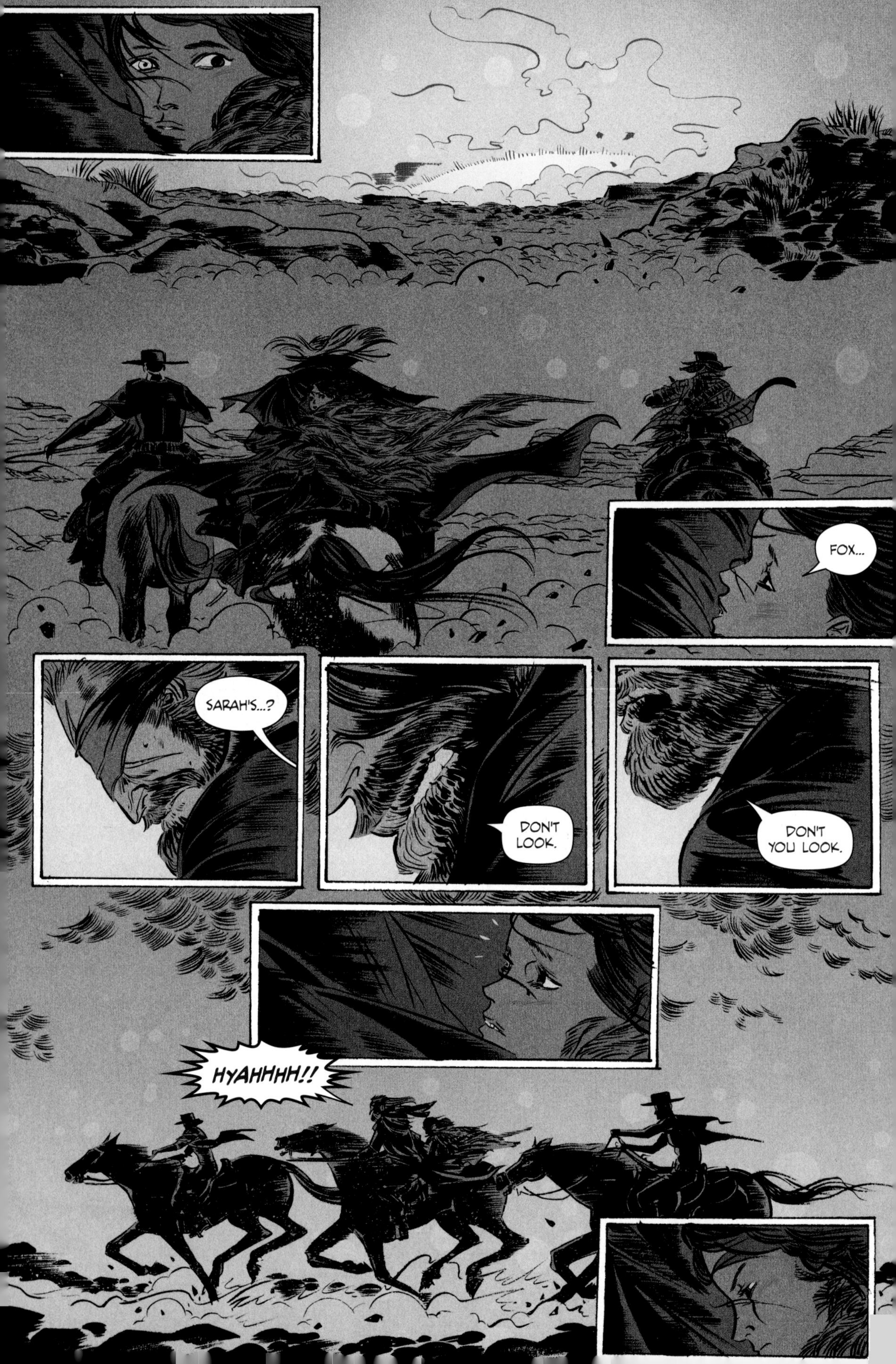
FOX...
SARAH'S...?
DON'T LOOK.
DON'T YOU LOOK.
HYAHHHH!!

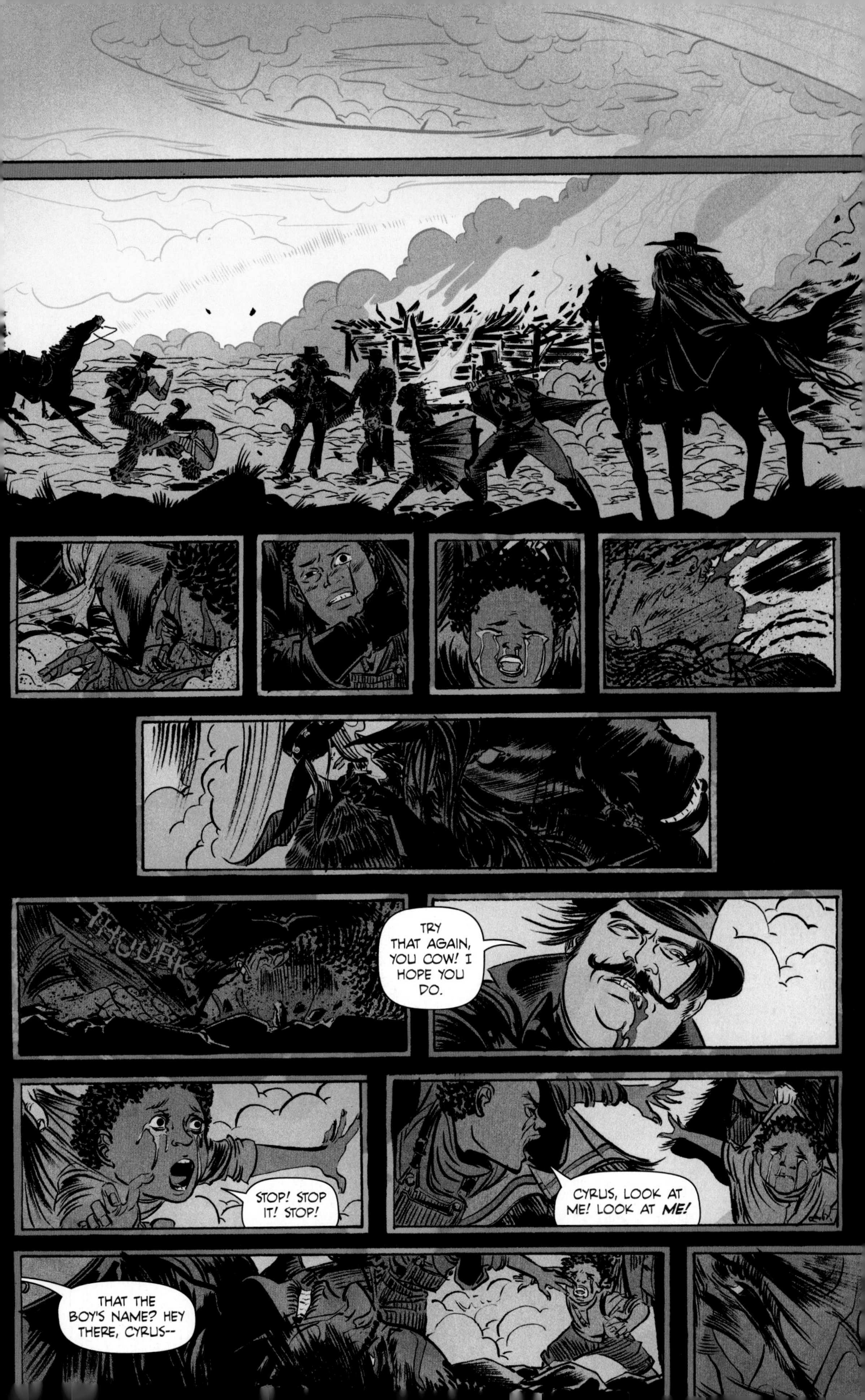
THUURK
TRY THAT AGAIN, YOU COW! I HOPE YOU DO.
STOP! STOP IT! STOP!
CYRUS, LOOK AT ME! LOOK AT ME!
THAT THE BOY'S NAME? HEY THERE, CYRUS--

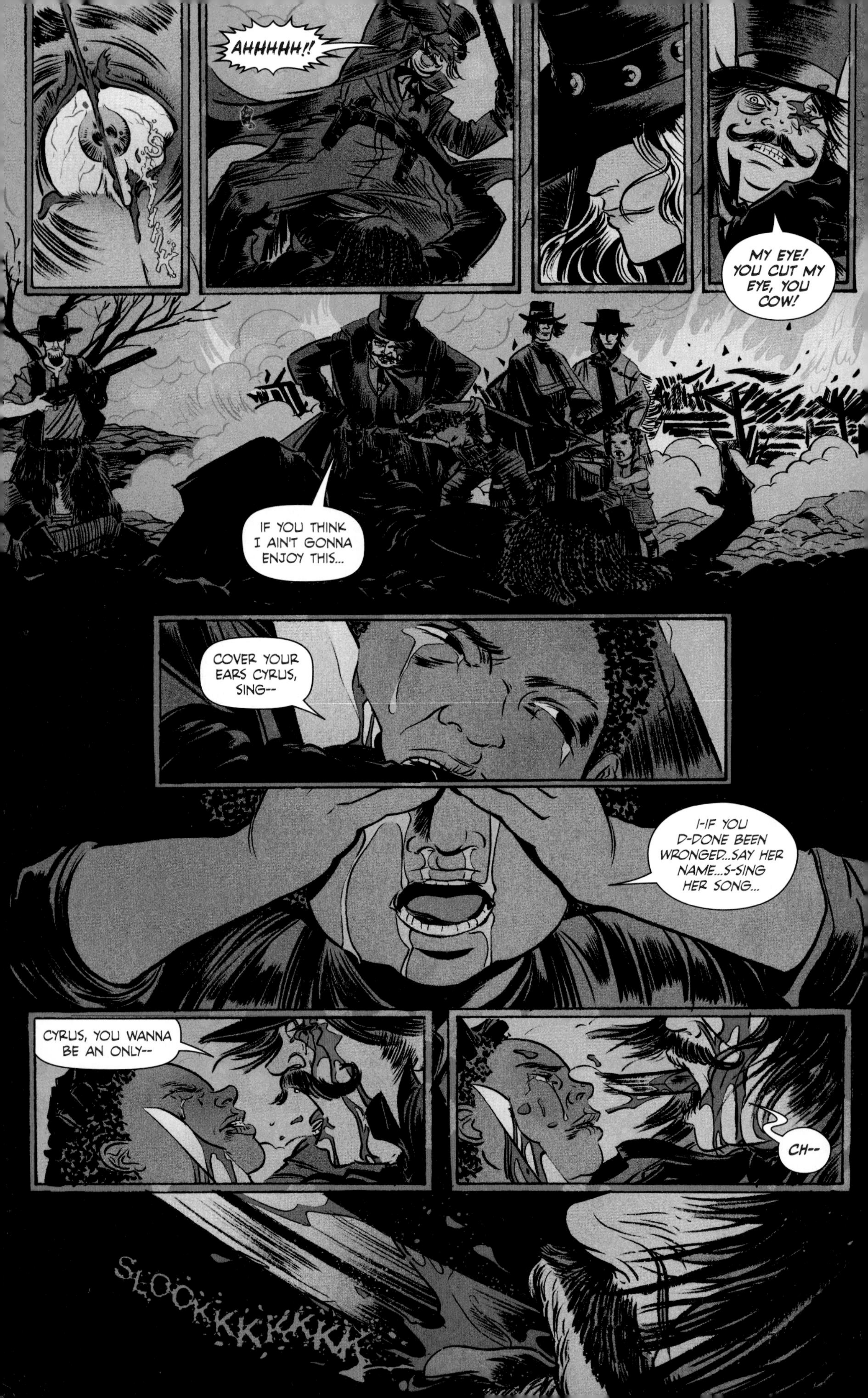
AHHHHH!!
MY EYE! YOU CUT MY EYE, YOU COW!
IF YOU THINK I AIN'T GONNA ENJOY THIS...
COVER YOUR EARS CYRUS, SING--
I-IF YOU D-DONE BEEN WRONGED...SAY HER NAME...S-SING HER SONG...
CYRUS, YOU WANNA BE AN ONLY--
CH--
SLOOKKKKKKK

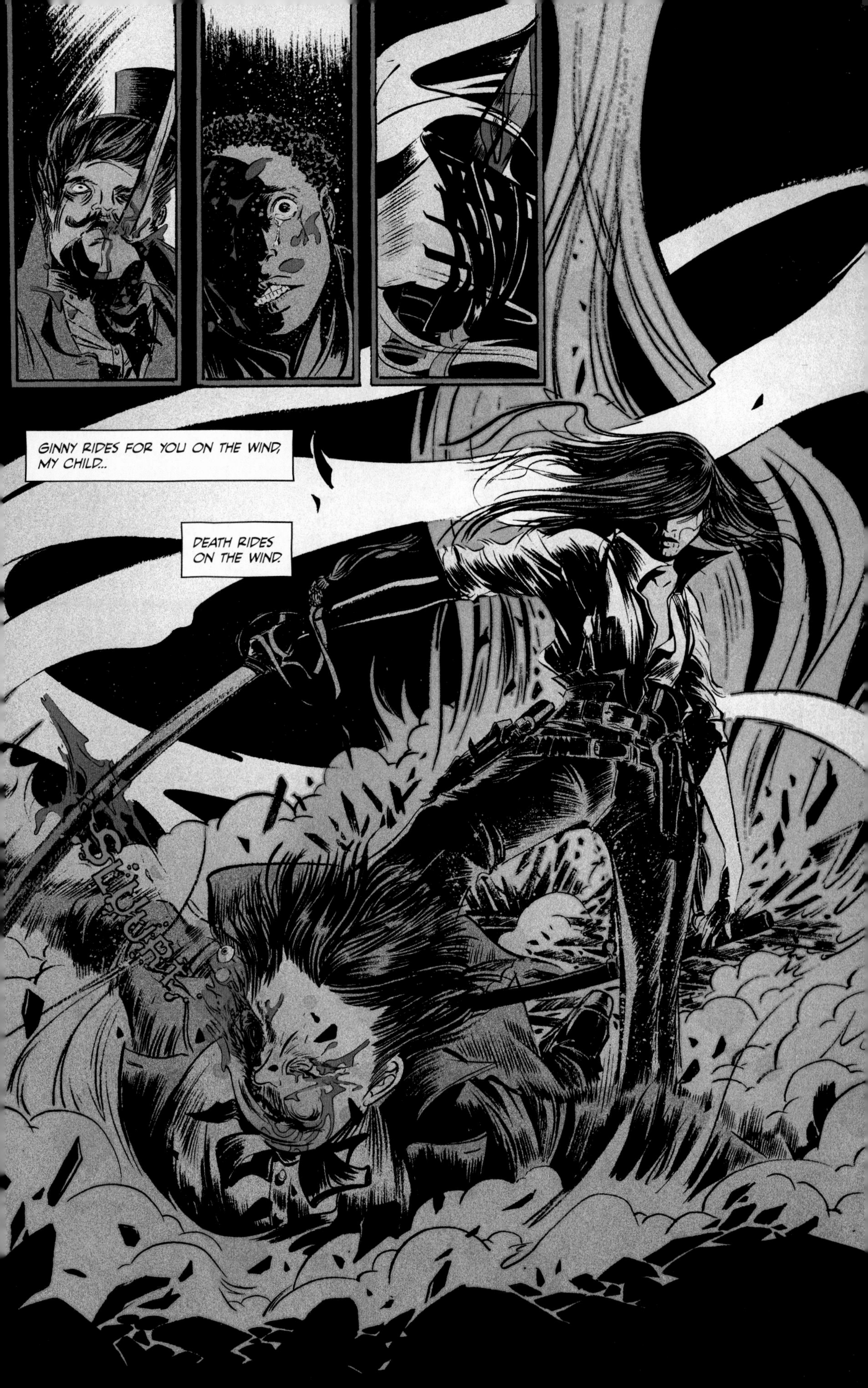
GINNY RIDES FOR YOU ON THE WIND, MY CHILD...
DEATH RIDES ON THE WIND.

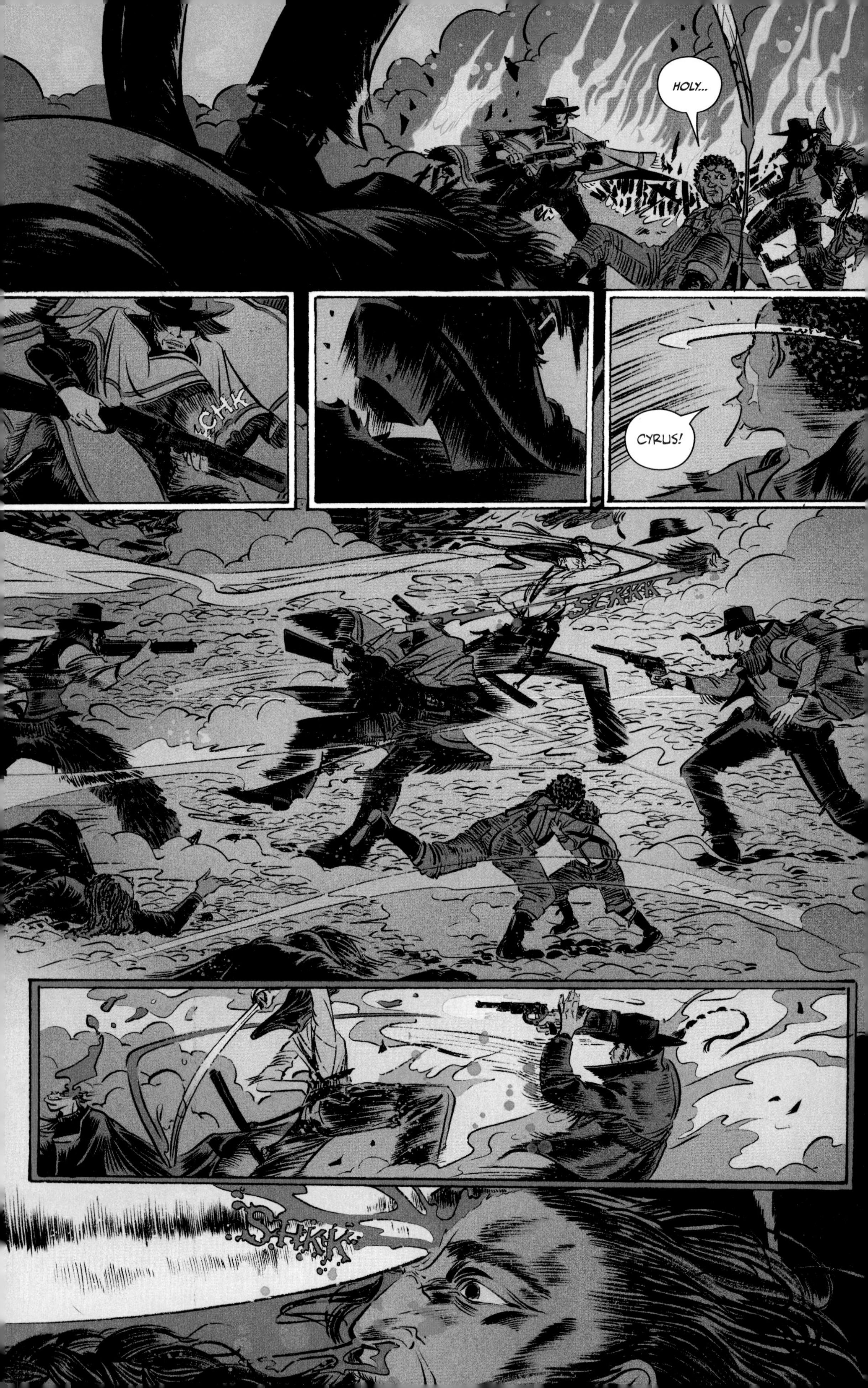
HOLY...
CHK
CYRUS!
SCRKK
SHKK

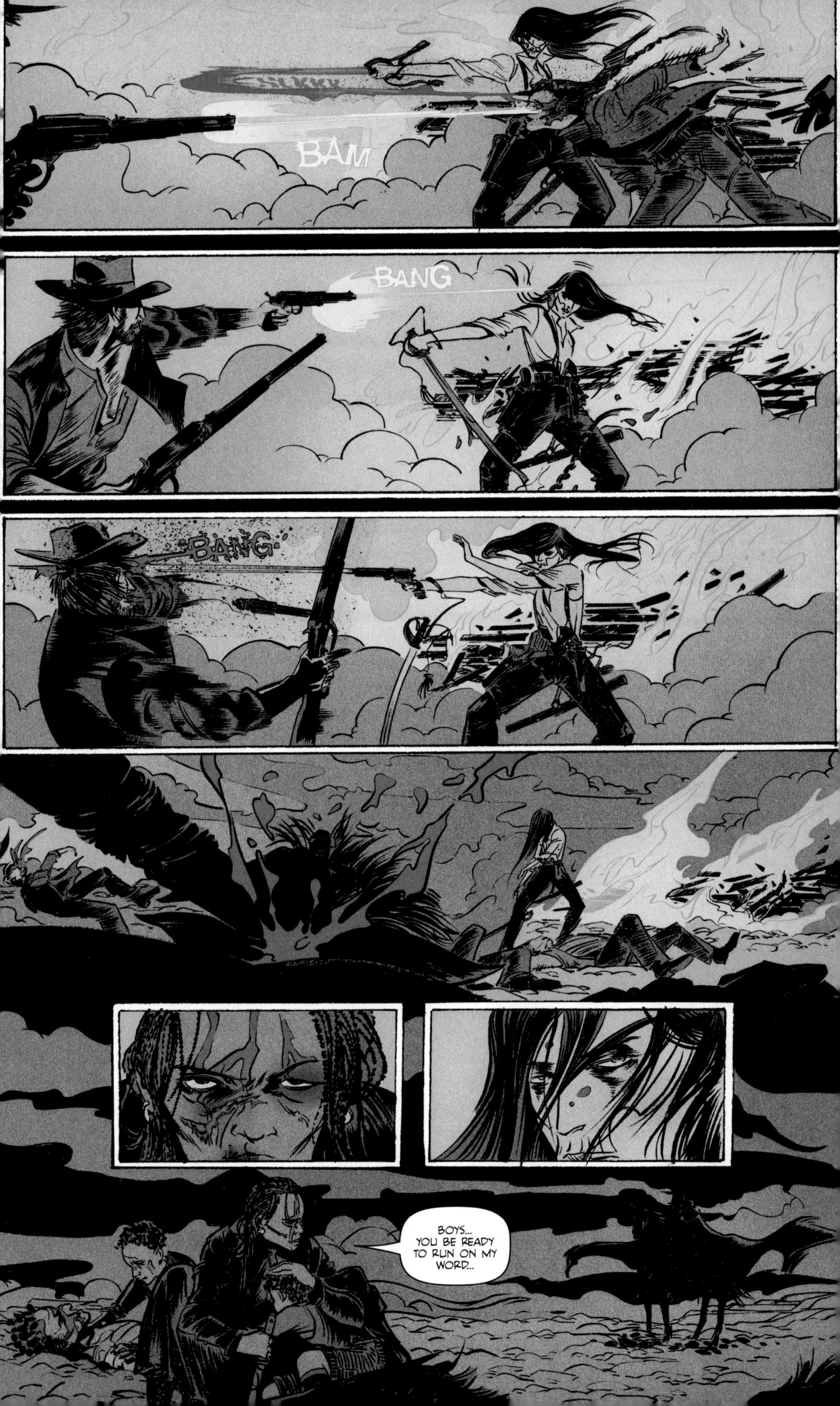

SHKKK
BAM
BANG
BANG
BOYS... YOU BE READY TO RUN ON MY WORD...

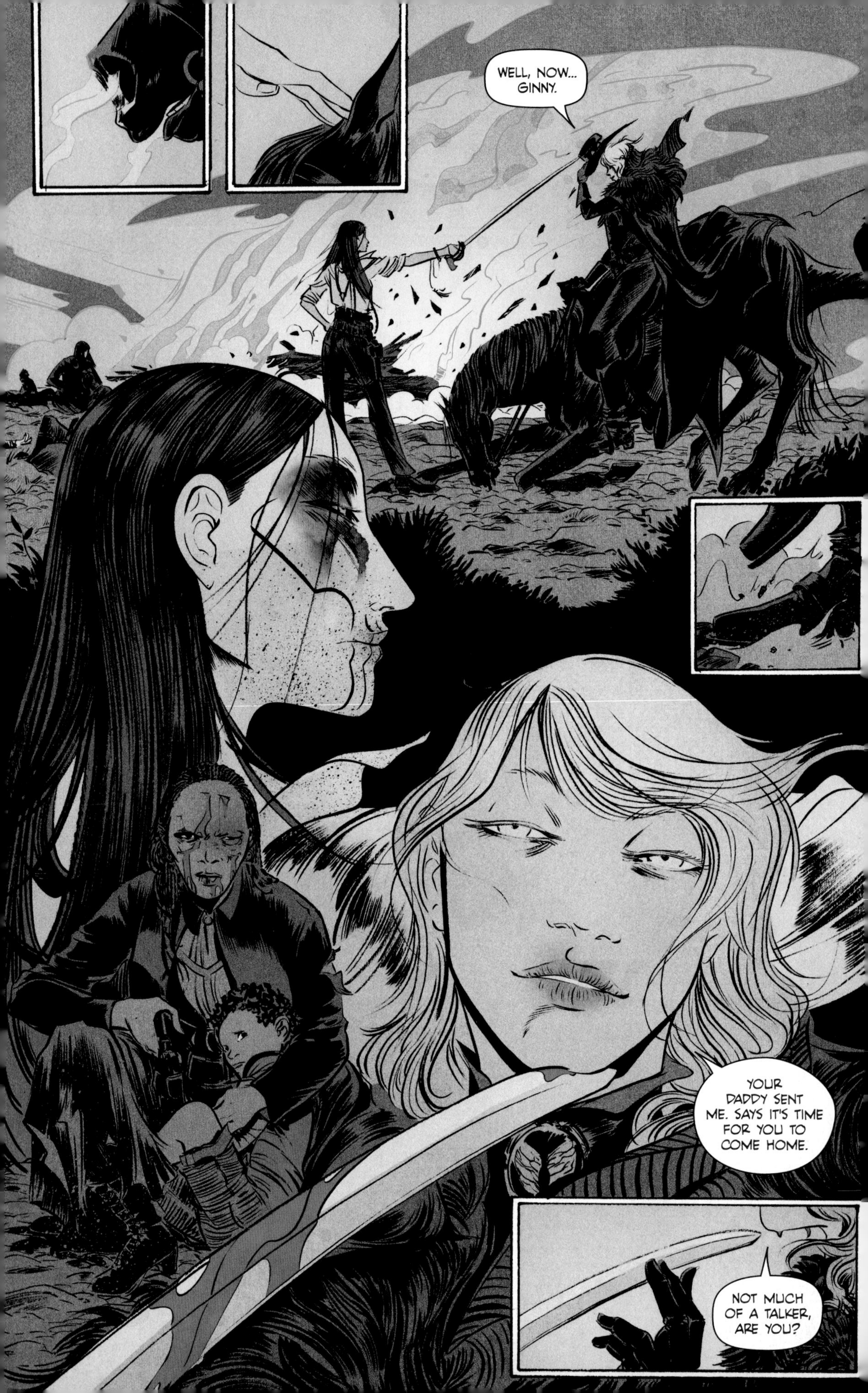
WELL, NOW... GINNY.
YOUR DADDY SENT ME. SAYS IT'S TIME FOR YOU TO COME HOME.
NOT MUCH OF A TALKER, ARE YOU?

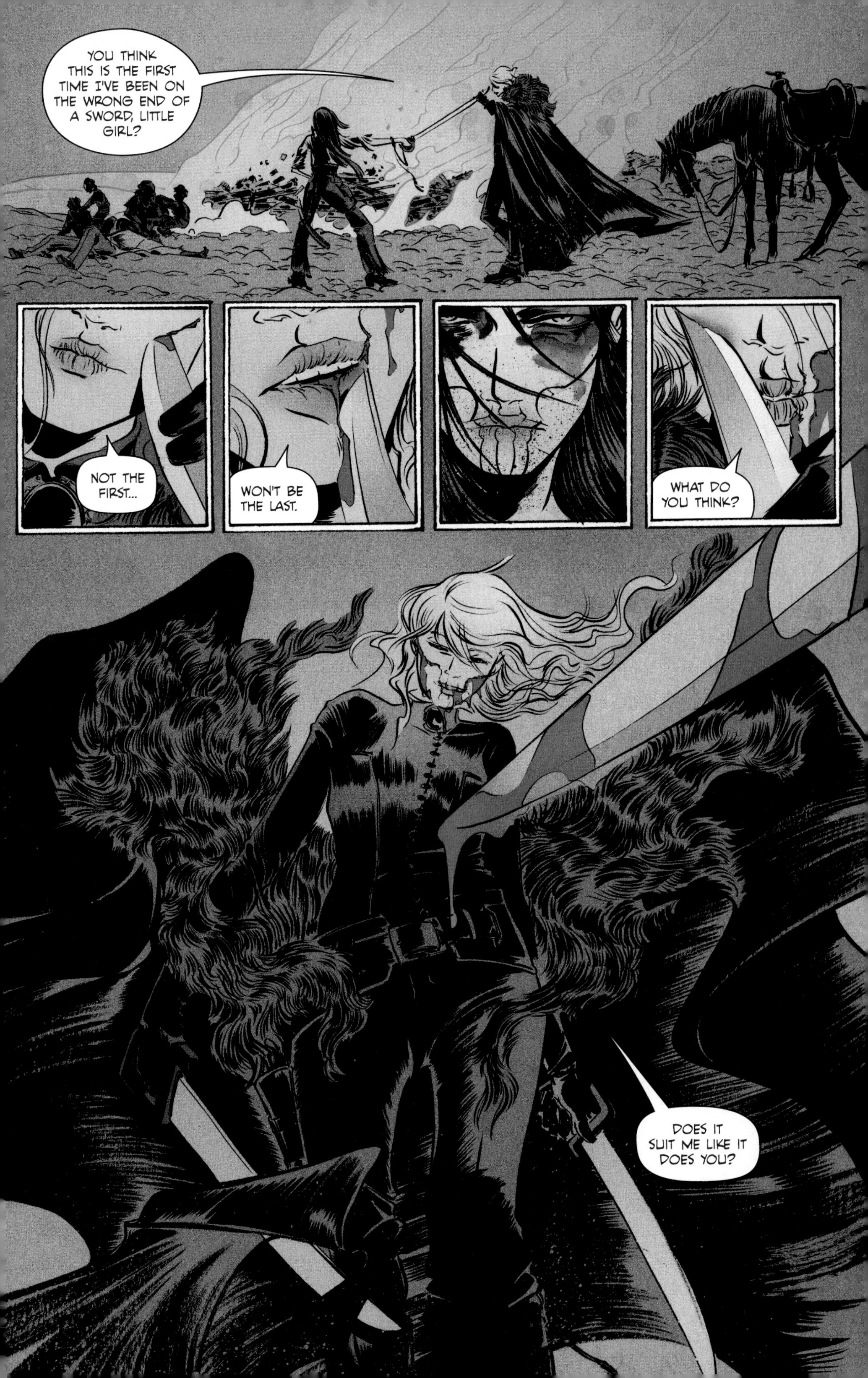
YOU THINK THIS IS THE FIRST TIME I'VE BEEN ON THE WRONG END OF A SWORD, LITTLE GIRL?
NOT THE FIRST...
WON'T BE THE LAST.
WHAT DO YOU THINK?
DOES IT SUIT ME LIKE IT DOES YOU?

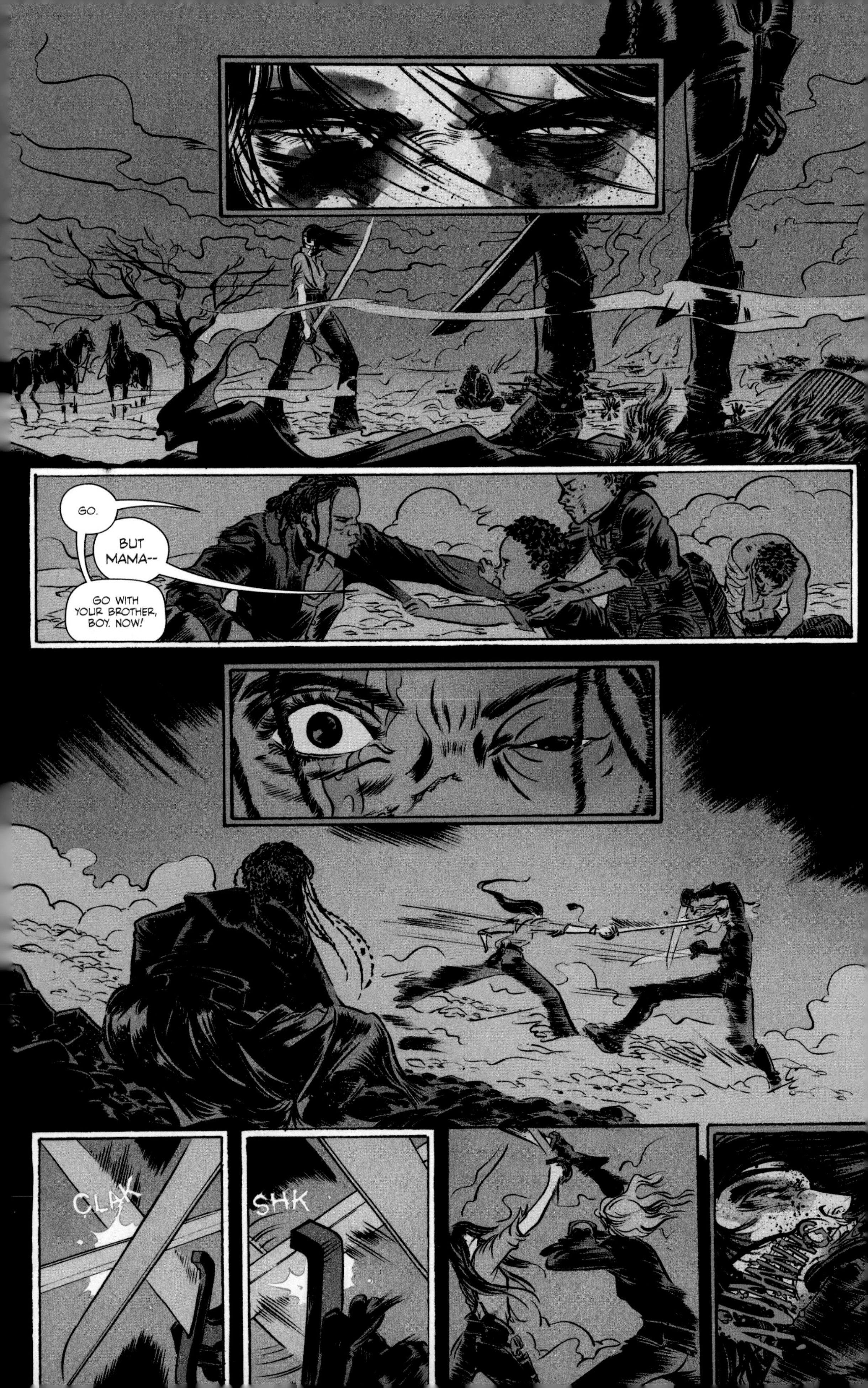
GO.
BUT MAMA--
GO WITH YOUR BROTHER, BOY. NOW!
CLAX
SHK

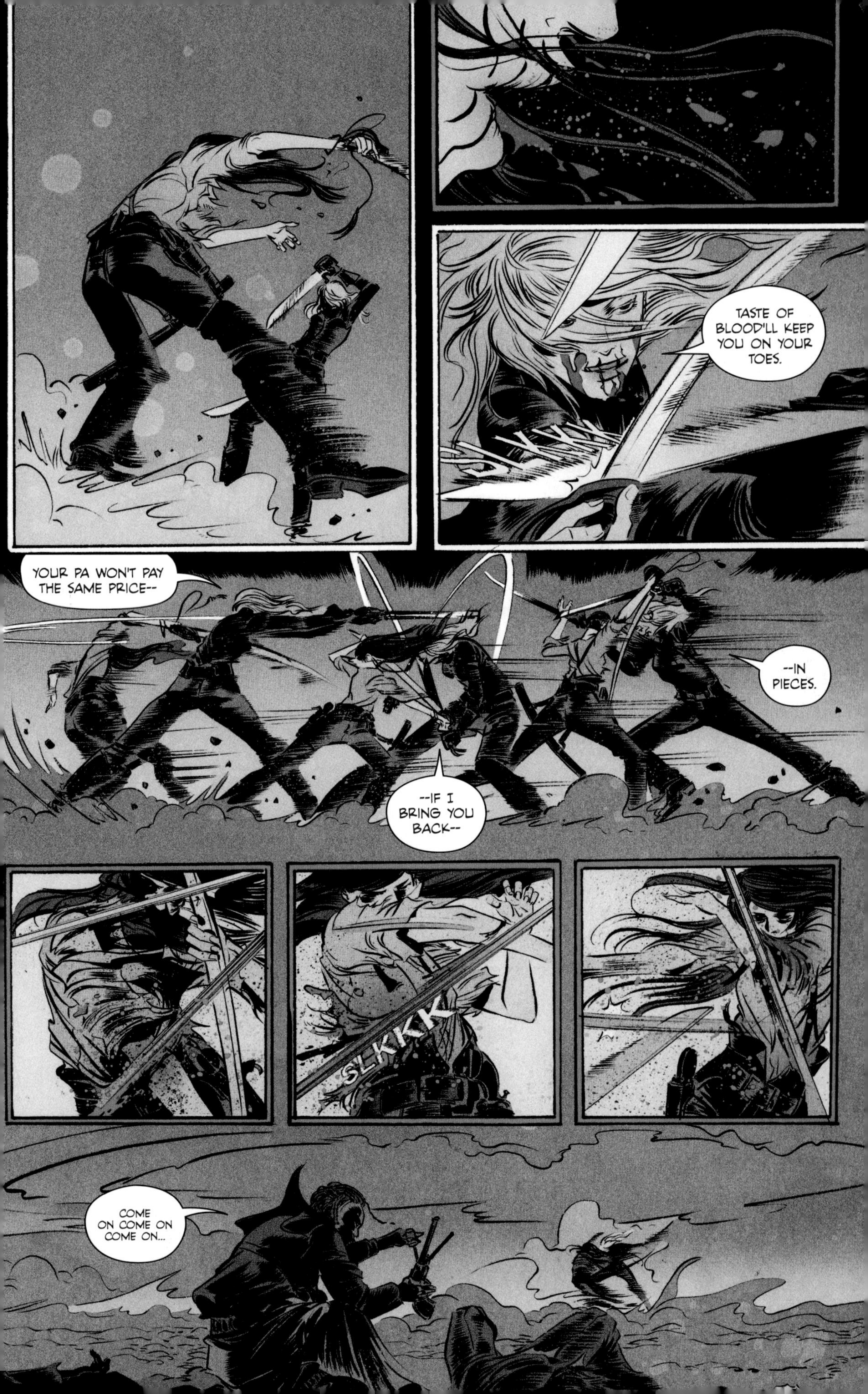
TASTE OF BLOOD'LL KEEP YOU ON YOUR TOES.
YOUR PA WON'T PAY THE SAME PRICE--
--IF I BRING YOU BACK--
--IN PIECES.
SLKKK
COME ON COME ON COME ON...

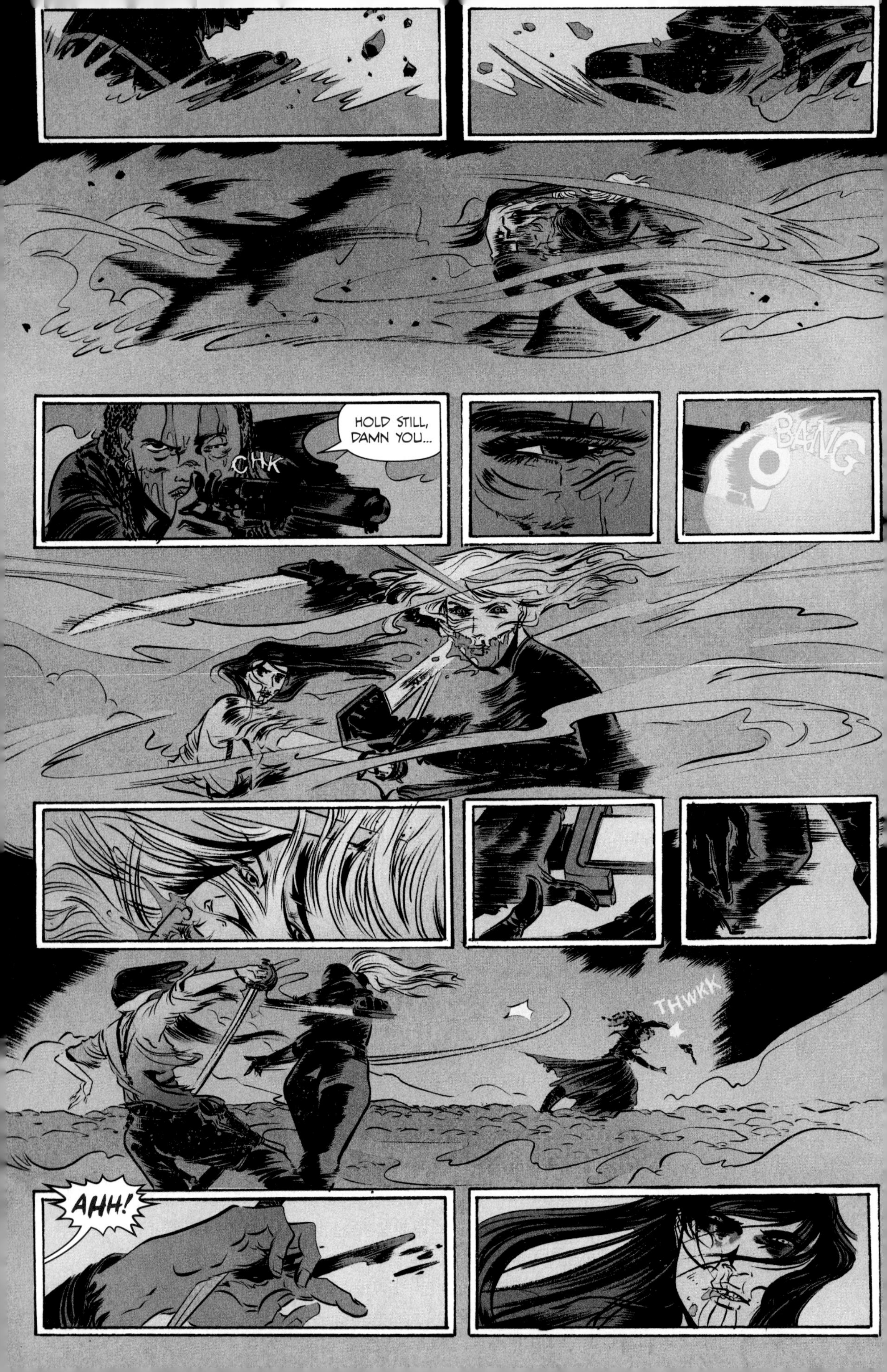
HOLD STILL, DAMN YOU...
CHK
BANG
THWKK
AHH!

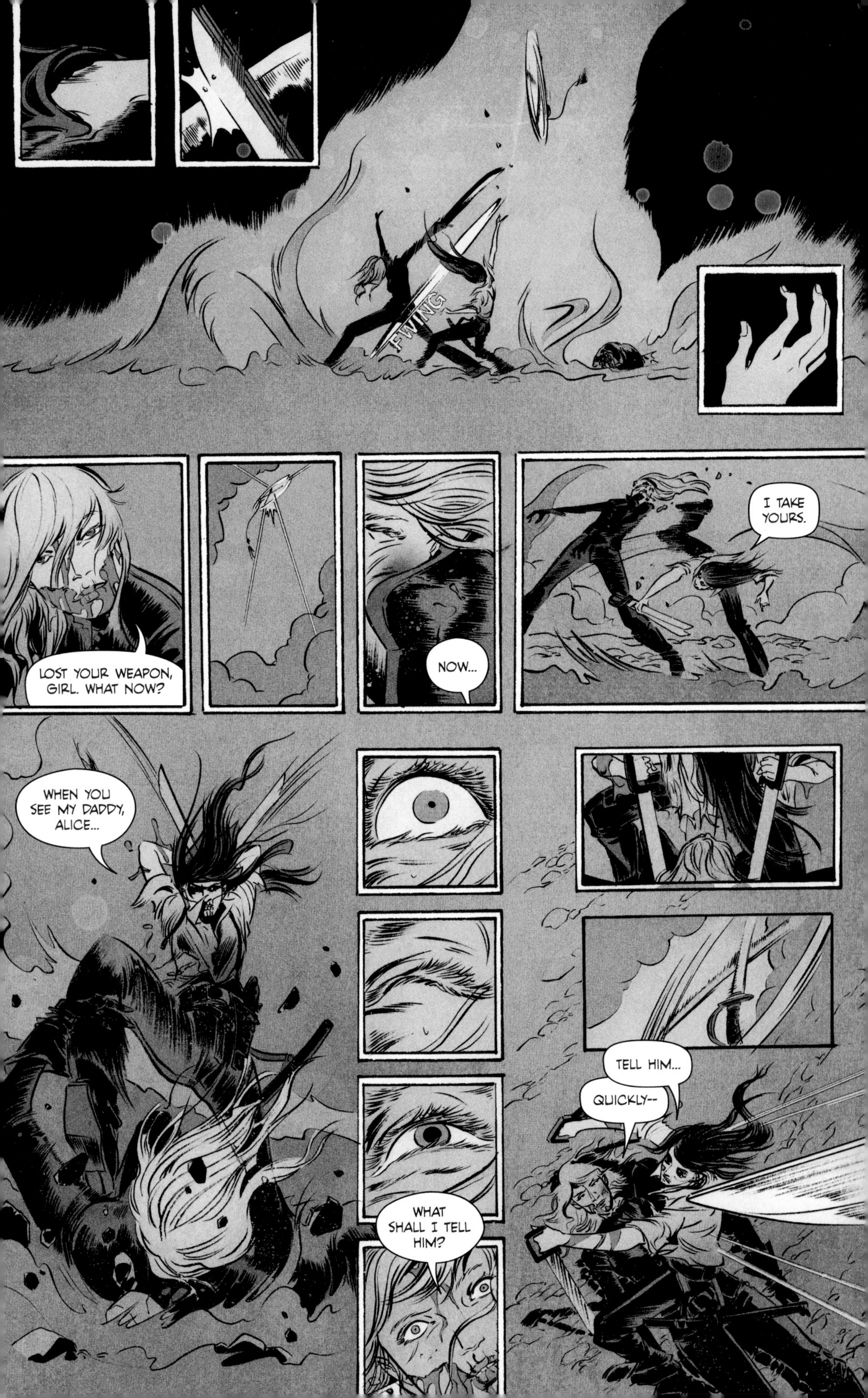
FWING
LOST YOUR WEAPON, GIRL. WHAT NOW?
NOW...
I TAKE YOURS.
WHEN YOU SEE MY DADDY, ALICE...
WHAT SHALL I TELL HIM?
TELL HIM...
QUICKLY--

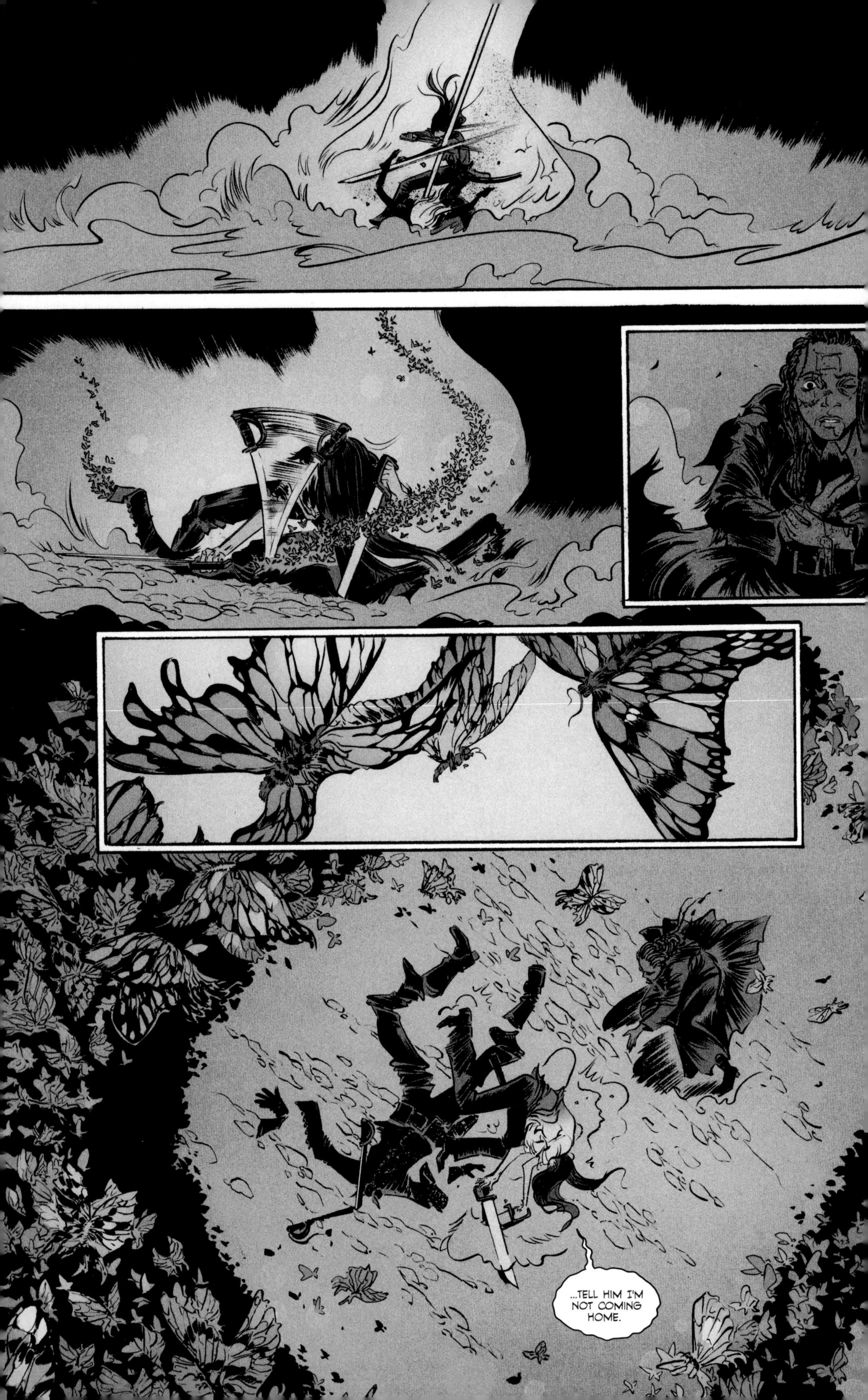
...TELL HIM I'M NOT COMING HOME.

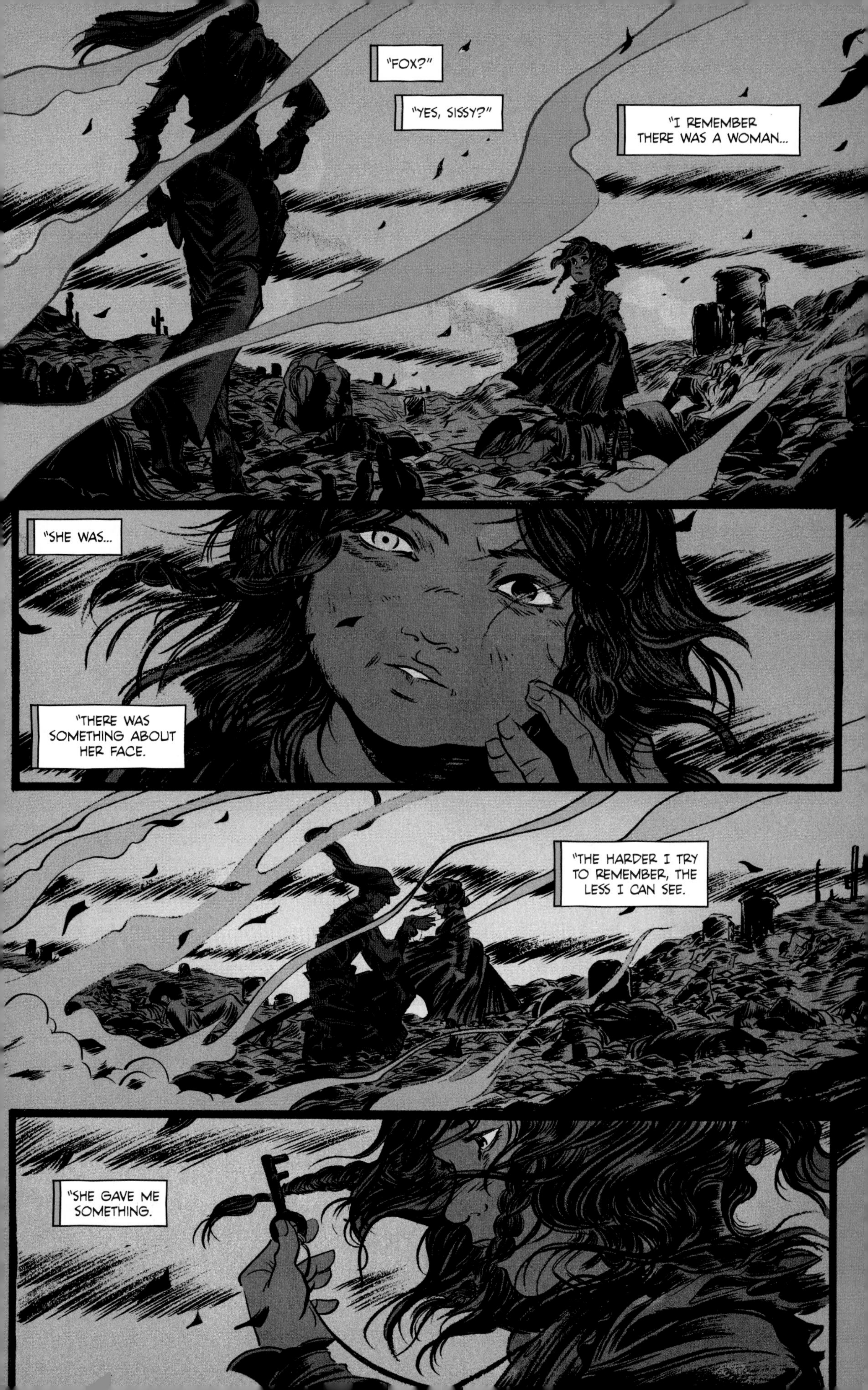
"FOX?"
"YES, SISSY?"
"I REMEMBER THERE WAS A WOMAN...
"SHE WAS...
"THERE WAS SOMETHING ABOUT HER FACE.
"THE HARDER I TRY TO REMEMBER, THE LESS I CAN SEE.
"SHE GAVE ME SOMETHING.

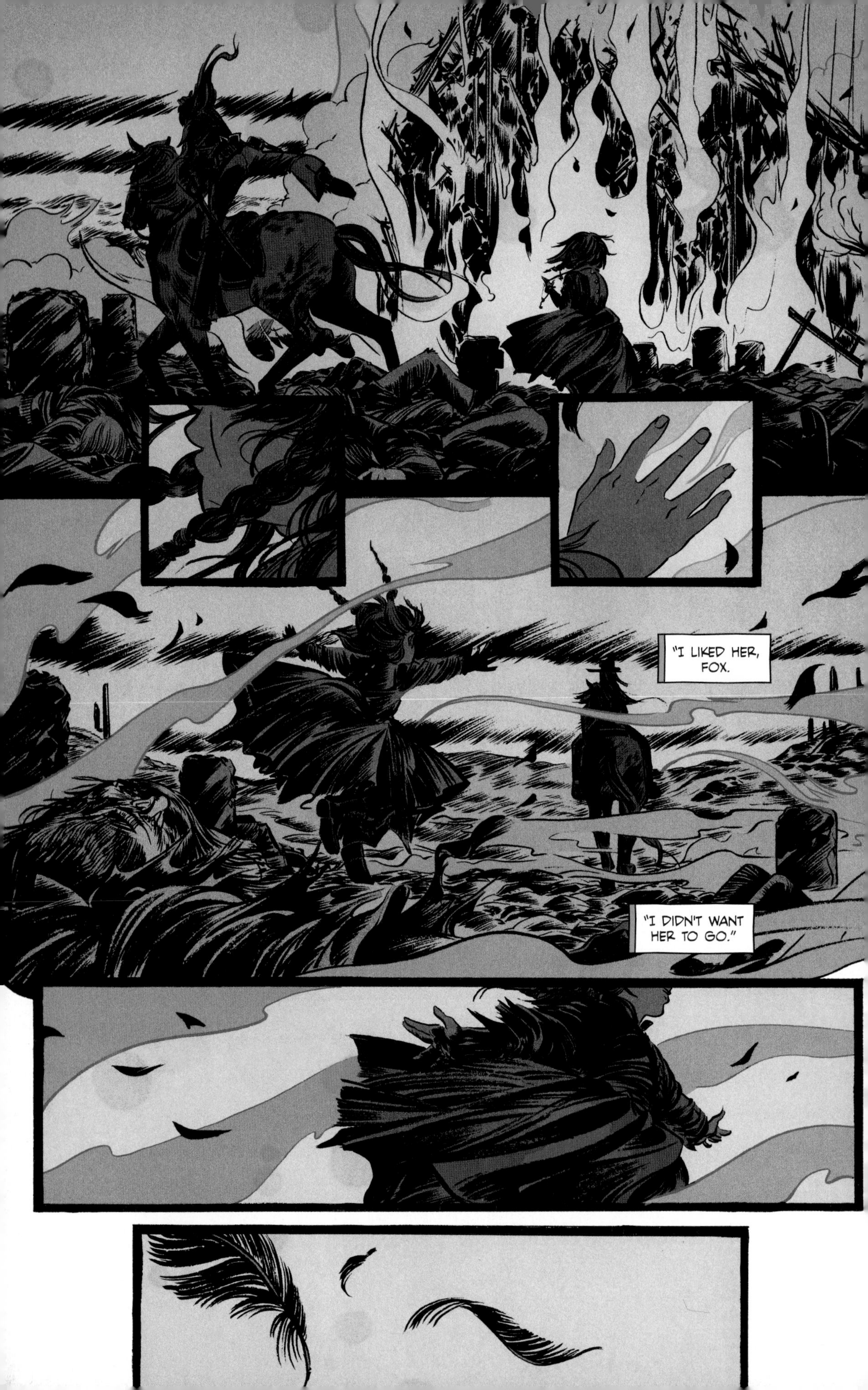
"I LIKED HER, FOX.
"I DIDN'T WANT HER TO GO."

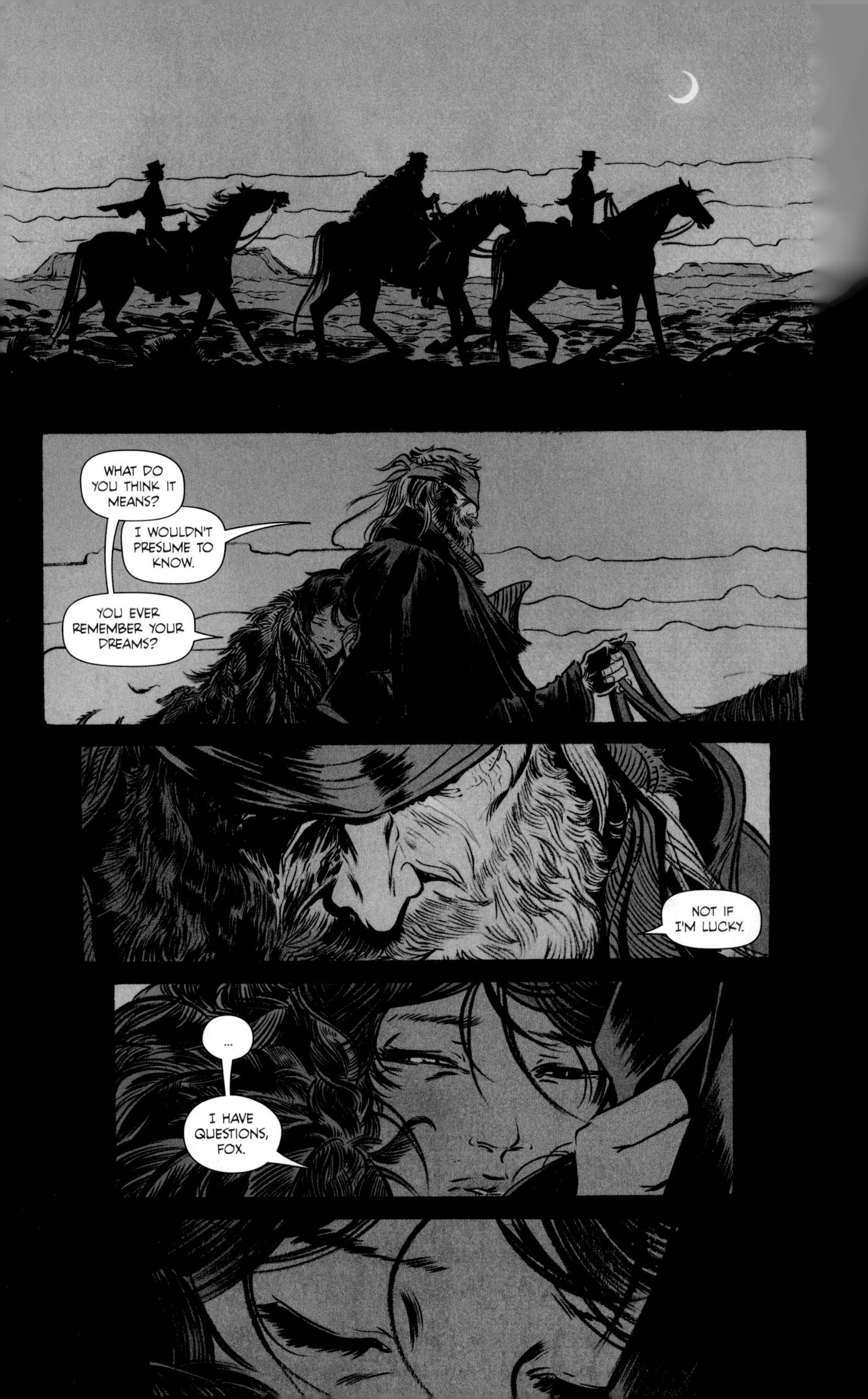
WHAT DO YOU THINK IT MEANS?
I WOULDN'T PRESUME TO KNOW.
YOU EVER REMEMBER YOUR DREAMS?
NOT IF I'M LUCKY.
...
I HAVE QUESTIONS, FOX.

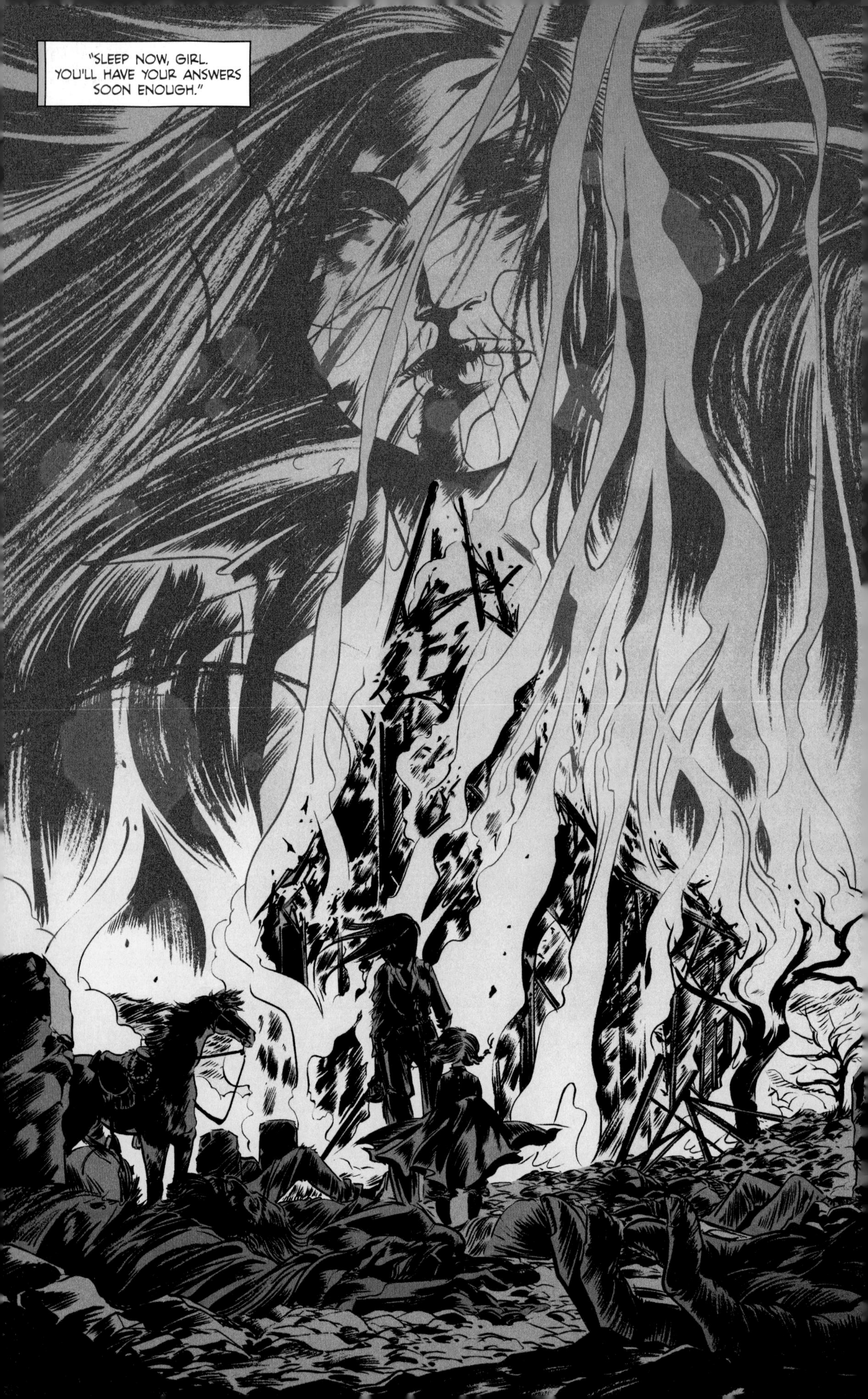
"SLEEP NOW, GIRL. YOU'LL HAVE YOUR ANSWERS SOON ENOUGH."

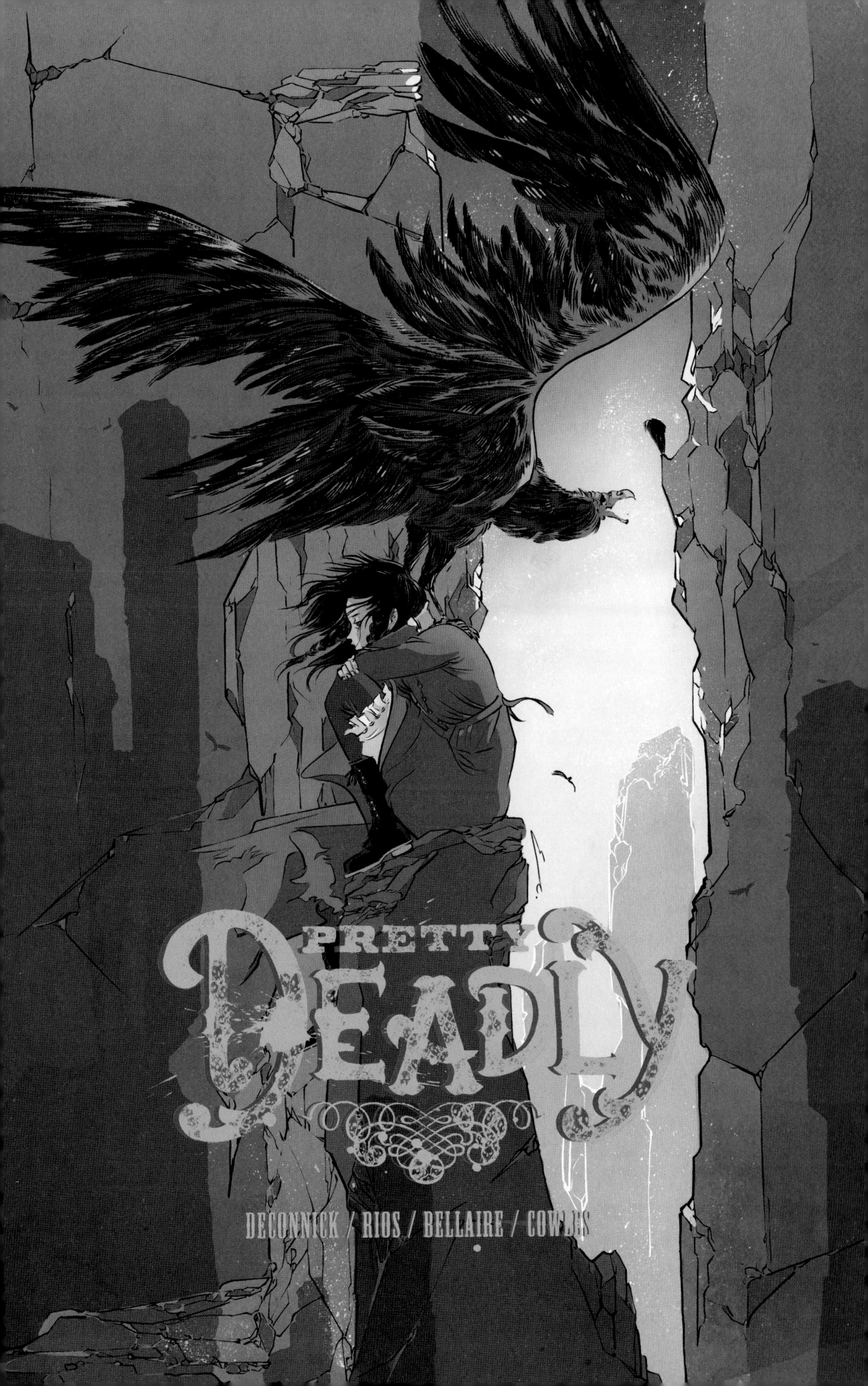
PRETTY DEADLY
DECONNICK / RIOS / BELLAIRE / COWLES

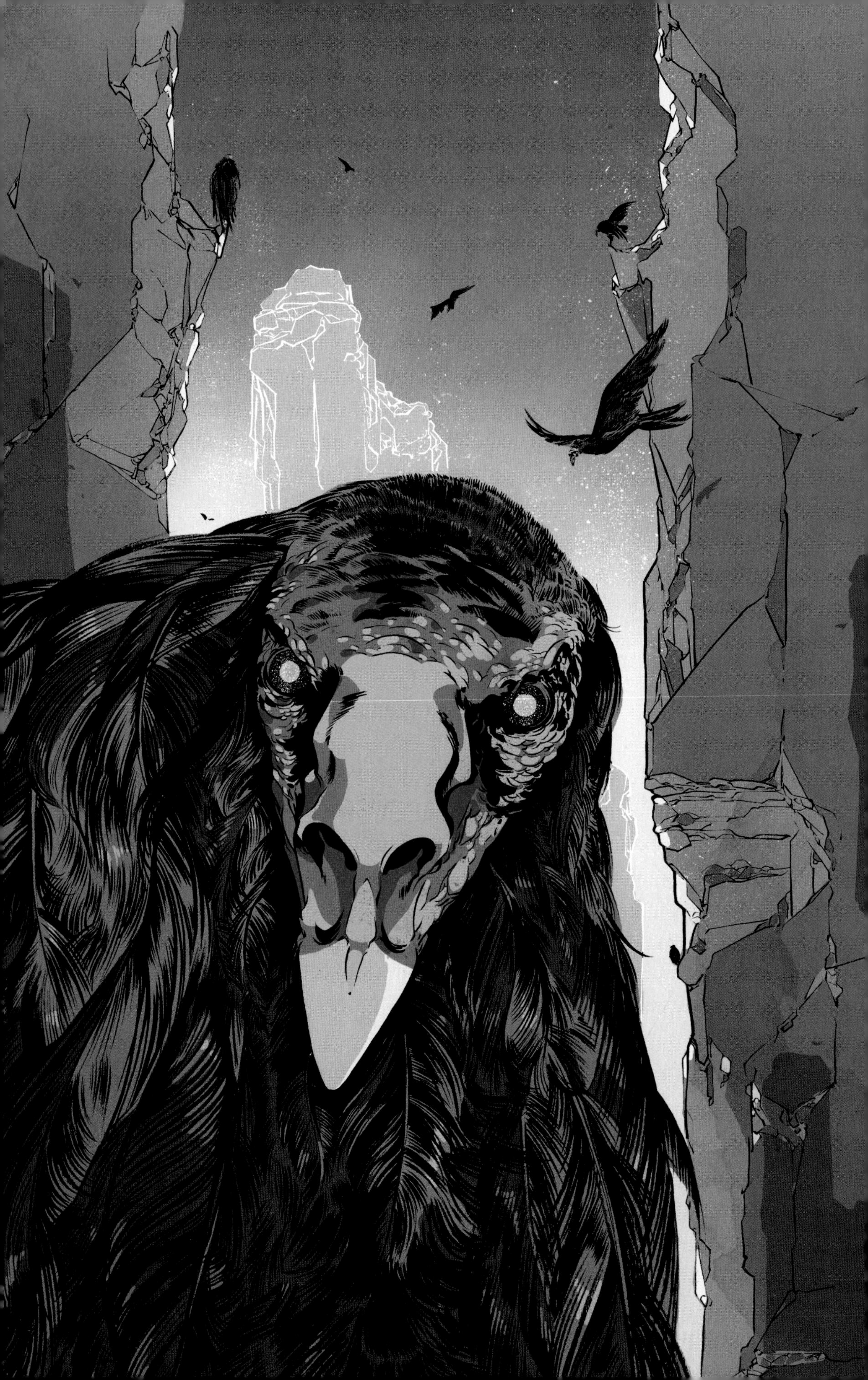

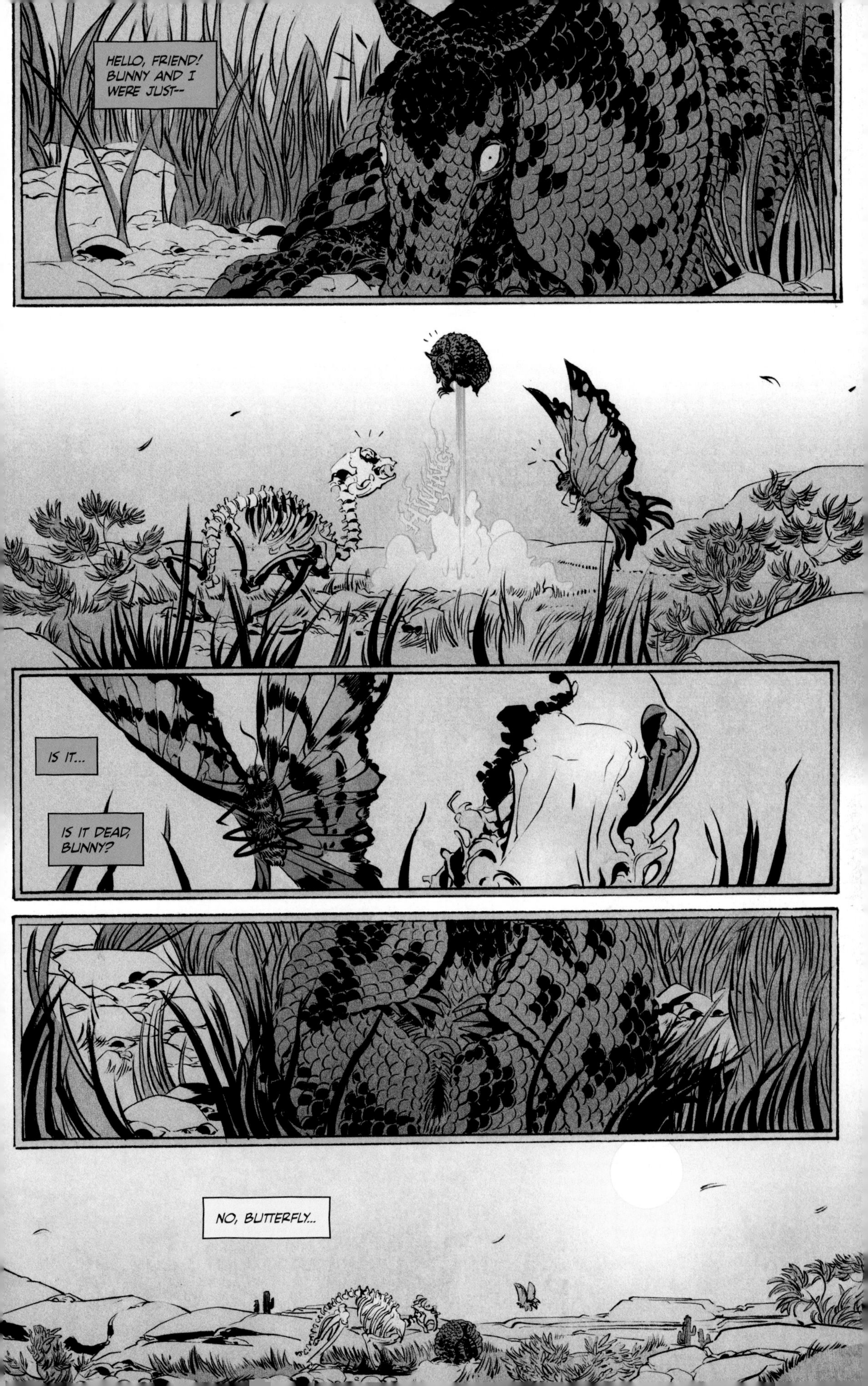
HELLO, FRIEND! BUNNY AND I WERE JUST--
IS IT...
IS IT DEAD, BUNNY?
NO, BUTTERFLY...

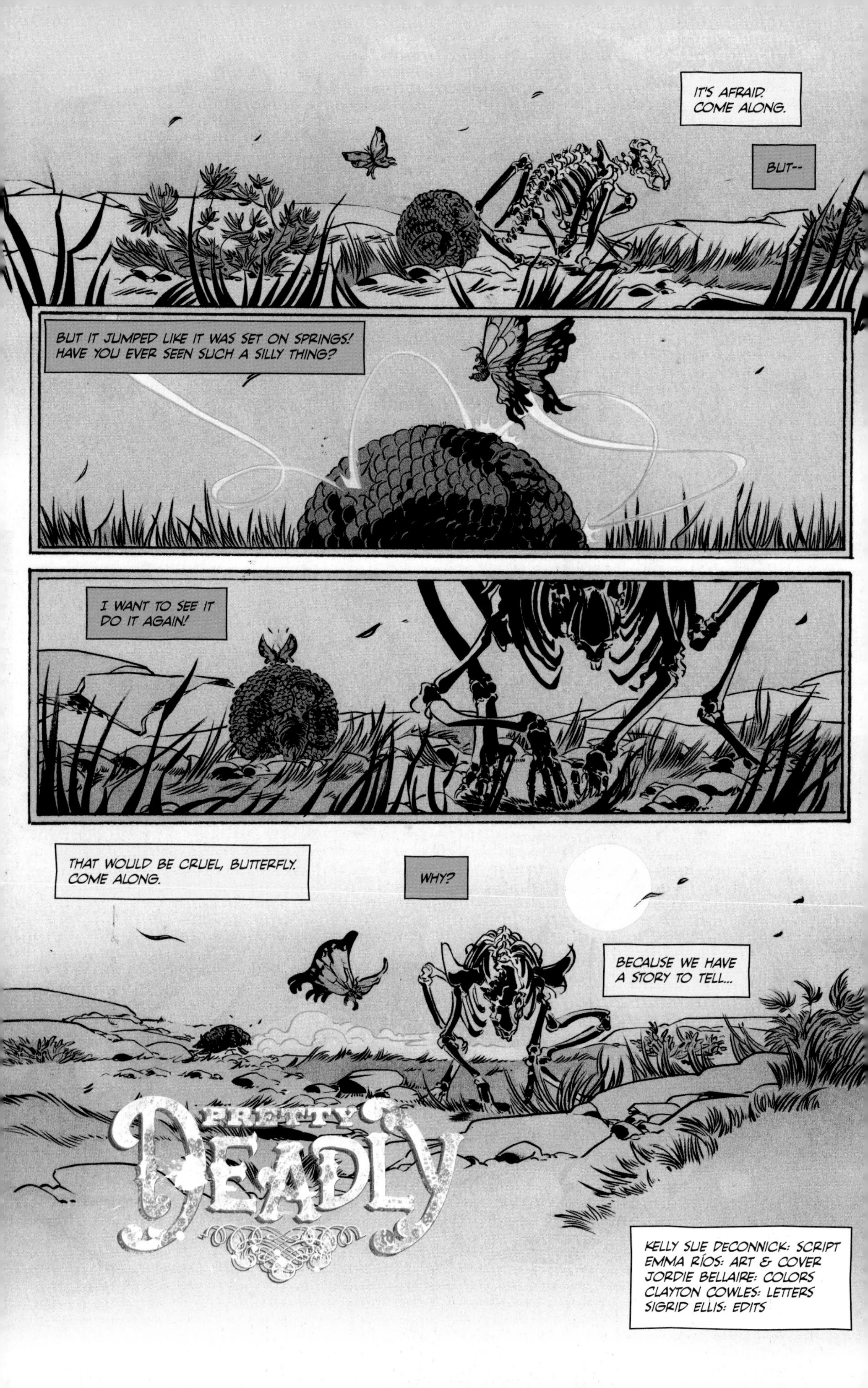
IT'S AFRAID. COME ALONG.
BUT--
BUT IT JUMPED LIKE IT WAS SET ON SPRINGS! HAVE YOU EVER SEEN SUCH A SILLY THING?
I WANT TO SEE IT DO IT AGAIN!
THAT WOULD BE CRUEL, BUTTERFLY. COME ALONG.
WHY?
BECAUSE WE HAVE A STORY TO TELL...
PRETTY DEADLY
KELLY SUE DECONNICK: SCRIPT
EMMA RÍOS: ART & COVER
JORDIE BELLAIRE: COLORS
CLAYTON COWLES: LETTERS
SIGRID ELLIS: EDITS

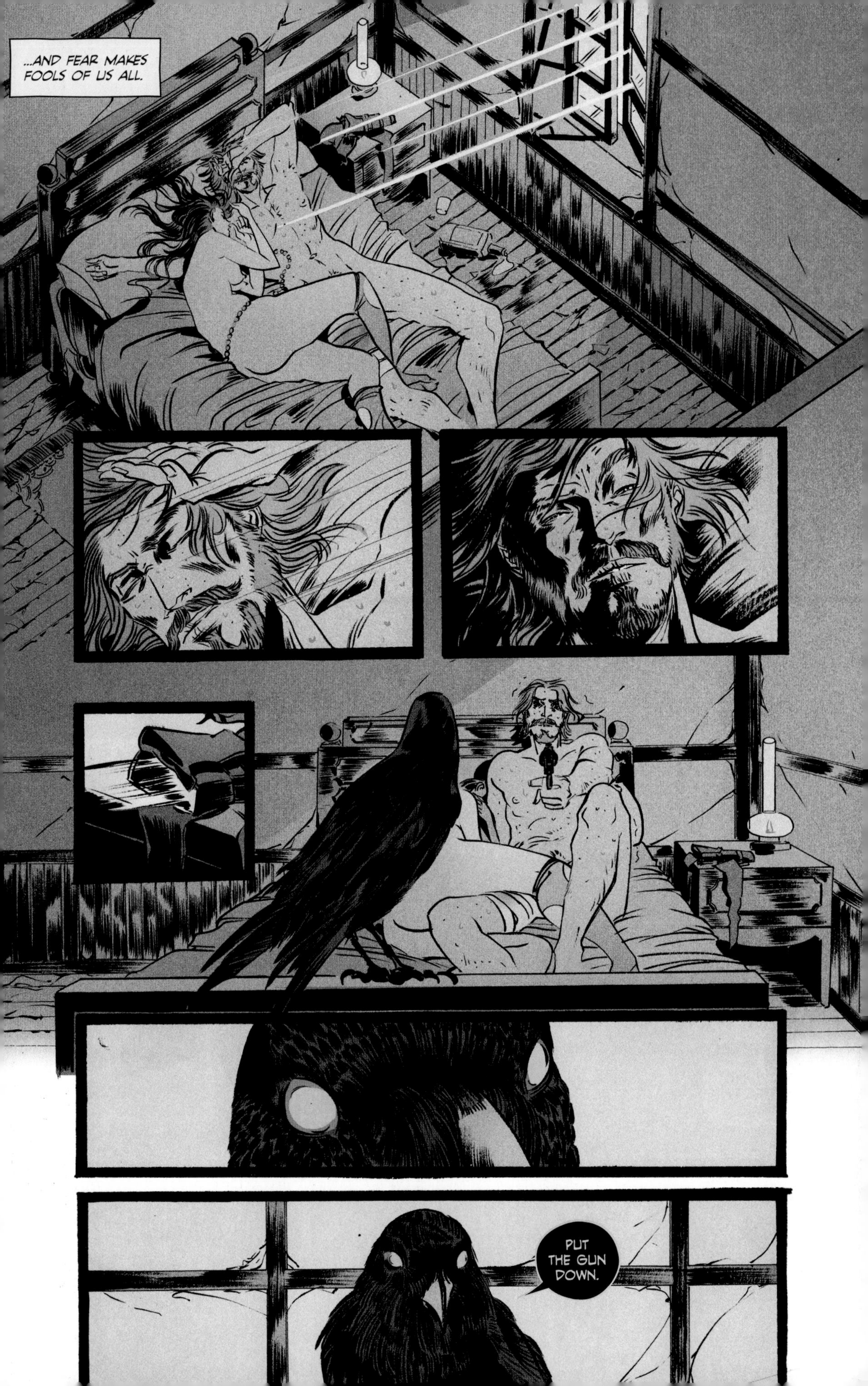
...AND FEAR MAKES FOOLS OF US ALL.
PUT THE GUN DOWN.

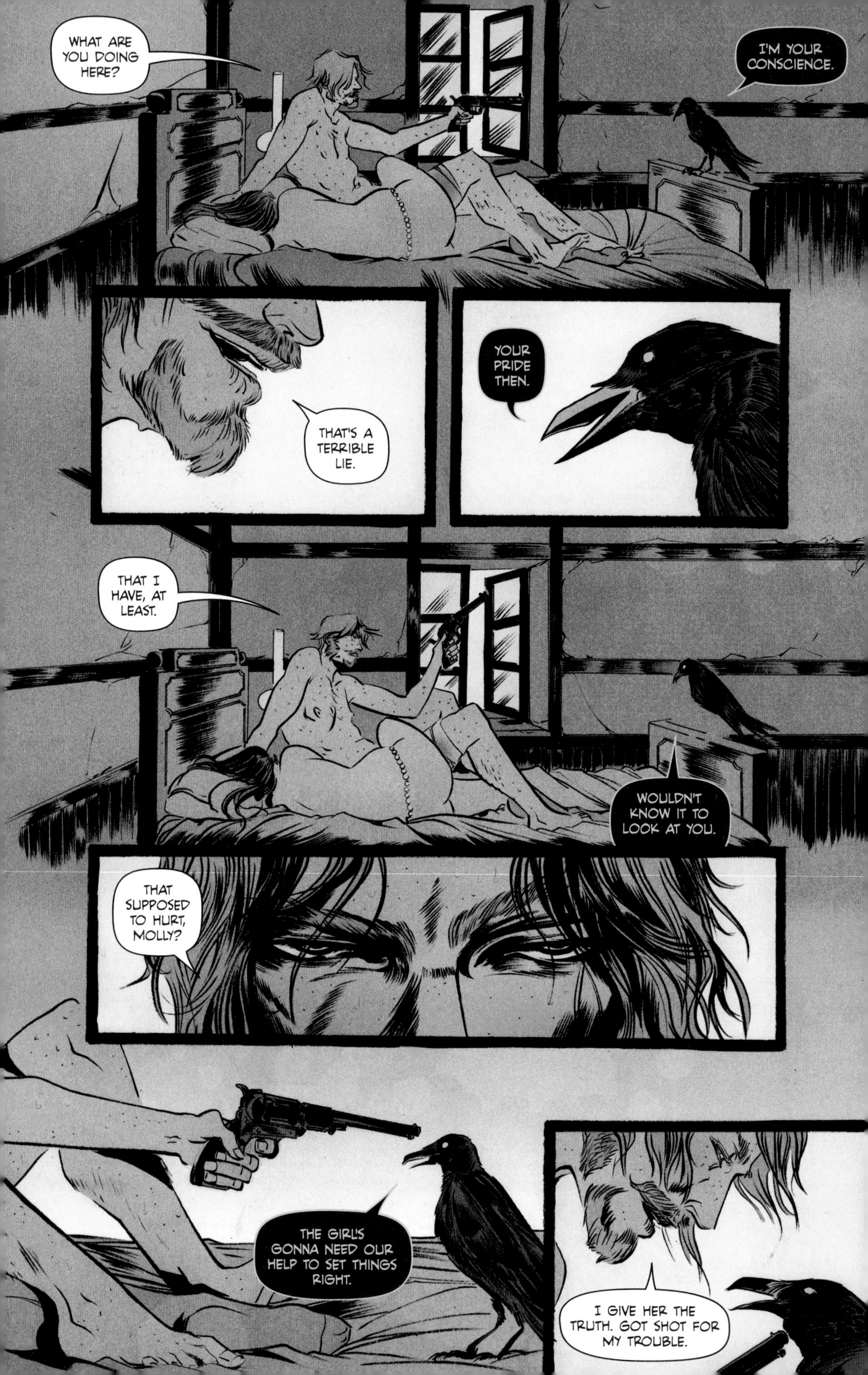
WHAT ARE YOU DOING HERE?
I'M YOUR CONSCIENCE.
THAT'S A TERRIBLE LIE.
YOUR PRIDE THEN.
THAT I HAVE, AT LEAST.
WOULDN'T KNOW IT TO LOOK AT YOU.
THAT SUPPOSED TO HURT, MOLLY?
THE GIRL'S GONNA NEED OUR HELP TO SET THINGS RIGHT.
I GIVE HER THE TRUTH. GOT SHOT FOR MY TROUBLE.

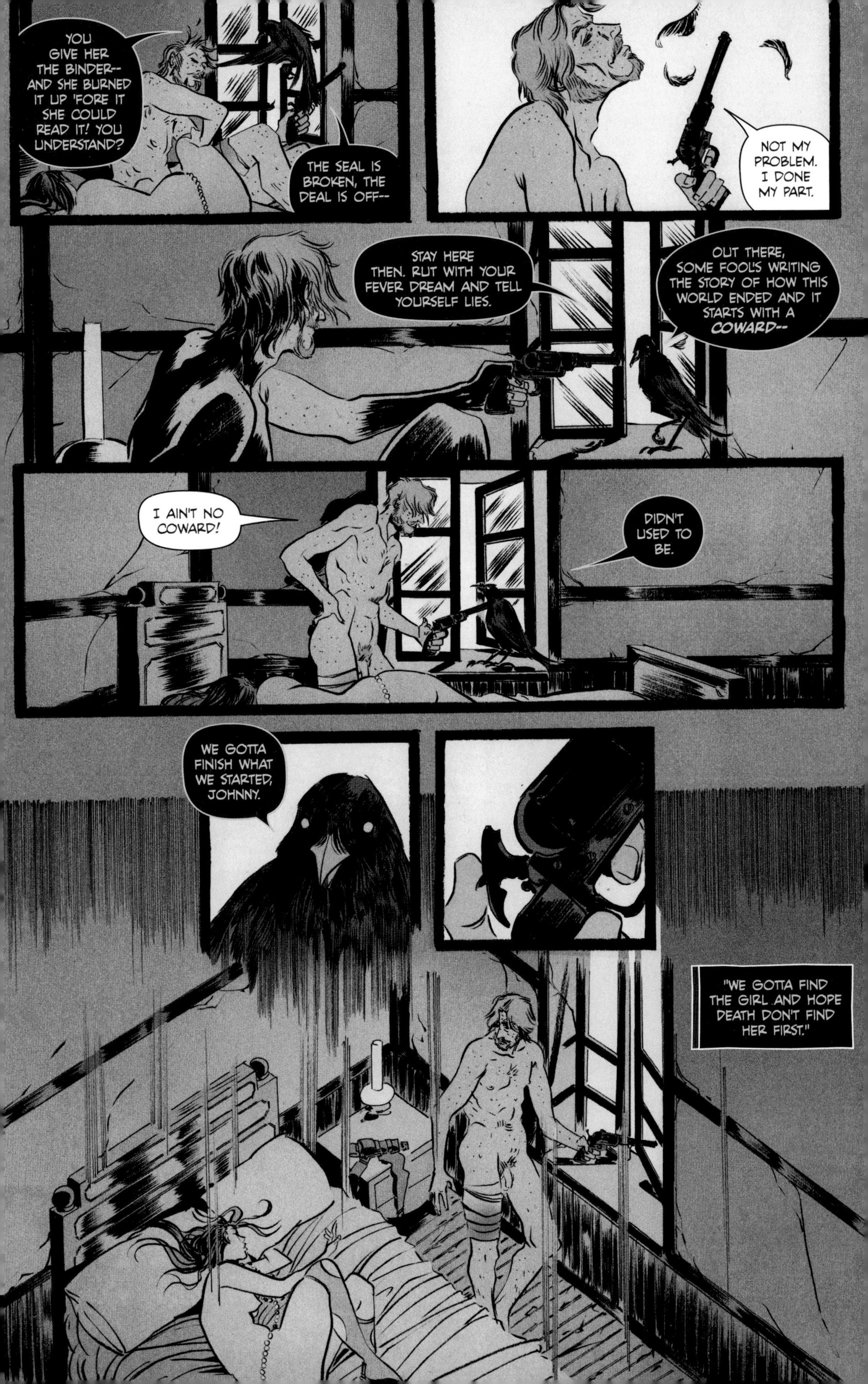
YOU GIVE HER THE BINDER-- AND SHE BURNED IT UP 'FORE IT SHE COULD READ IT! YOU UNDERSTAND?
THE SEAL IS BROKEN, THE DEAL IS OFF--
NOT MY PROBLEM. I DONE MY PART.
STAY HERE THEN. RUT WITH YOUR FEVER DREAM AND TELL YOURSELF LIES.
OUT THERE, SOME FOOL'S WRITING THE STORY OF HOW THIS WORLD ENDED AND IT STARTS WITH A COWARD--
I AIN'T NO COWARD!
DIDN'T USED TO BE.
WE GOTTA FINISH WHAT WE STARTED, JOHNNY.
"WE GOTTA FIND THE GIRL AND HOPE DEATH DON'T FIND HER FIRST."

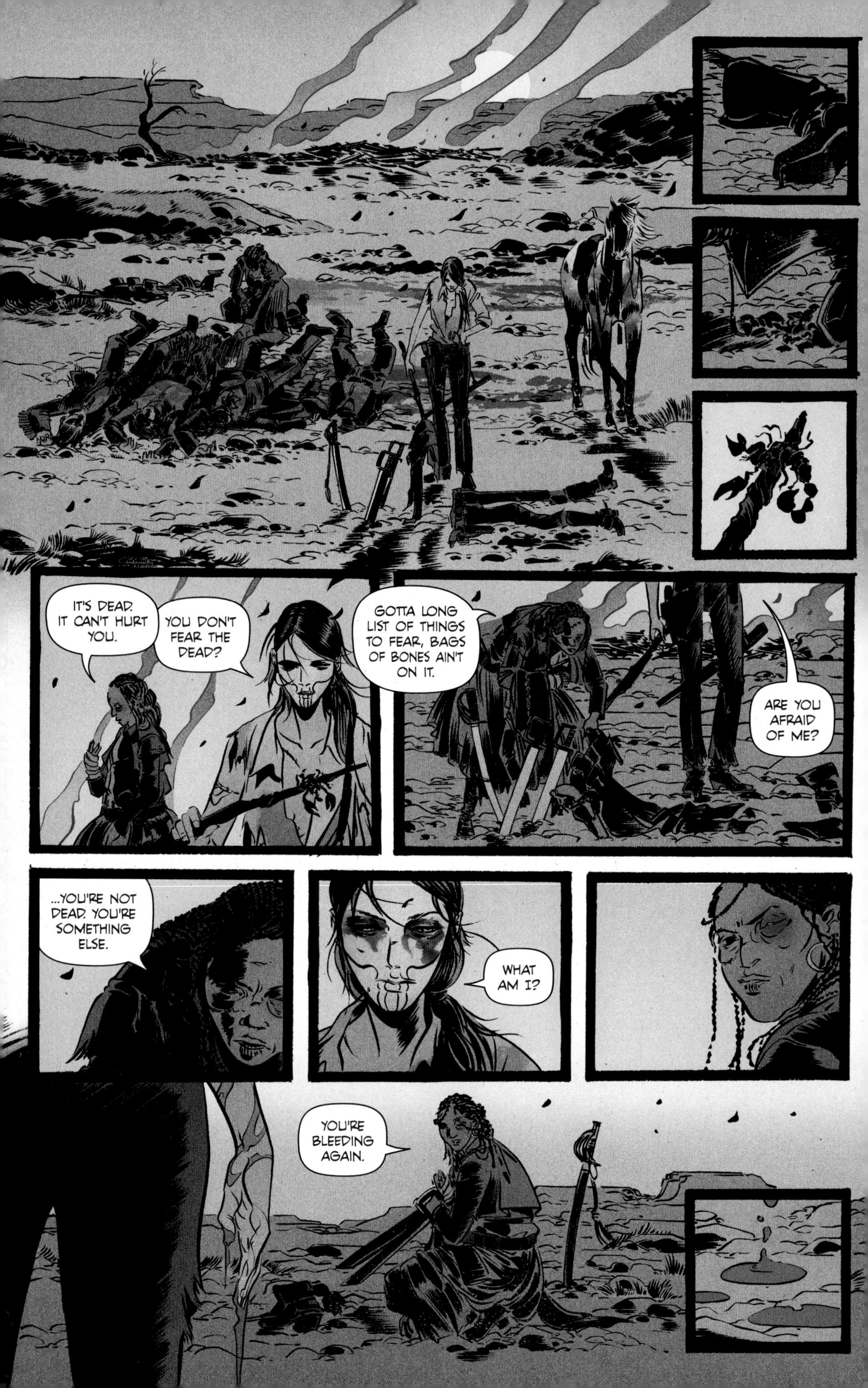
IT'S DEAD. IT CAN'T HURT YOU.
YOU DON'T FEAR THE DEAD?
GOTTA LONG LIST OF THINGS TO FEAR, BAGS OF BONES AIN'T ON IT.
ARE YOU AFRAID OF ME?
...YOU'RE NOT DEAD. YOU'RE SOMETHING ELSE.
WHAT AM I?
YOU'RE BLEEDING AGAIN.

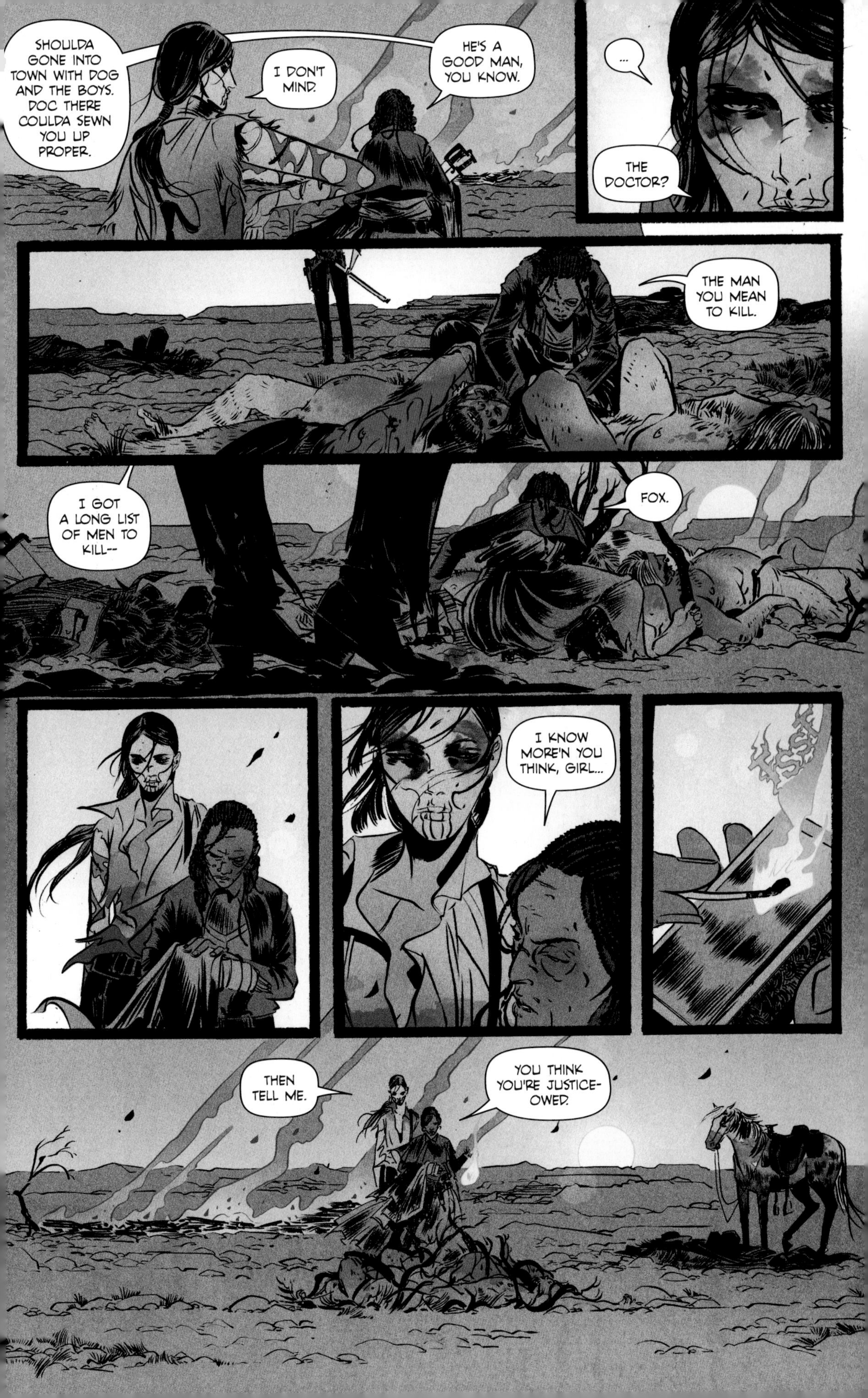
SHOULDA GONE INTO TOWN WITH DOG AND THE BOYS. DOC THERE COULDA SEWN YOU UP PROPER.
I DON'T MIND.
HE'S A GOOD MAN, YOU KNOW.
...
THE DOCTOR?
THE MAN YOU MEAN TO KILL.
I GOT A LONG LIST OF MEN TO KILL--
FOX.
I KNOW MORE'N YOU THINK, GIRL...
THEN TELL ME.
YOU THINK YOU'RE JUSTICE-OWED.

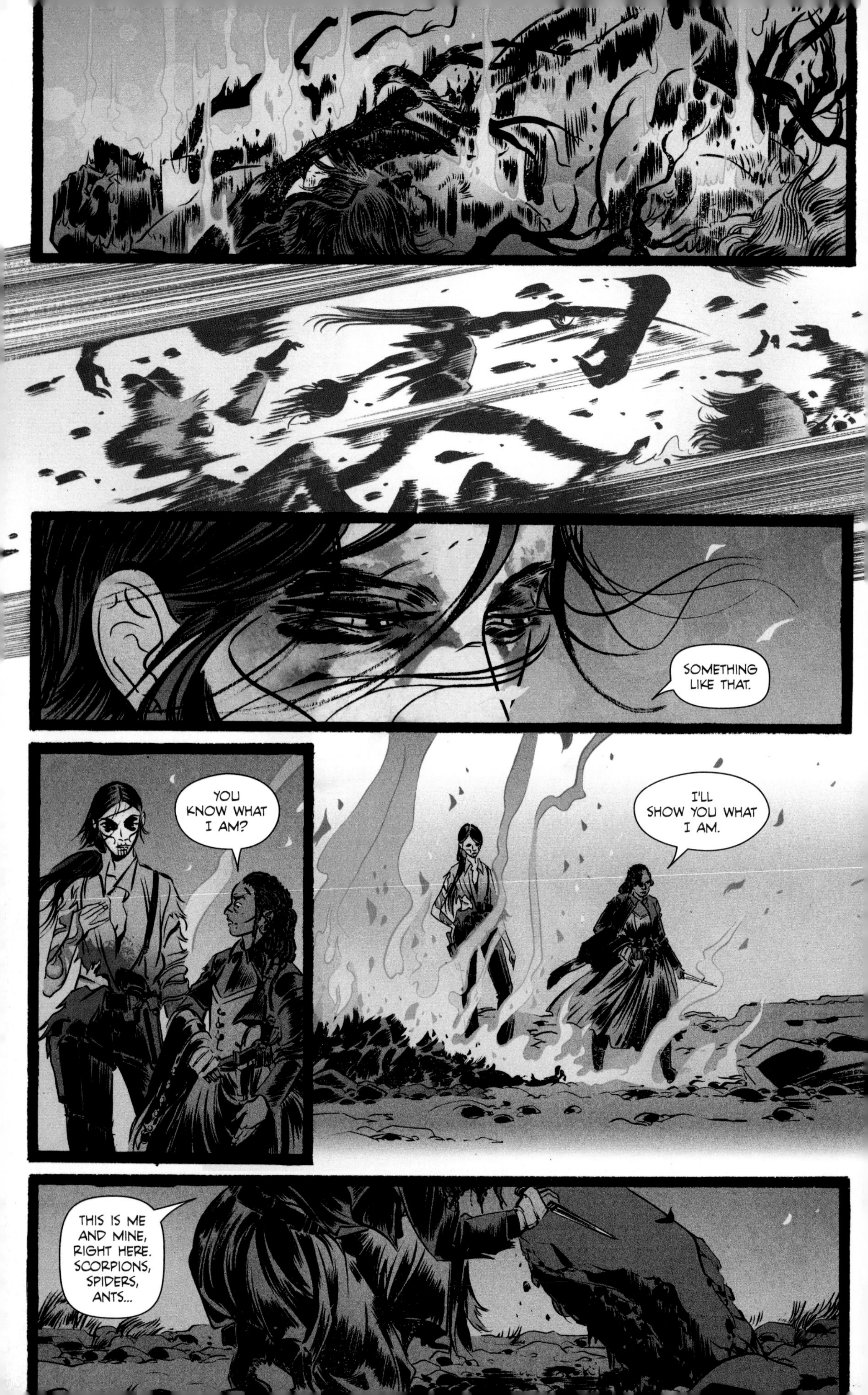
SOMETHING LIKE THAT.
YOU KNOW WHAT I AM?
I'LL SHOW YOU WHAT I AM.
THIS IS ME AND MINE, RIGHT HERE. SCORPIONS, SPIDERS, ANTS...

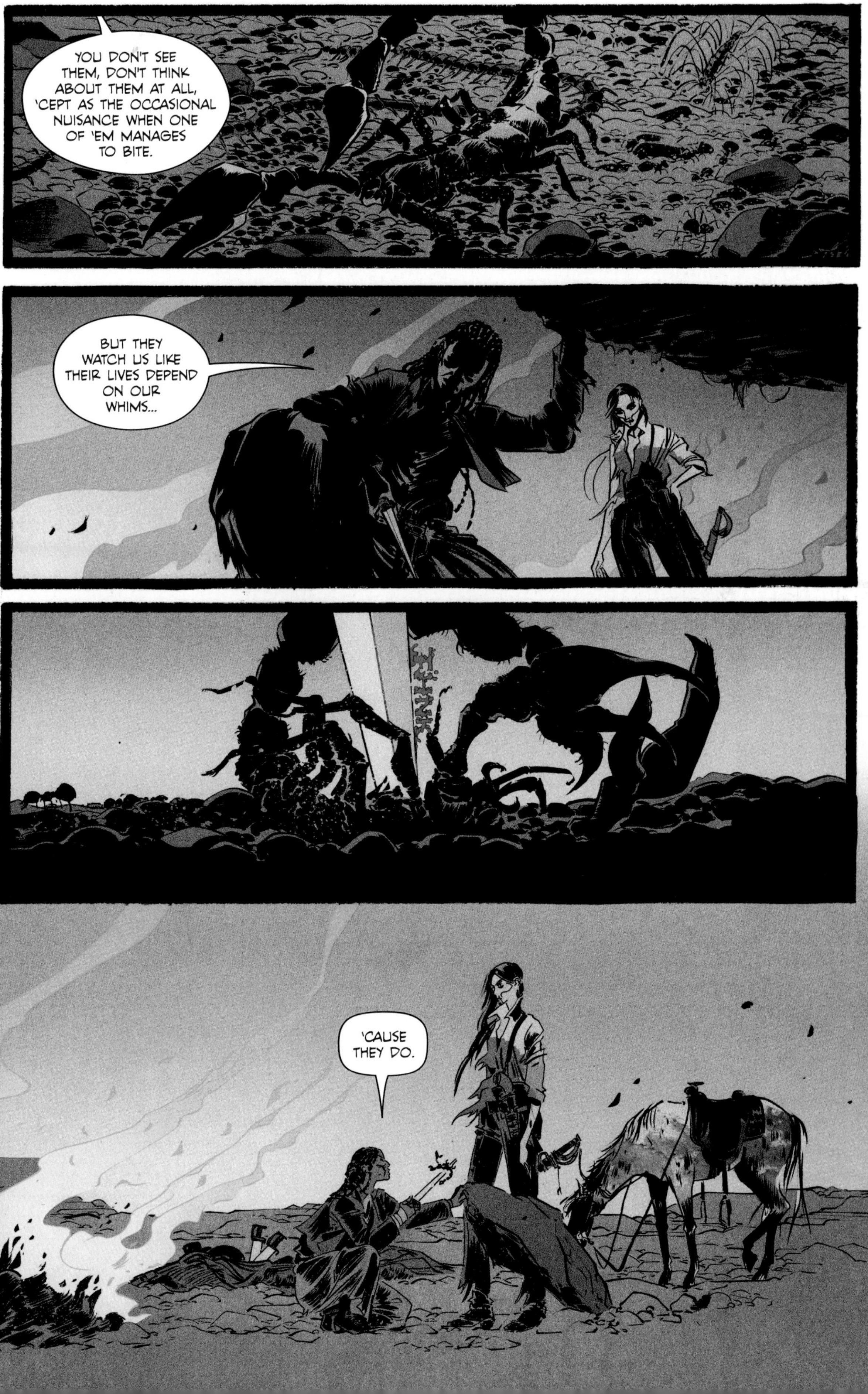
YOU DON'T SEE THEM, DON'T THINK ABOUT THEM AT ALL, 'CEPT AS THE OCCASIONAL NUISANCE WHEN ONE OF 'EM MANAGES TO BITE.
BUT THEY WATCH US LIKE THEIR LIVES DEPEND ON OUR WHIMS...
'CAUSE THEY DO.

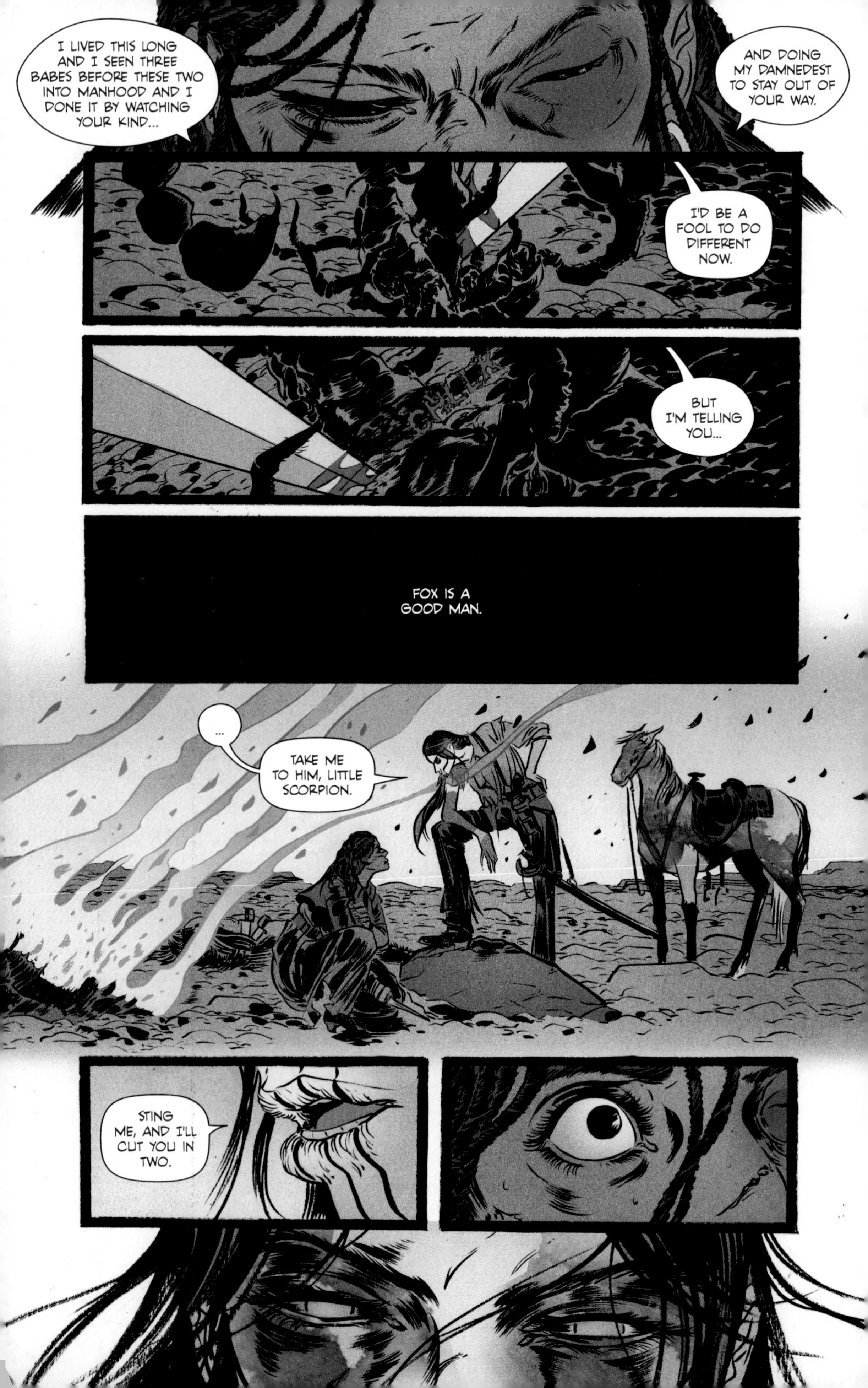

I LIVED THIS LONG AND I SEEN THREE BABES BEFORE THESE TWO INTO MANHOOD AND I DONE IT BY WATCHING YOUR KIND...
AND DOING MY DAMNEDEST TO STAY OUT OF YOUR WAY.
I'D BE A FOOL TO DO DIFFERENT NOW.
BUT I'M TELLING YOU...
FOX IS A GOOD MAN.
...
TAKE ME TO HIM, LITTLE SCORPION.
STING ME, AND I'LL CUT YOU IN TWO.

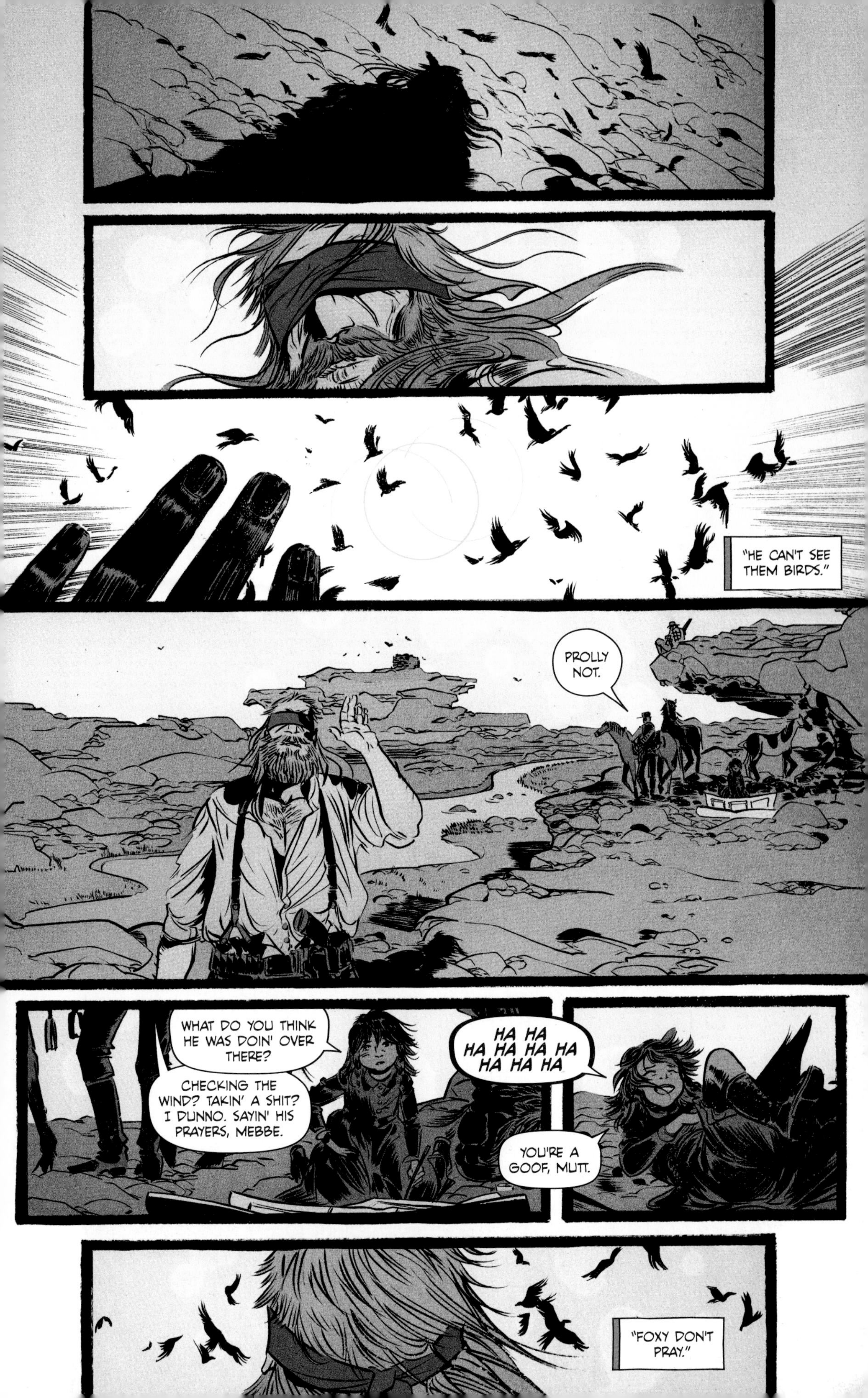
"HE CAN'T SEE THEM BIRDS."
PROLLY NOT.
WHAT DO YOU THINK HE WAS DOIN' OVER THERE?
CHECKING THE WIND? TAKIN' A SHIT? I DUNNO. SAYIN' HIS PRAYERS, MEBBE.
HA HA HA HA HA HA HA HA HA
YOU'RE A GOOF, MUTT.
"FOXY DON'T PRAY."

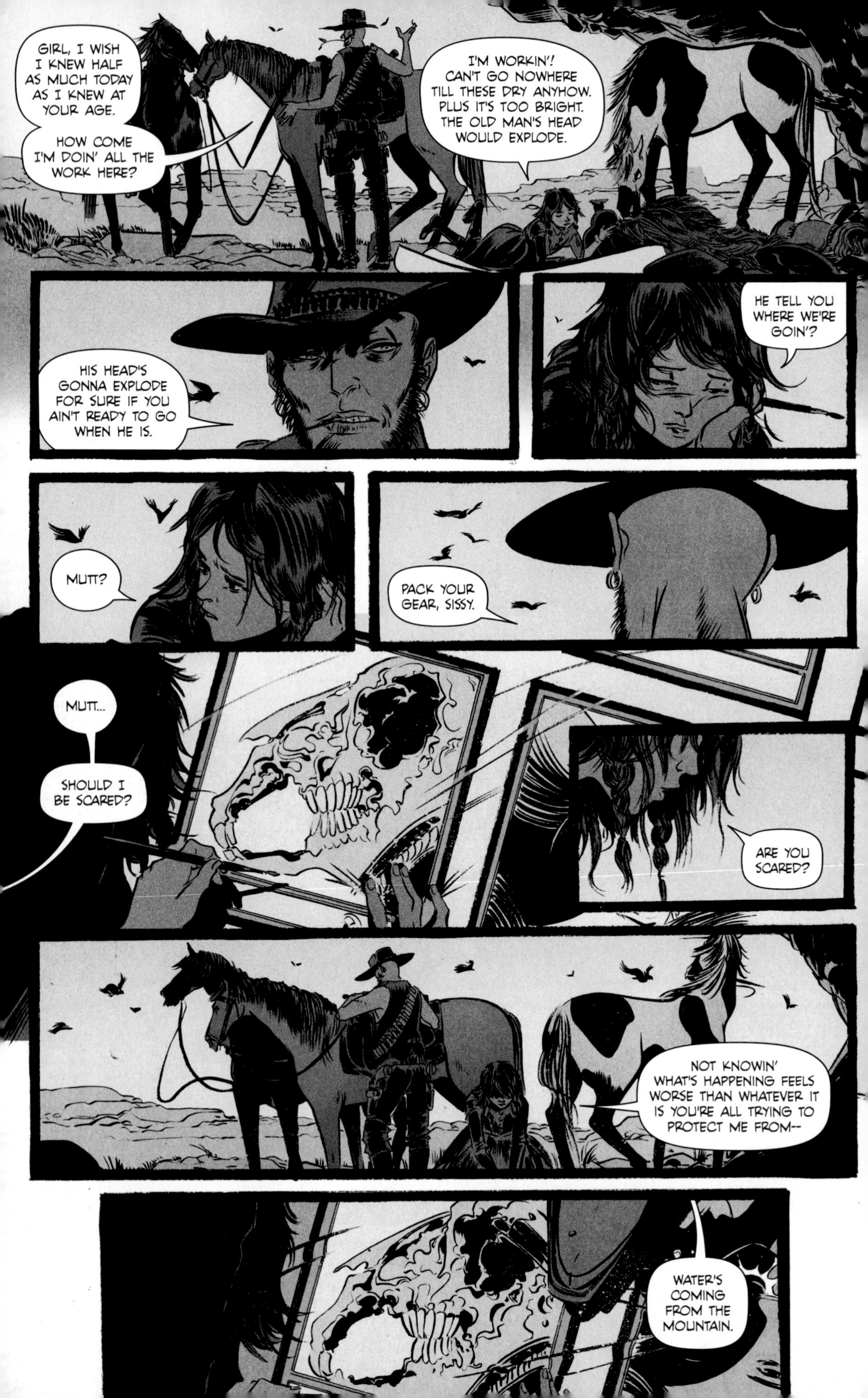
GIRL, I WISH I KNEW HALF AS MUCH TODAY AS I KNEW AT YOUR AGE.
HOW COME I'M DOIN' ALL THE WORK HERE?
I'M WORKIN'! CAN'T GO NOWHERE TILL THESE DRY ANYHOW. PLUS IT'S TOO BRIGHT. THE OLD MAN'S HEAD WOULD EXPLODE.
HIS HEAD'S GONNA EXPLODE FOR SURE IF YOU AIN'T READY TO GO WHEN HE IS.
HE TELL YOU WHERE WE'RE GOIN'?
MUTT?
PACK YOUR GEAR, SISSY.
MUTT...
SHOULD I BE SCARED?
ARE YOU SCARED?
NOT KNOWIN' WHAT'S HAPPENING FEELS WORSE THAN WHATEVER IT IS YOU'RE ALL TRYING TO PROTECT ME FROM--
WATER'S COMING FROM THE MOUNTAIN.

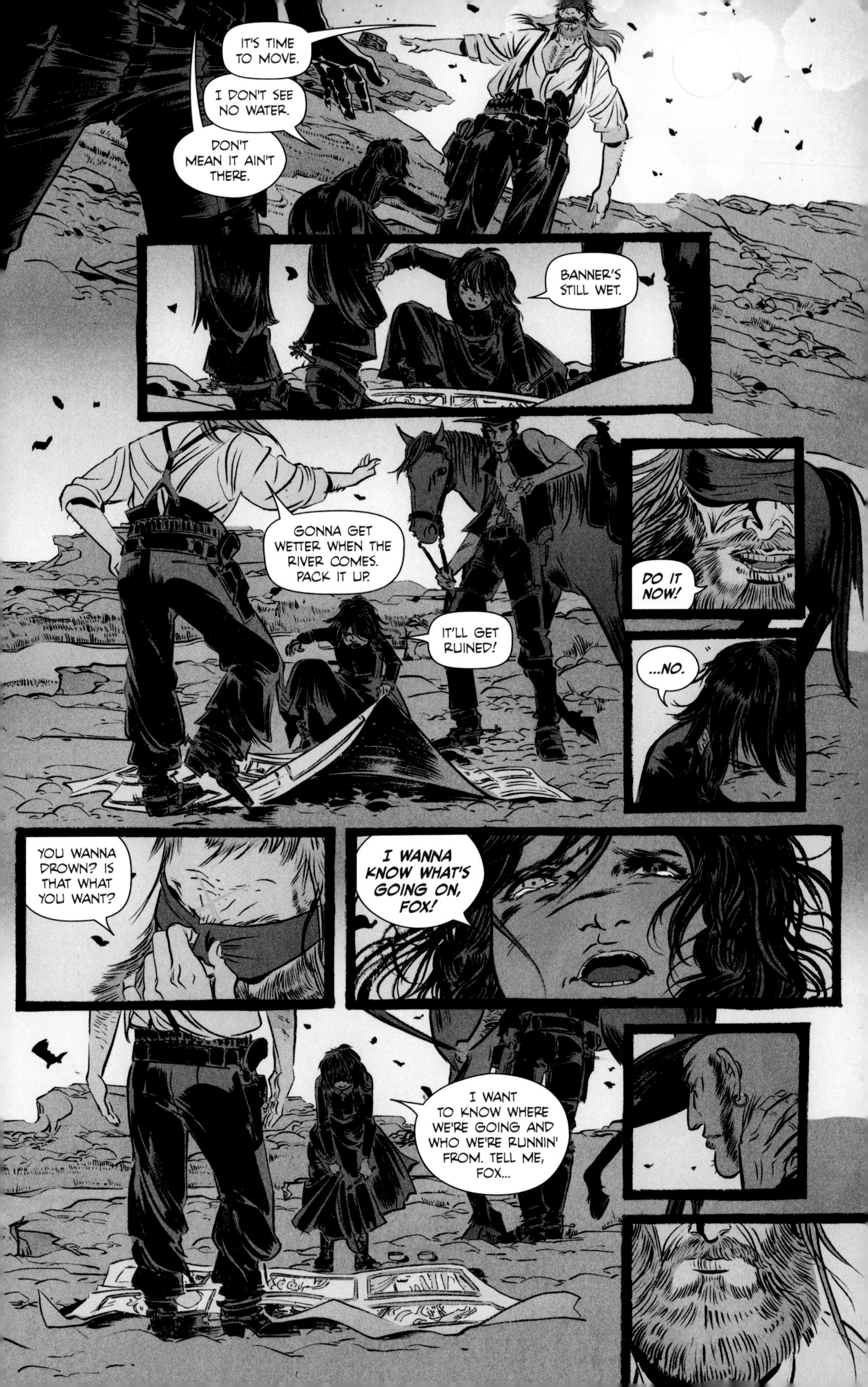
IT'S TIME TO MOVE.
I DON'T SEE NO WATER.
DON'T MEAN IT AIN'T THERE.
BANNER'S STILL WET.
GONNA GET WETTER WHEN THE RIVER COMES. PACK IT UP.
IT'LL GET RUINED!
DO IT NOW!
...NO.
YOU WANNA DROWN? IS THAT WHAT YOU WANT?
I WANNA KNOW WHAT'S GOING ON, FOX!
I WANT TO KNOW WHERE WE'RE GOING AND WHO WE'RE RUNNIN' FROM. TELL ME, FOX...

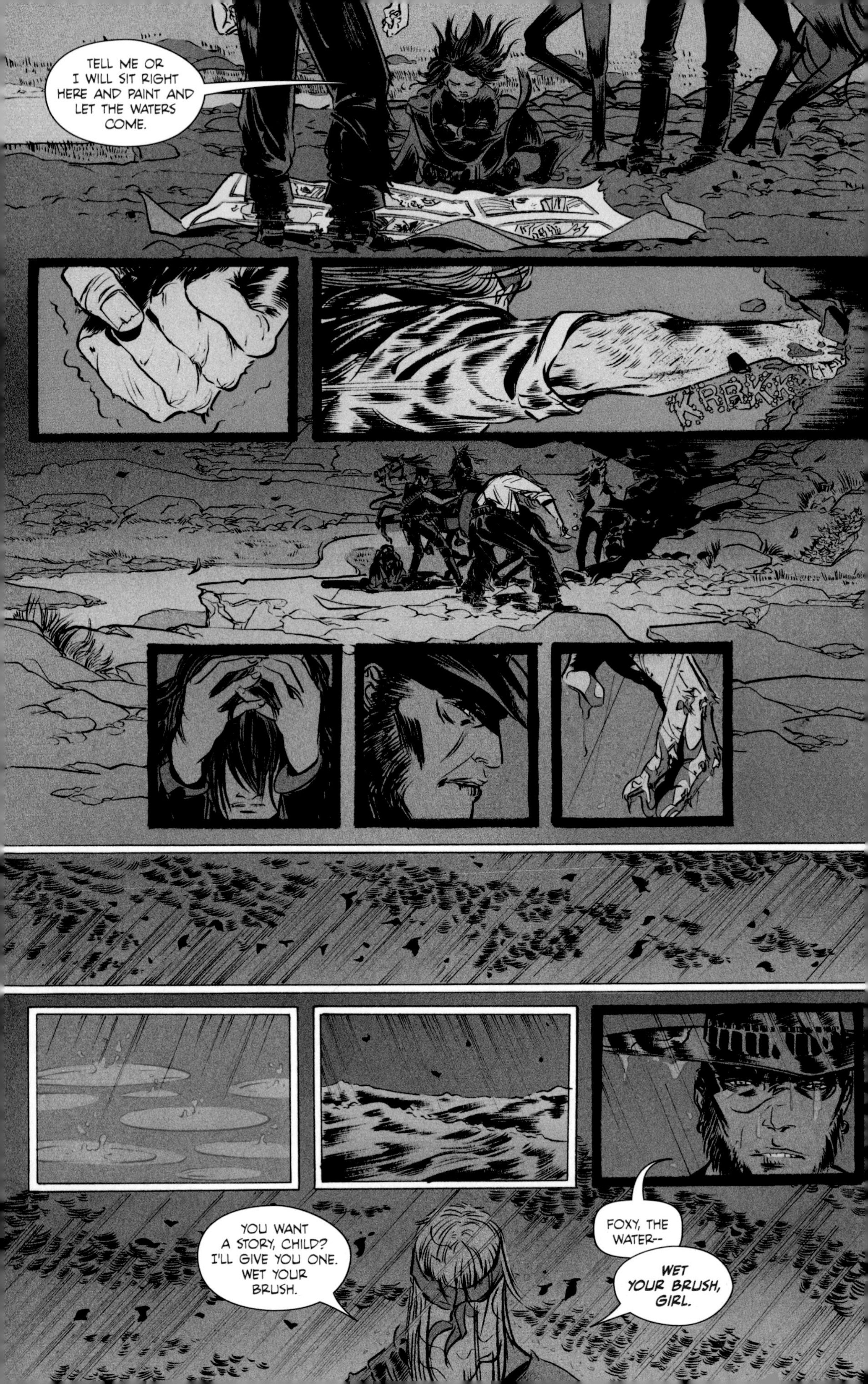
TELL ME OR I WILL SIT RIGHT HERE AND PAINT AND LET THE WATERS COME.
KRBKK
YOU WANT A STORY, CHILD? I'LL GIVE YOU ONE. WET YOUR BRUSH.
FOXY, THE WATER--
WET YOUR BRUSH, GIRL.

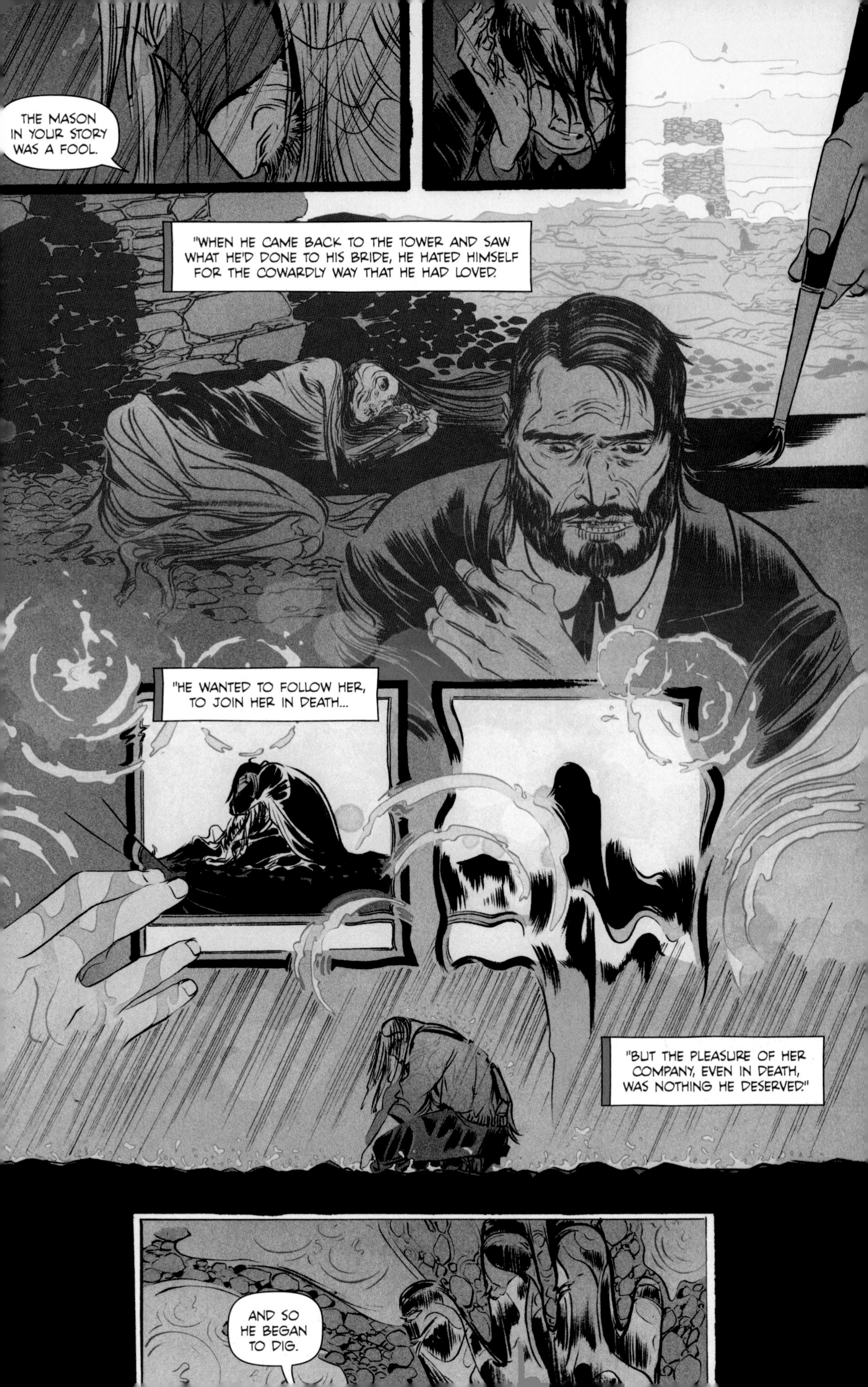
THE MASON IN YOUR STORY WAS A FOOL.
"WHEN HE CAME BACK TO THE TOWER AND SAW WHAT HE'D DONE TO HIS BRIDE, HE HATED HIMSELF FOR THE COWARDLY WAY THAT HE HAD LOVED.
"HE WANTED TO FOLLOW HER, TO JOIN HER IN DEATH...
"BUT THE PLEASURE OF HER COMPANY, EVEN IN DEATH, WAS NOTHING HE DESERVED."
AND SO HE BEGAN TO DIG.

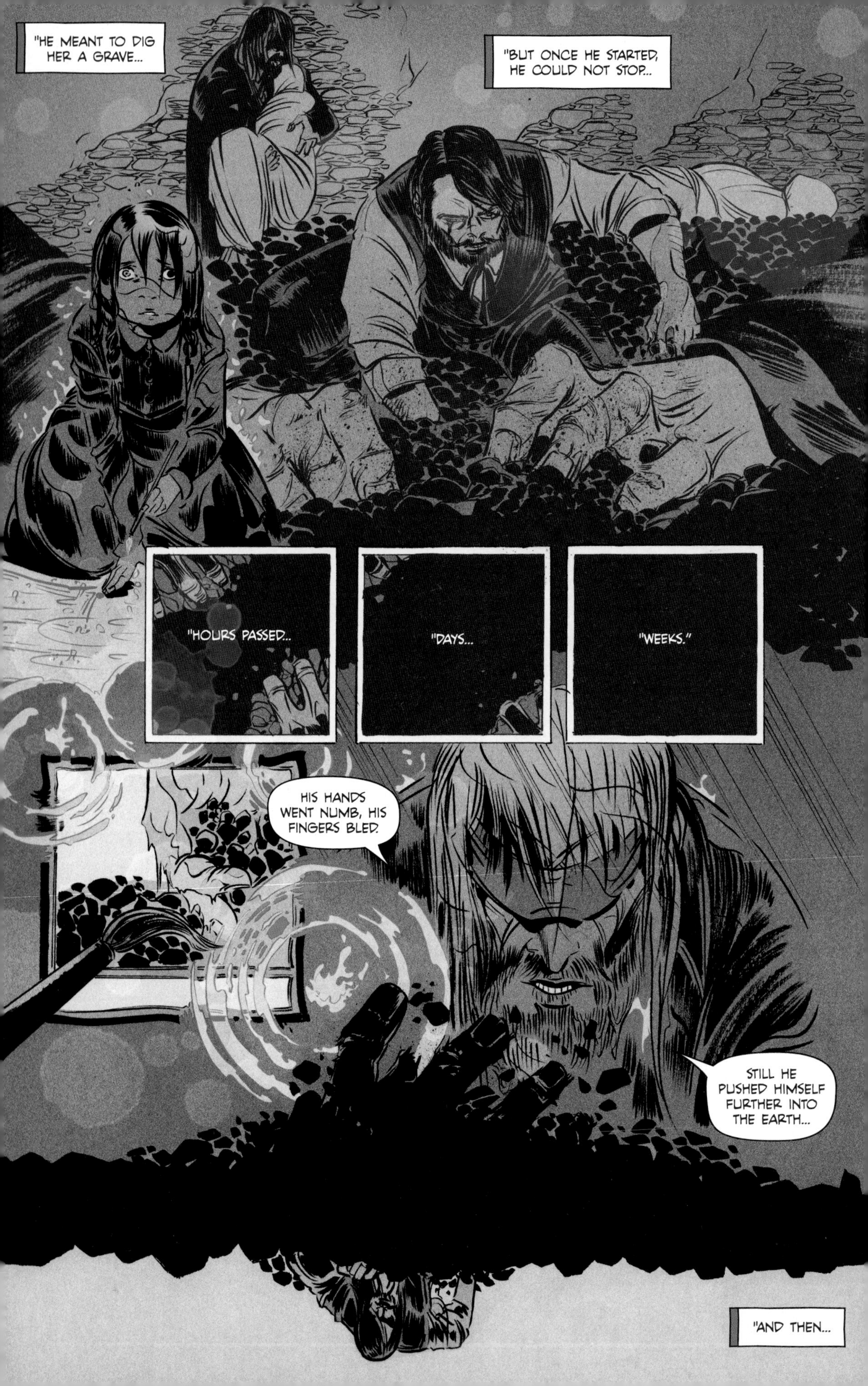
"HE MEANT TO DIG HER A GRAVE...
"BUT ONCE HE STARTED, HE COULD NOT STOP...
"HOURS PASSED...
"DAYS...
"WEEKS."
HIS HANDS WENT NUMB, HIS FINGERS BLED.
STILL HE PUSHED HIMSELF FURTHER INTO THE EARTH...
"AND THEN...

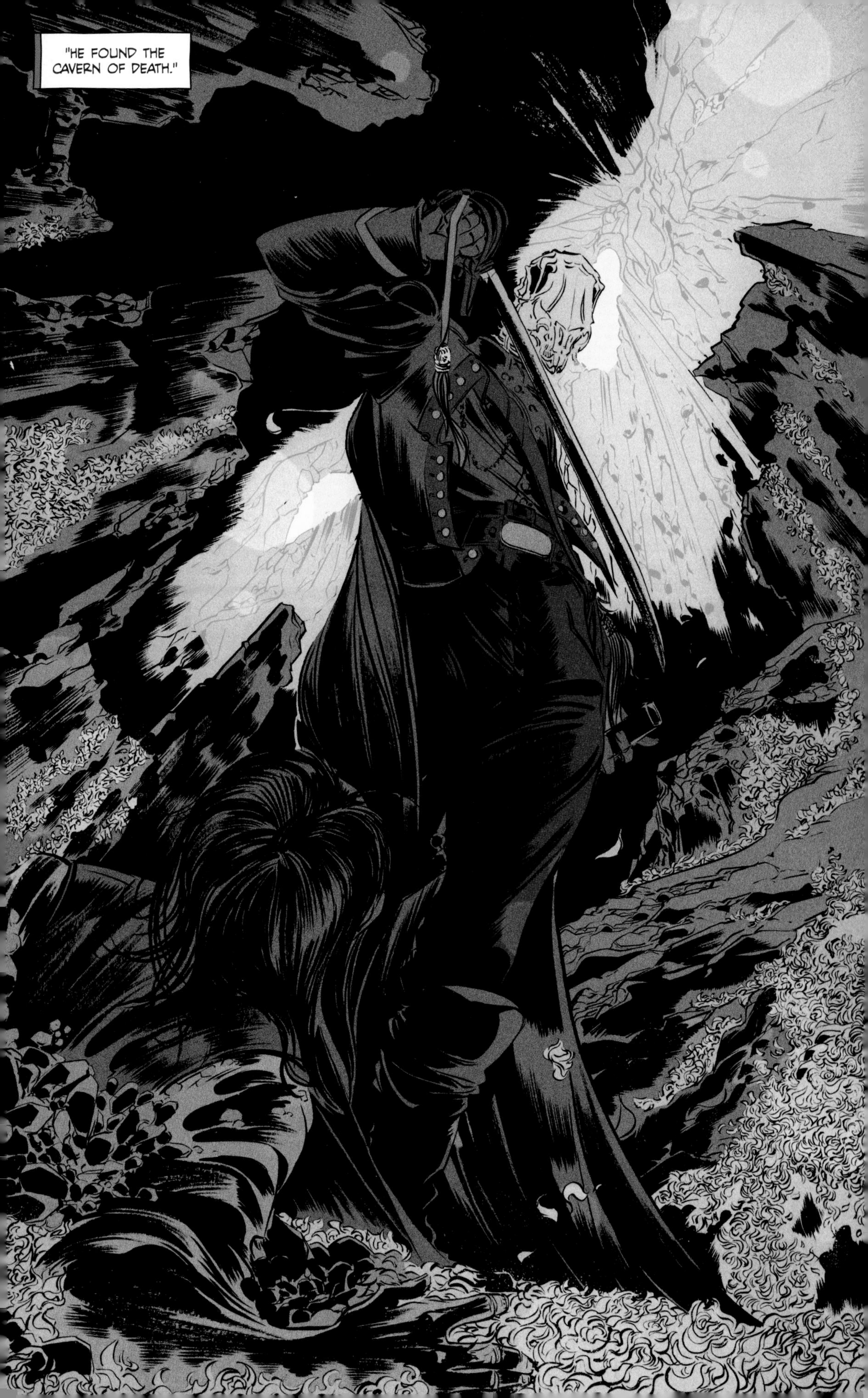
"HE FOUND THE CAVERN OF DEATH."

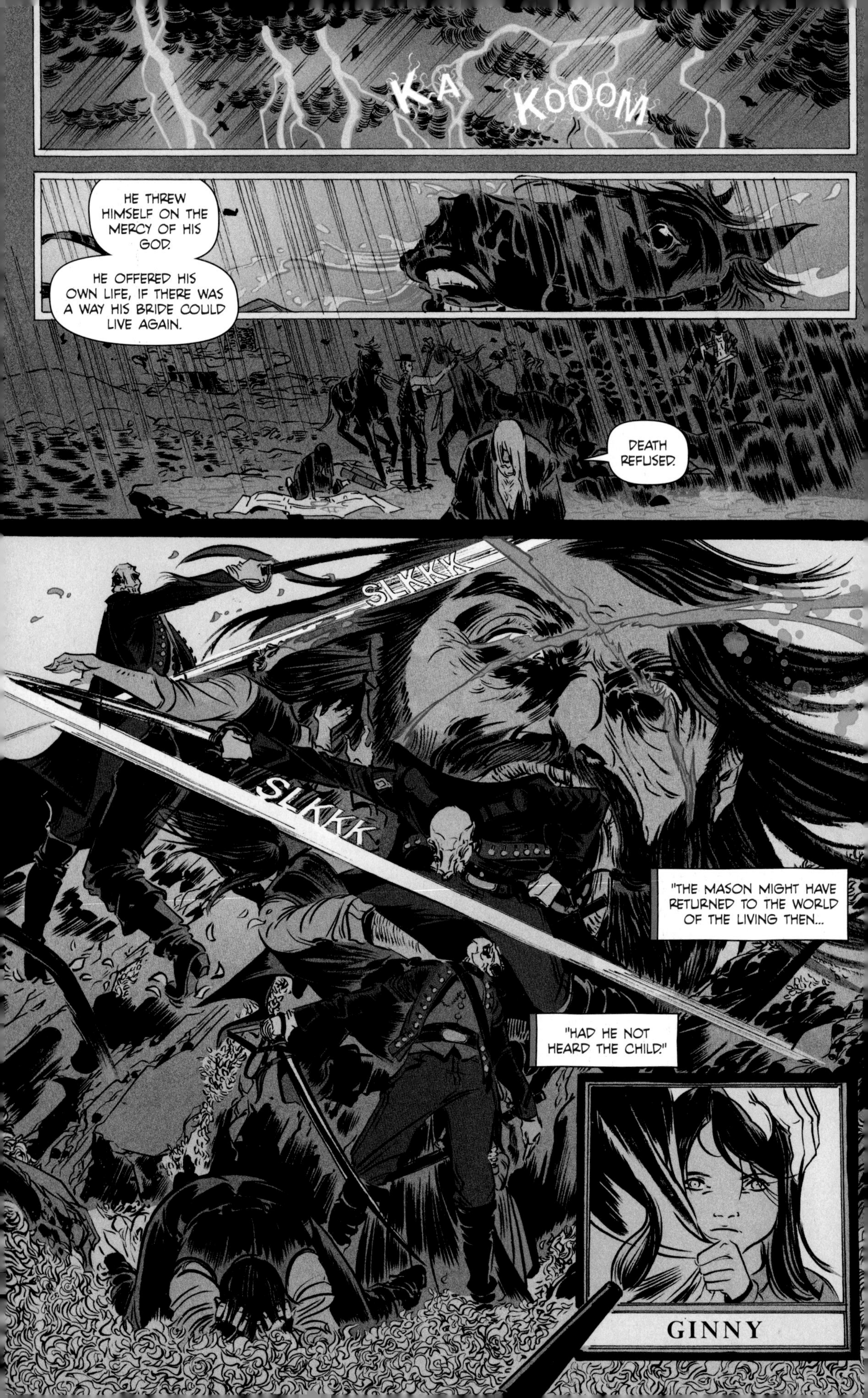
KA KOOOM
HE THREW HIMSELF ON THE MERCY OF HIS GOD.
HE OFFERED HIS OWN LIFE, IF THERE WAS A WAY HIS BRIDE COULD LIVE AGAIN.
DEATH REFUSED.
SLKKK
SLKKK
"THE MASON MIGHT HAVE RETURNED TO THE WORLD OF THE LIVING THEN...
"HAD HE NOT HEARD THE CHILD."
GINNY

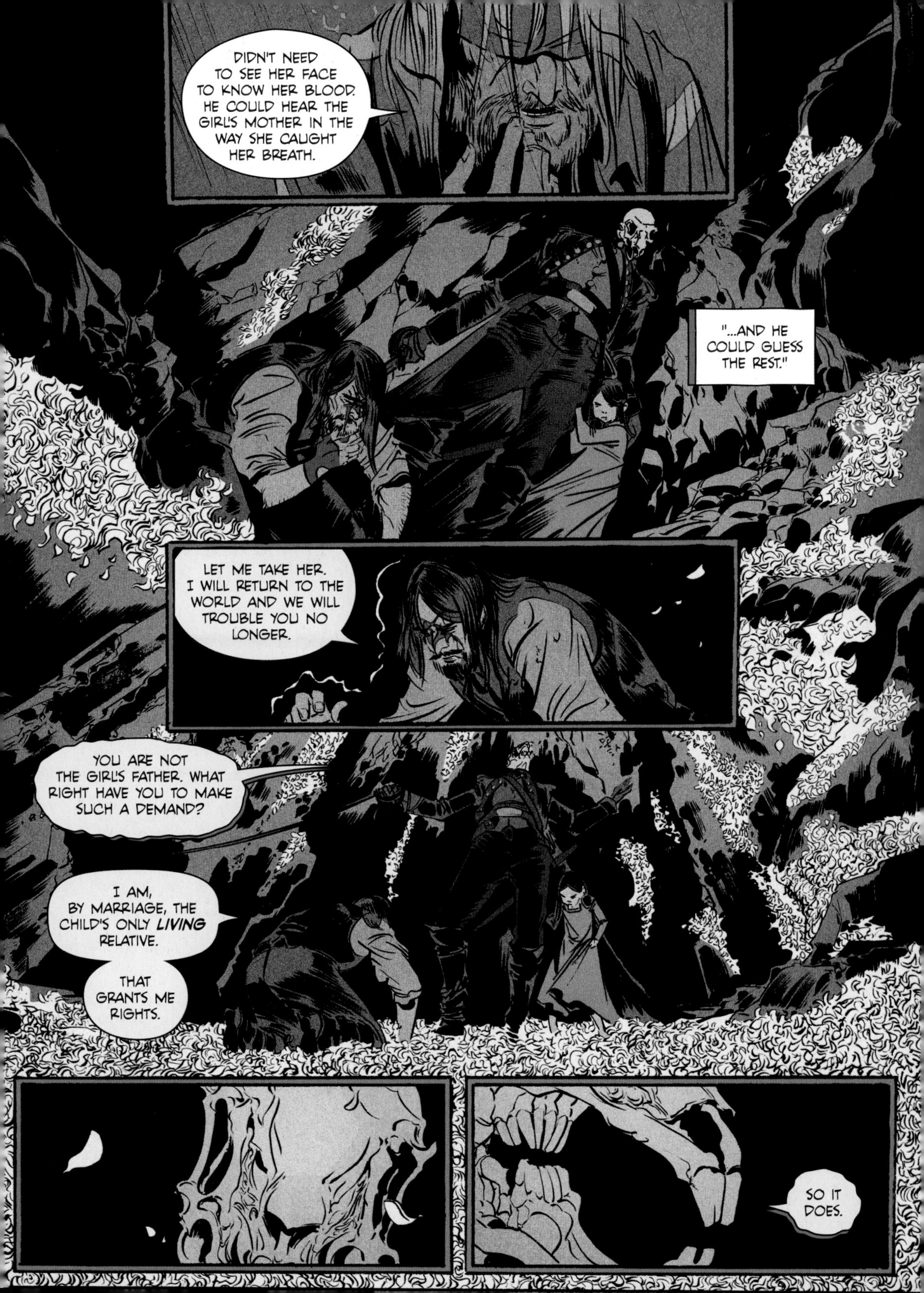
DIDN'T NEED TO SEE HER FACE TO KNOW HER BLOOD. HE COULD HEAR THE GIRL'S MOTHER IN THE WAY SHE CAUGHT HER BREATH.
"...AND HE COULD GUESS THE REST."
LET ME TAKE HER. I WILL RETURN TO THE WORLD AND WE WILL TROUBLE YOU NO LONGER.
YOU ARE NOT THE GIRL'S FATHER. WHAT RIGHT HAVE YOU TO MAKE SUCH A DEMAND?
I AM, BY MARRIAGE, THE CHILD'S ONLY *LIVING* RELATIVE.
THAT GRANTS ME RIGHTS.
SO IT DOES.

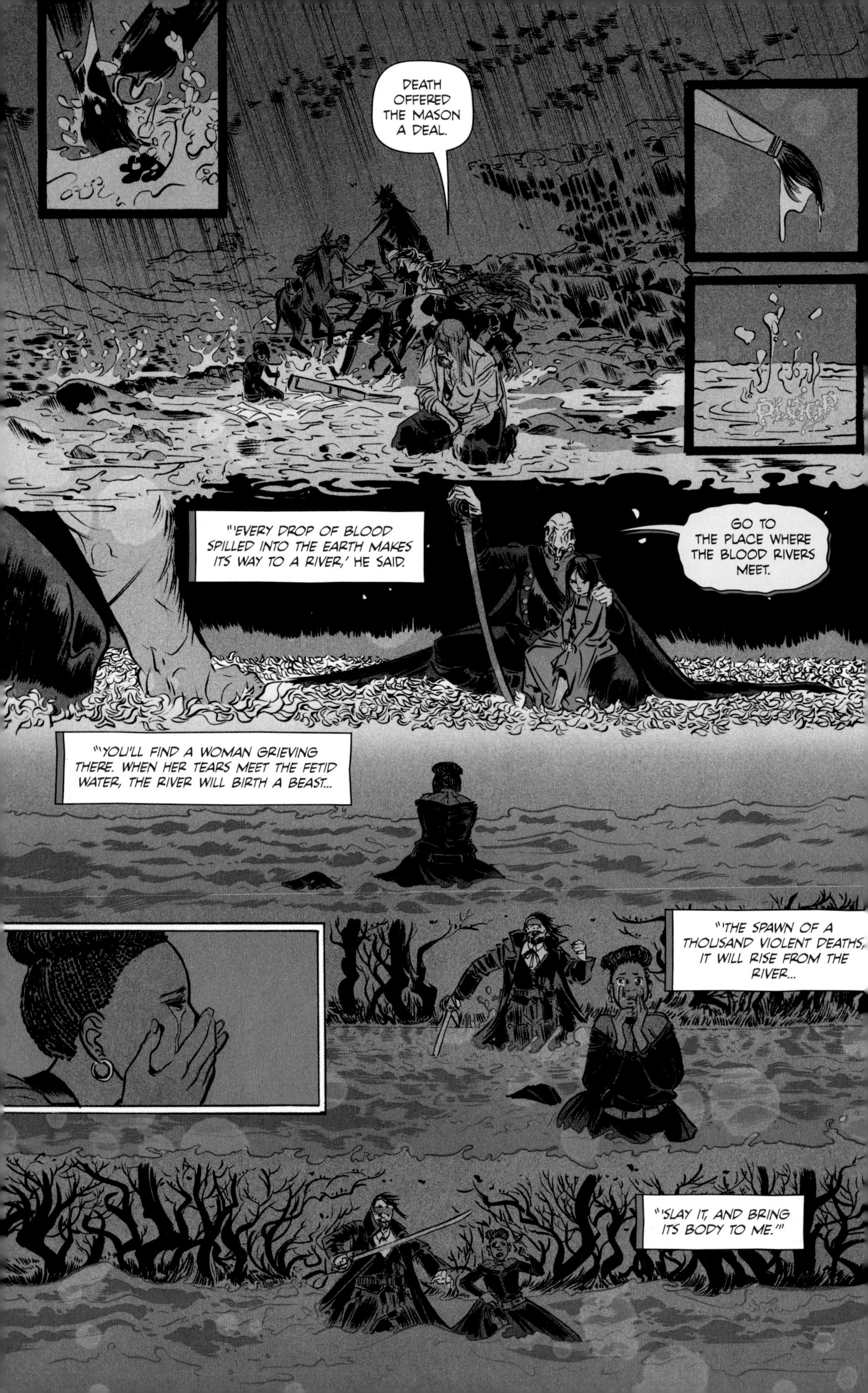
DEATH OFFERED THE MASON A DEAL.
"'EVERY DROP OF BLOOD SPILLED INTO THE EARTH MAKES ITS WAY TO A RIVER,' HE SAID.
GO TO THE PLACE WHERE THE BLOOD RIVERS MEET.
"YOU'LL FIND A WOMAN GRIEVING THERE. WHEN HER TEARS MEET THE FETID WATER, THE RIVER WILL BIRTH A BEAST...
"'THE SPAWN OF A THOUSAND VIOLENT DEATHS, IT WILL RISE FROM THE RIVER...
"SLAY IT, AND BRING ITS BODY TO ME.'"

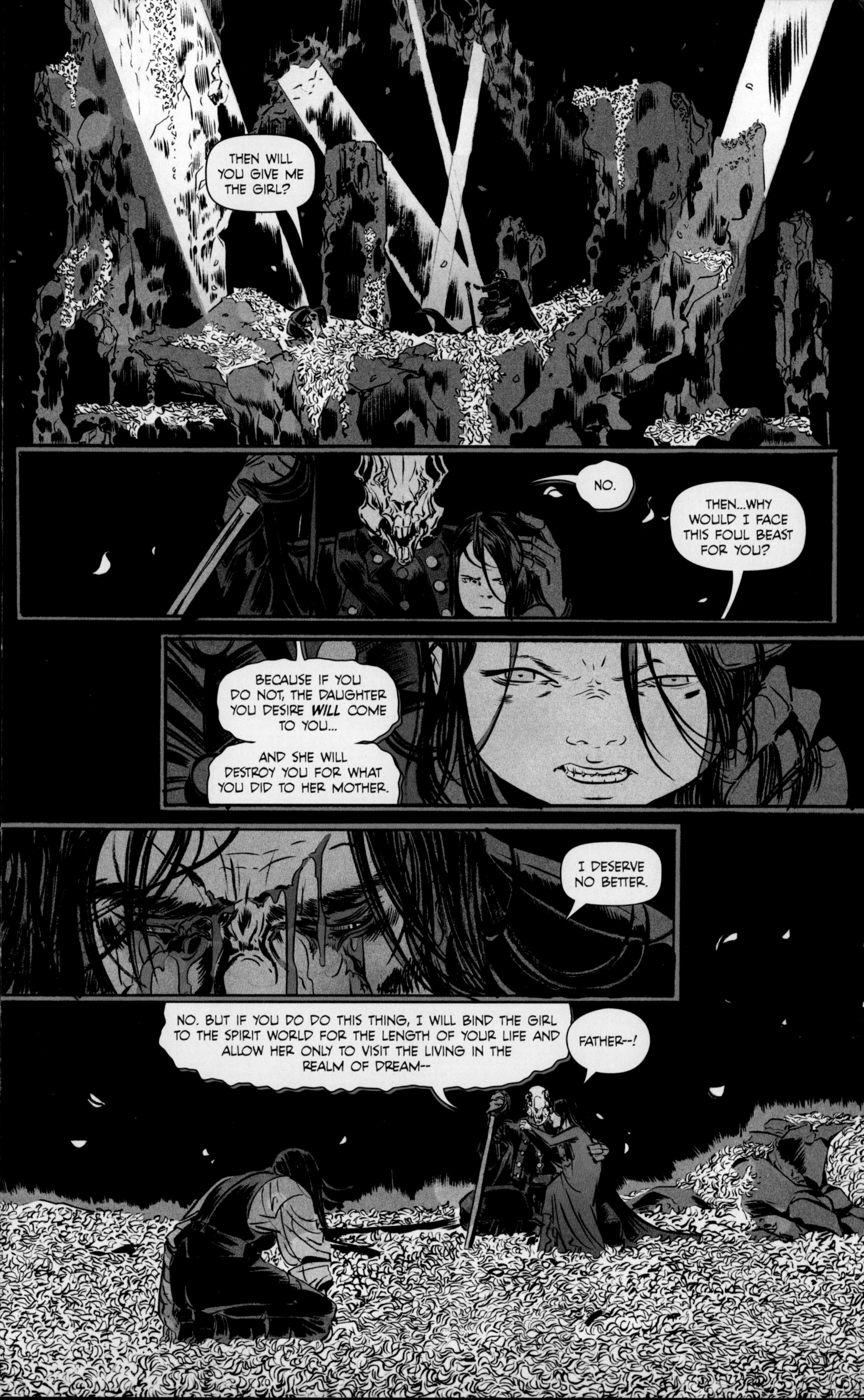
THEN WILL YOU GIVE ME THE GIRL?
NO.
THEN...WHY WOULD I FACE THIS FOUL BEAST FOR YOU?
BECAUSE IF YOU DO NOT, THE DAUGHTER YOU DESIRE WILL COME TO YOU...
AND SHE WILL DESTROY YOU FOR WHAT YOU DID TO HER MOTHER.
I DESERVE NO BETTER.
NO. BUT IF YOU DO DO THIS THING, I WILL BIND THE GIRL TO THE SPIRIT WORLD FOR THE LENGTH OF YOUR LIFE AND ALLOW HER ONLY TO VISIT THE LIVING IN THE REALM OF DREAM--
FATHER--!

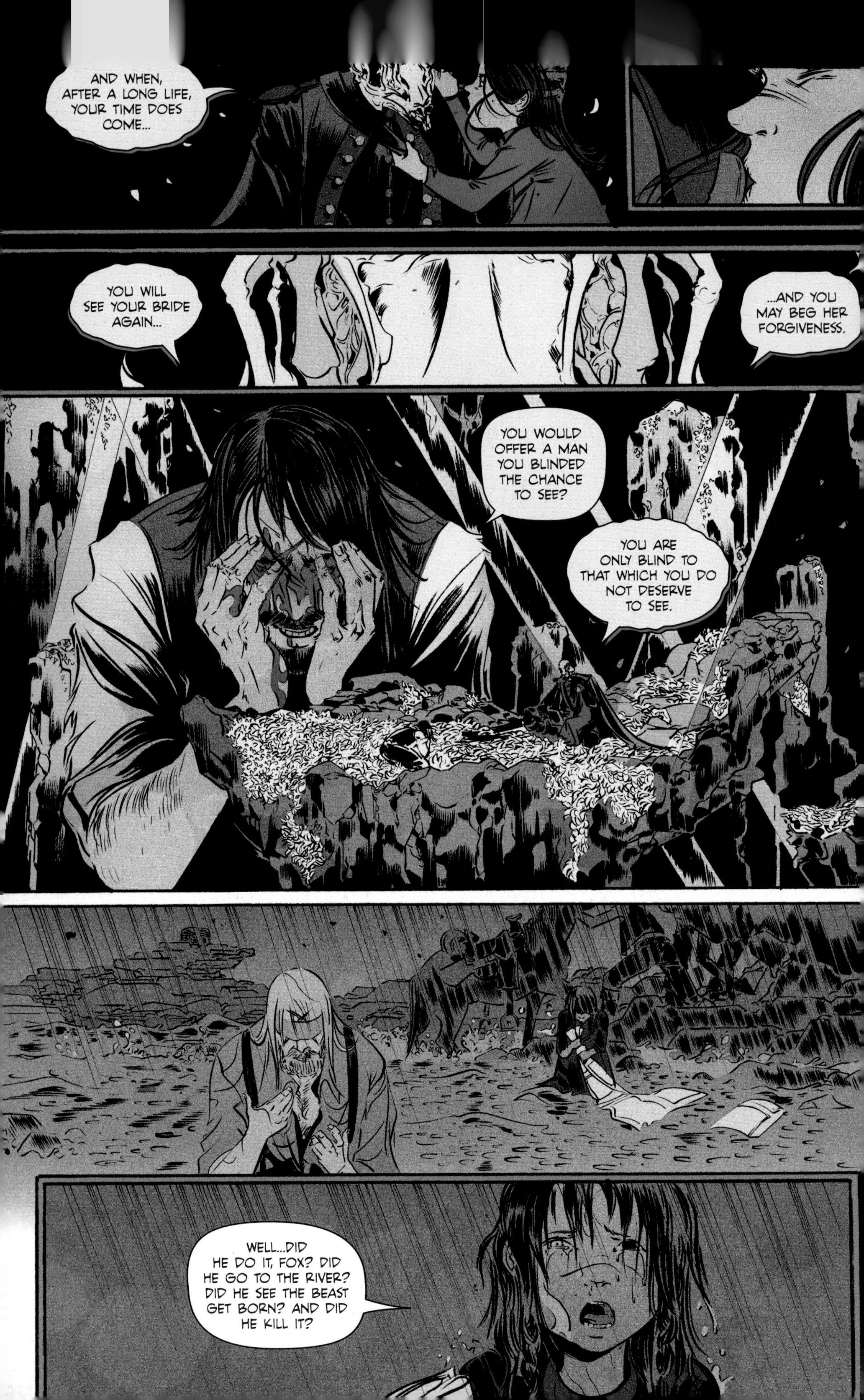
AND WHEN, AFTER A LONG LIFE, YOUR TIME DOES COME...
YOU WILL SEE YOUR BRIDE AGAIN...
...AND YOU MAY BEG HER FORGIVENESS.
YOU WOULD OFFER A MAN YOU BLINDED THE CHANCE TO SEE?
YOU ARE ONLY BLIND TO THAT WHICH YOU DO NOT DESERVE TO SEE.
WELL...DID HE DO IT, FOX? DID HE GO TO THE RIVER? DID HE SEE THE BEAST GET BORN? AND DID HE KILL IT?

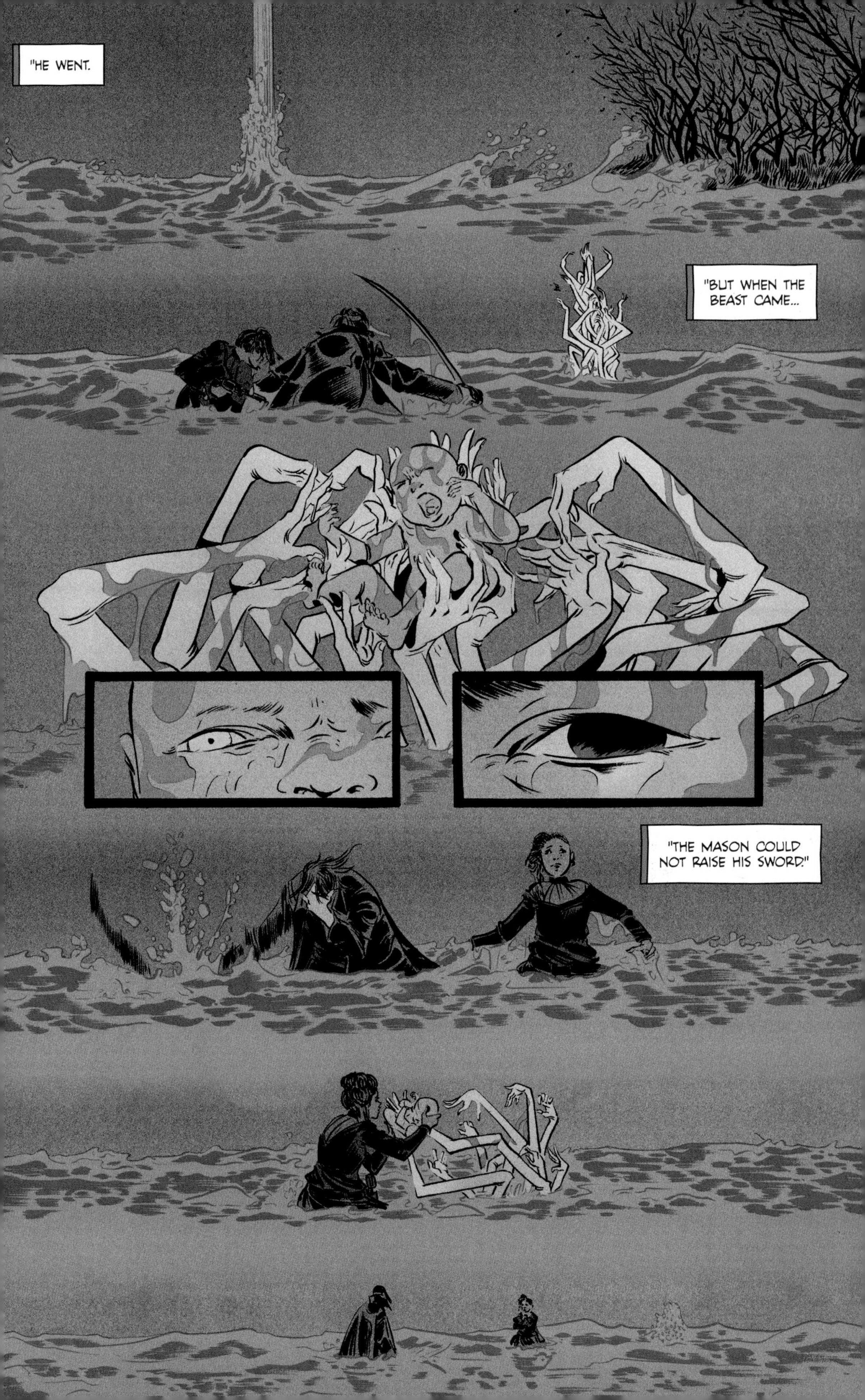
"HE WENT.
"BUT WHEN THE BEAST CAME...
"THE MASON COULD NOT RAISE HIS SWORD."

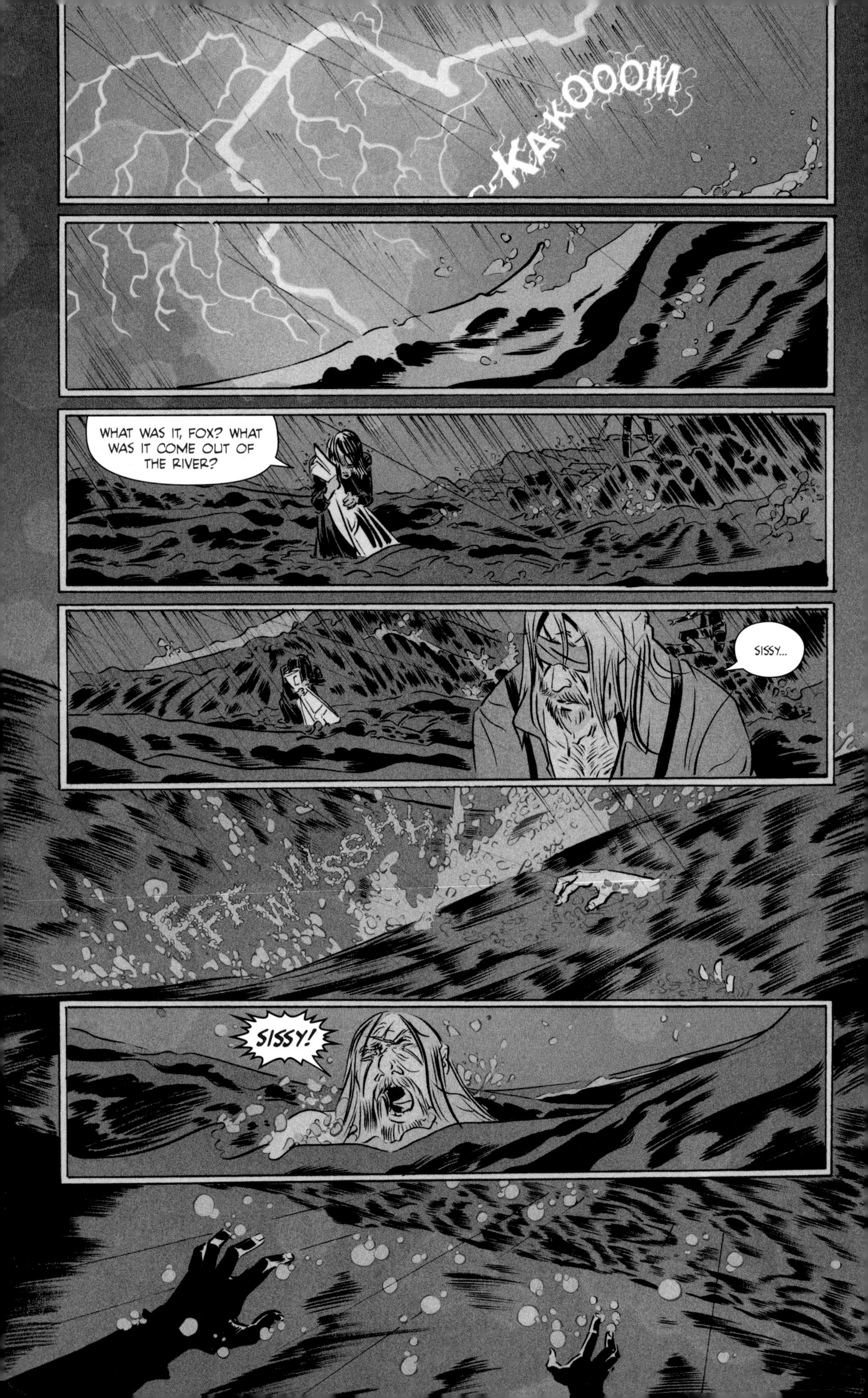
KAKOOOM
WHAT WAS IT, FOX? WHAT WAS IT COME OUT OF THE RIVER?
SISSY...
SISSY!

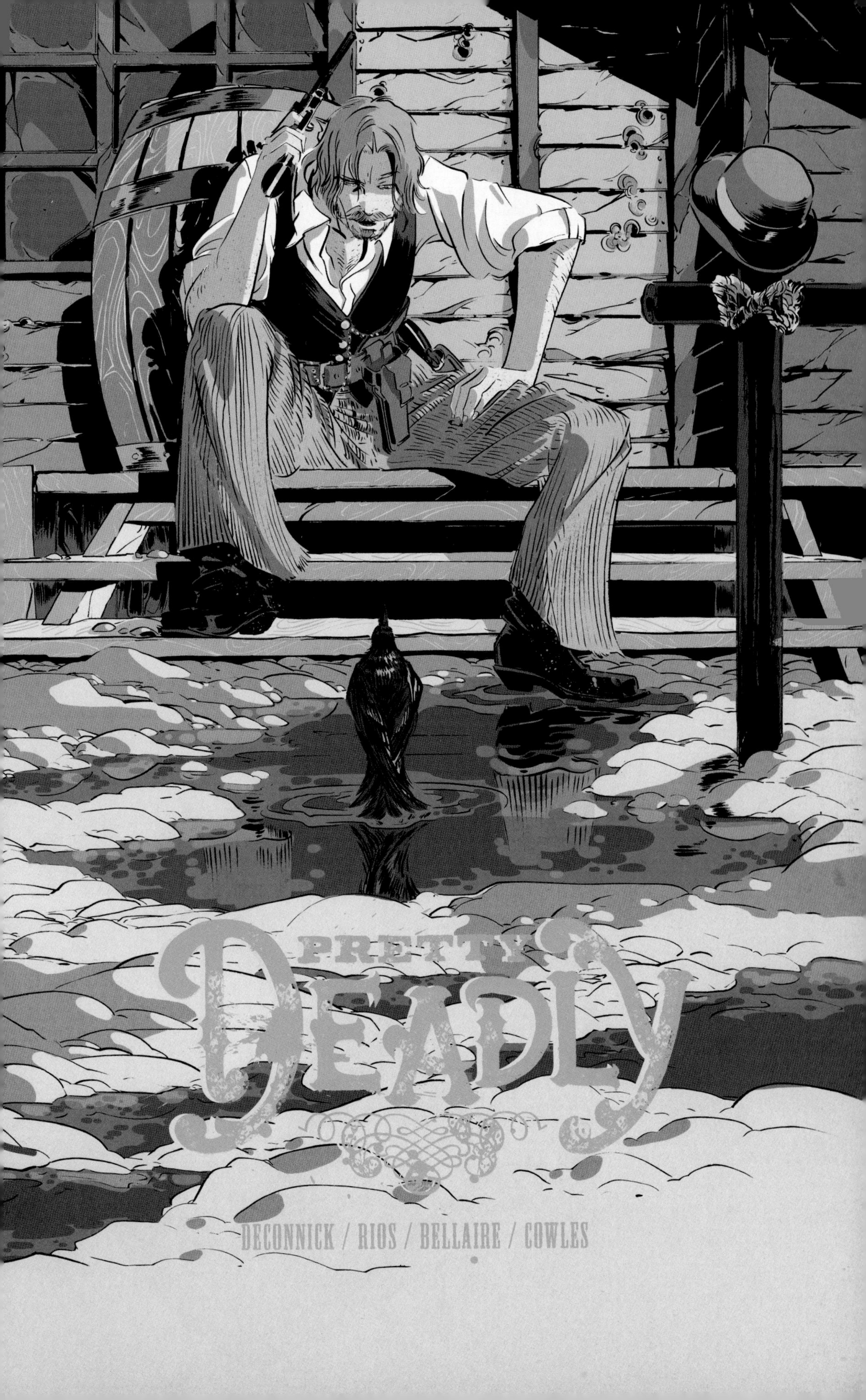
PRETTY DEADLY
DECONNICK / RIOS / BELLAIRE / COWLES

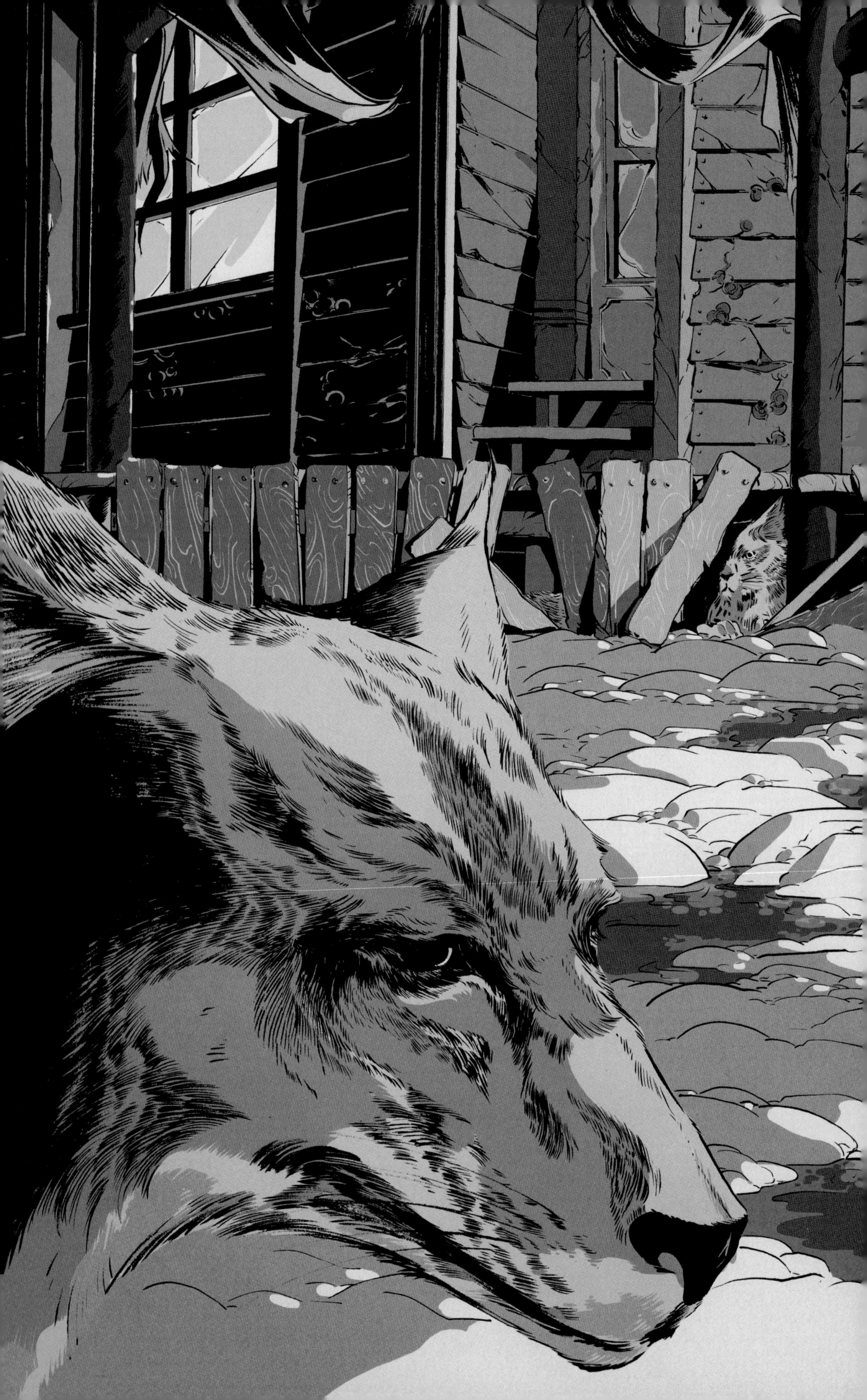

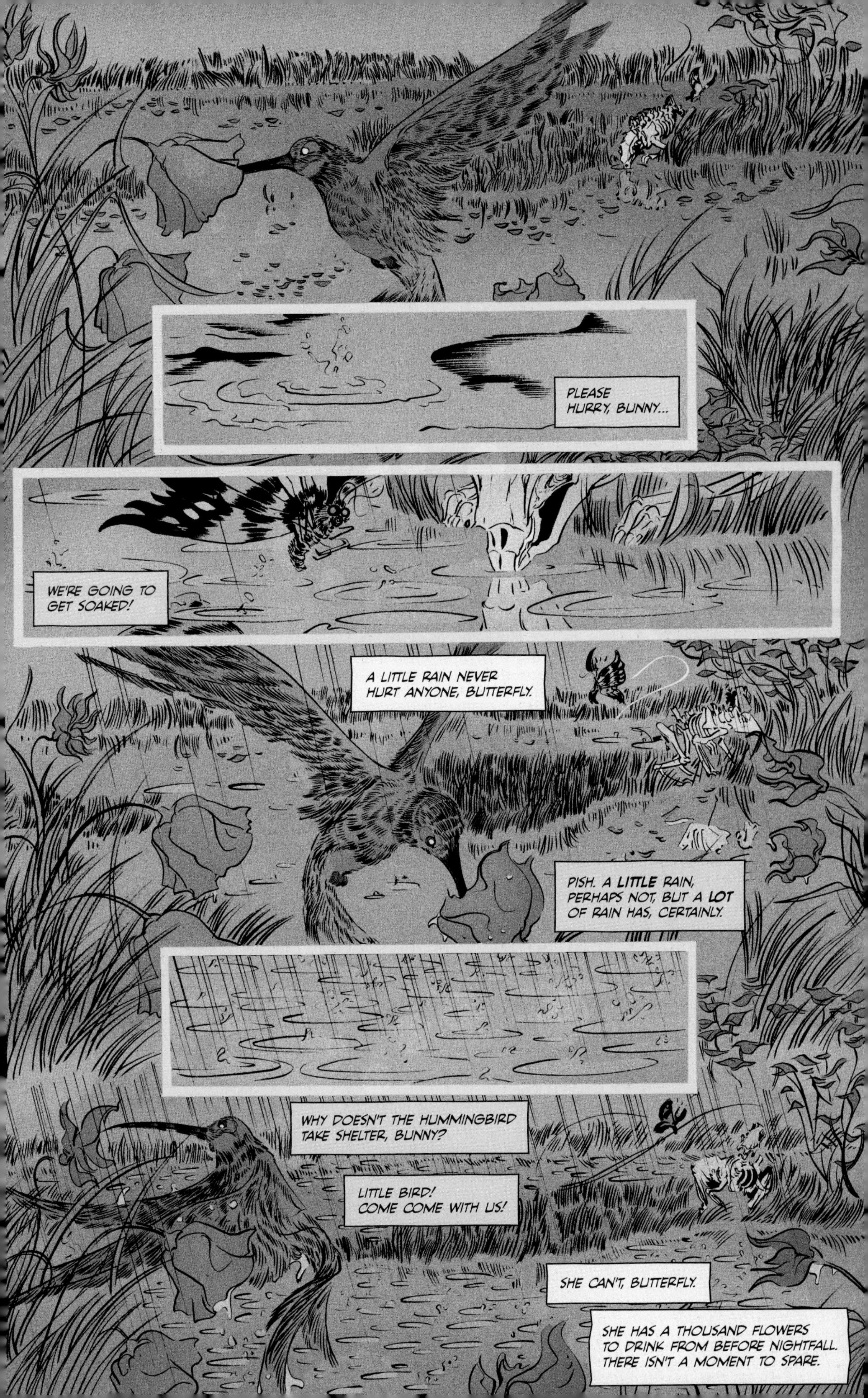
PLEASE HURRY, BUNNY...
WE'RE GOING TO GET SOAKED!
A LITTLE RAIN NEVER HURT ANYONE, BUTTERFLY.
PISH. A **LITTLE** RAIN, PERHAPS NOT, BUT A **LOT** OF RAIN HAS, CERTAINLY.
WHY DOESN'T THE HUMMINGBIRD TAKE SHELTER, BUNNY?
LITTLE BIRD! COME COME WITH US!
SHE CAN'T, BUTTERFLY.
SHE HAS A THOUSAND FLOWERS TO DRINK FROM BEFORE NIGHTFALL. THERE ISN'T A MOMENT TO SPARE.

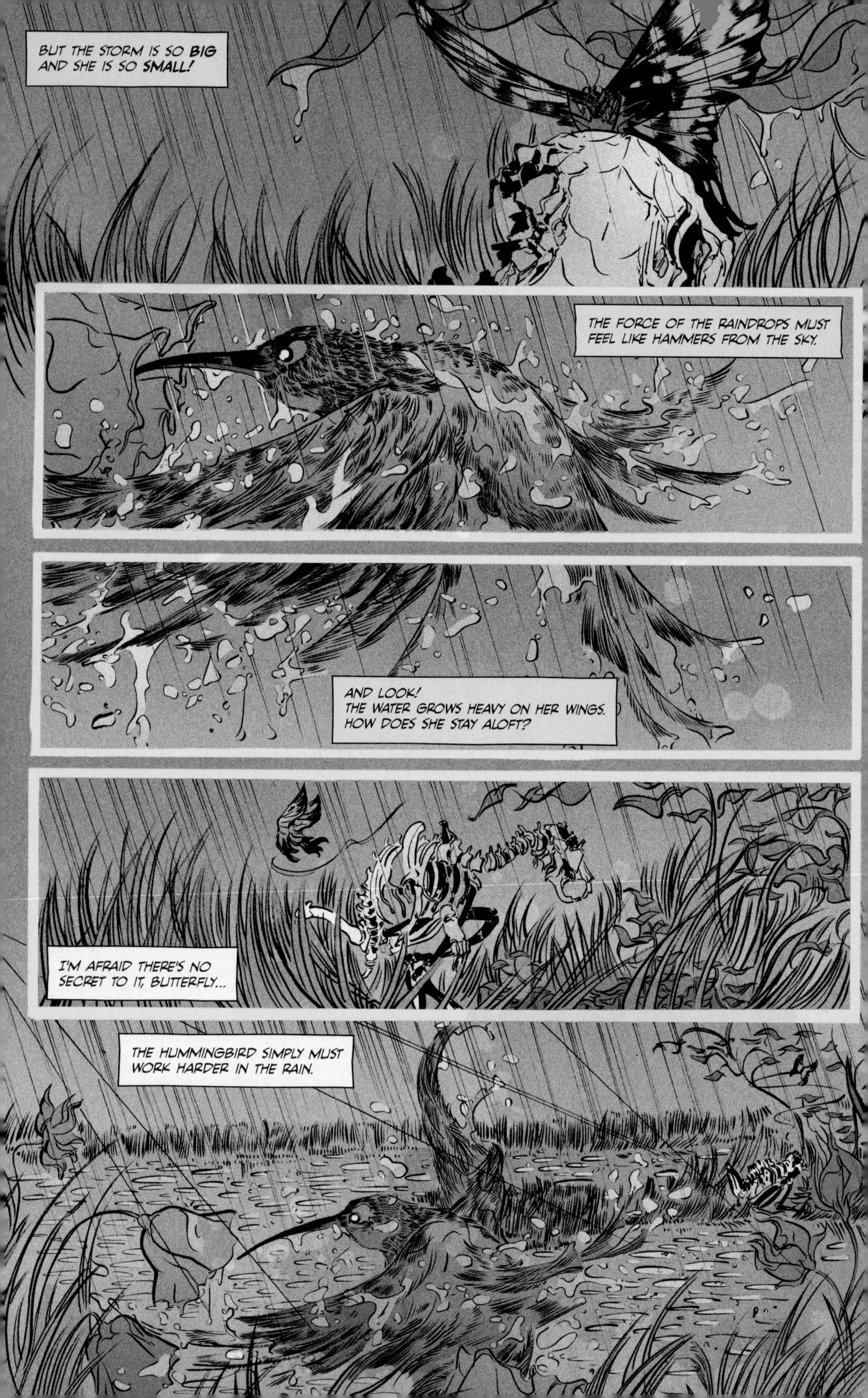
BUT THE STORM IS SO **BIG** AND SHE IS SO **SMALL!**
THE FORCE OF THE RAINDROPS MUST FEEL LIKE HAMMERS FROM THE SKY.
AND LOOK! THE WATER GROWS HEAVY ON HER WINGS. HOW DOES SHE STAY ALOFT?
I'M AFRAID THERE'S NO SECRET TO IT, BUTTERFLY...
THE HUMMINGBIRD SIMPLY MUST WORK HARDER IN THE RAIN.

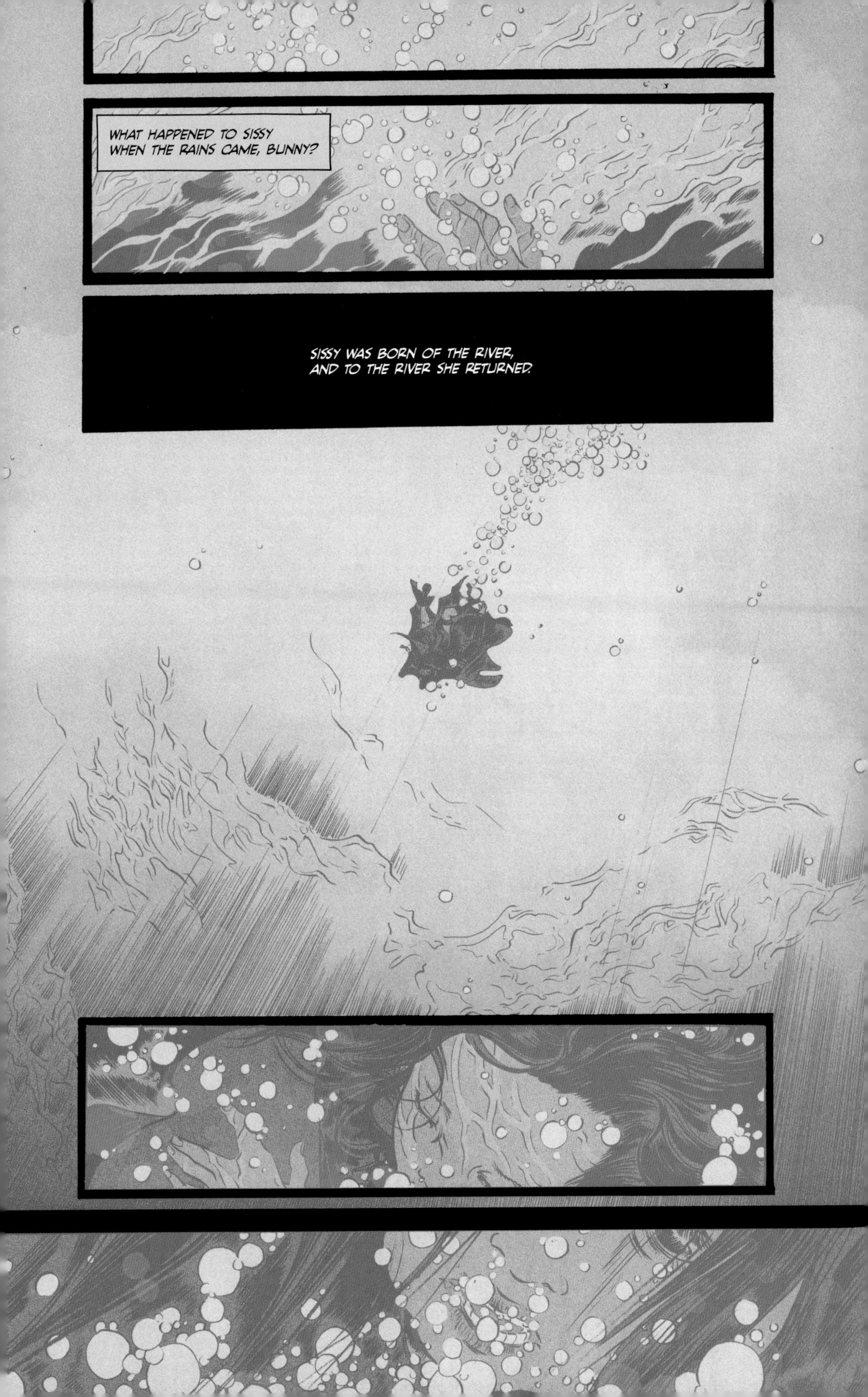
WHAT HAPPENED TO SISSY WHEN THE RAINS CAME, BUNNY?
SISSY WAS BORN OF THE RIVER, AND TO THE RIVER SHE RETURNED.

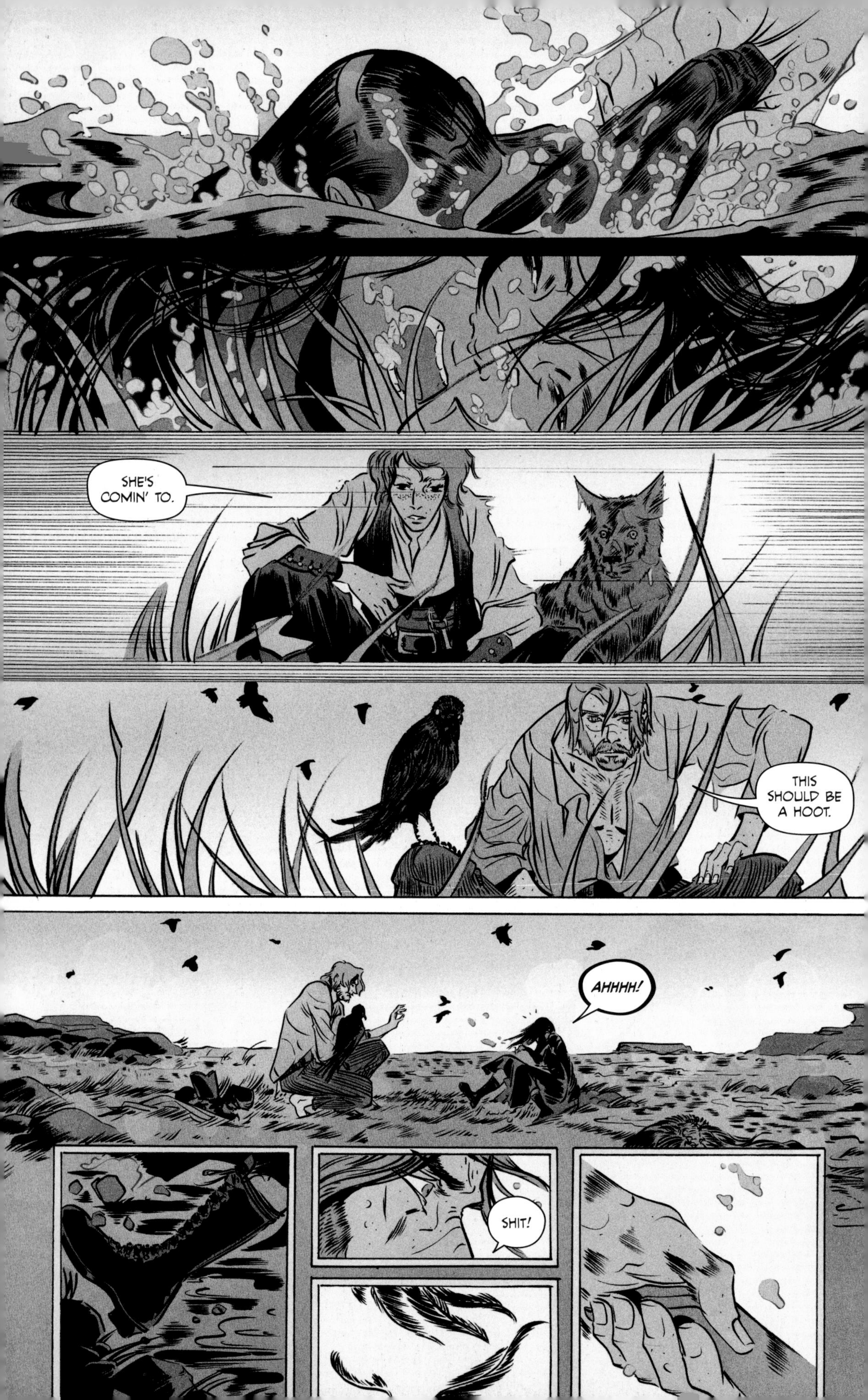
SHE'S COMIN' TO.
THIS SHOULD BE A HOOT.
AHHHH!
SHIT!

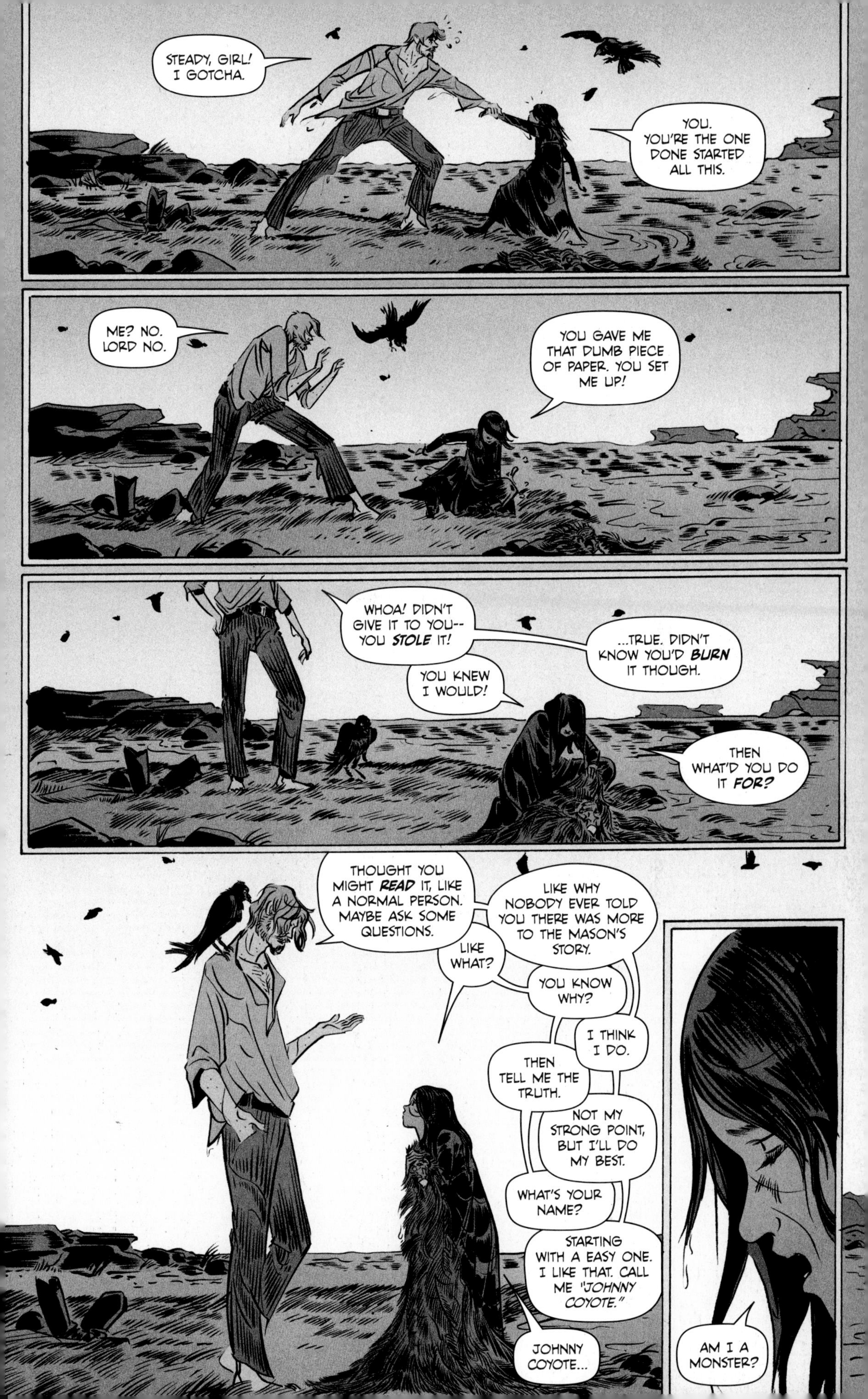
STEADY, GIRL! I GOTCHA.
YOU. YOU'RE THE ONE DONE STARTED ALL THIS.
ME? NO. LORD NO.
YOU GAVE ME THAT DUMB PIECE OF PAPER. YOU SET ME UP!
WHOA! DIDN'T GIVE IT TO YOU-- YOU STOLE IT!
YOU KNEW I WOULD!
...TRUE. DIDN'T KNOW YOU'D BURN IT THOUGH.
THEN WHAT'D YOU DO IT FOR?
THOUGHT YOU MIGHT READ IT, LIKE A NORMAL PERSON. MAYBE ASK SOME QUESTIONS.
LIKE WHAT?
LIKE WHY NOBODY EVER TOLD YOU THERE WAS MORE TO THE MASON'S STORY.
YOU KNOW WHY?
I THINK I DO.
THEN TELL ME THE TRUTH.
NOT MY STRONG POINT, BUT I'LL DO MY BEST.
WHAT'S YOUR NAME?
STARTING WITH A EASY ONE. I LIKE THAT. CALL ME "JOHNNY COYOTE."
JOHNNY COYOTE...
AM I A MONSTER?

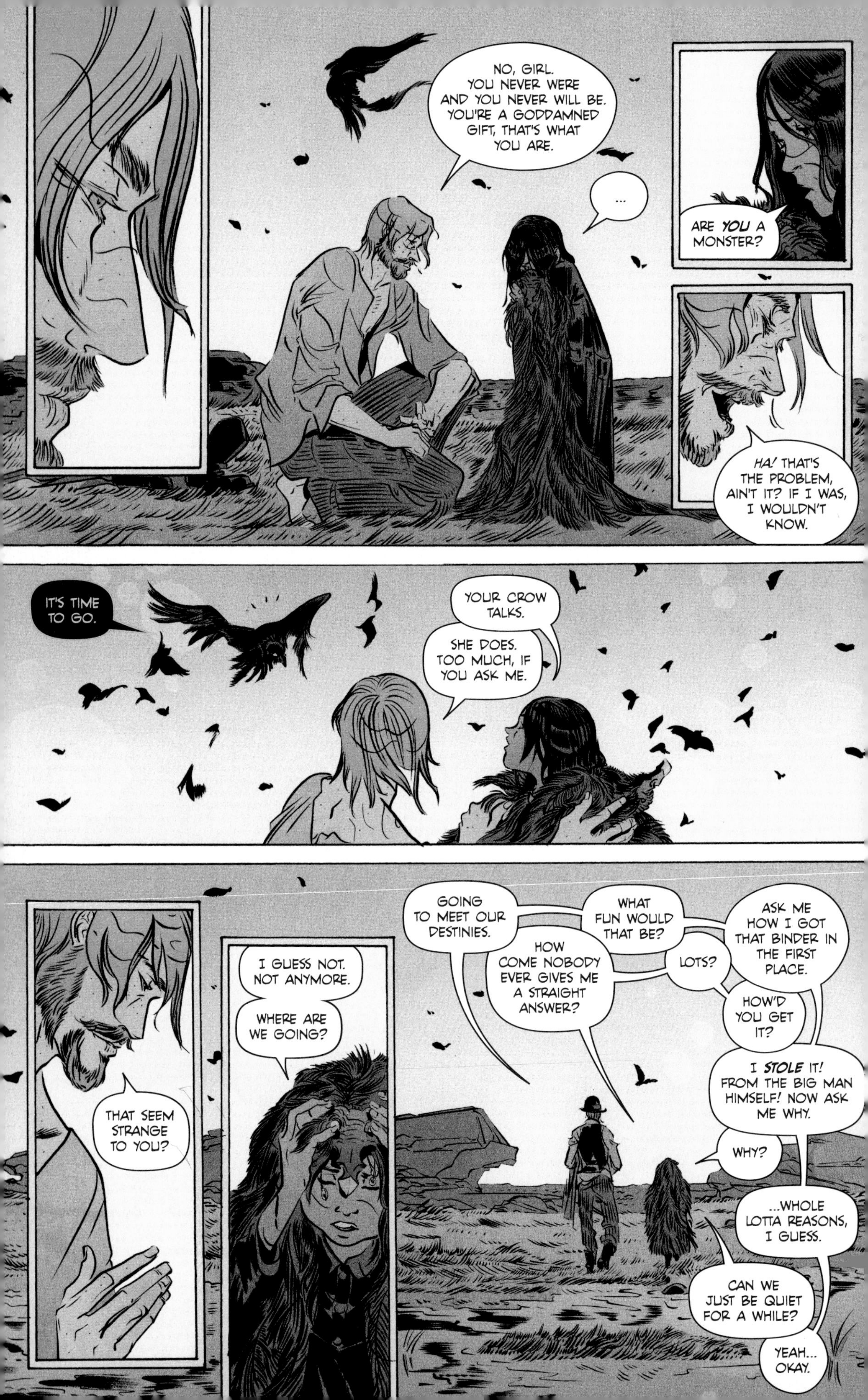
NO, GIRL. YOU NEVER WERE AND YOU NEVER WILL BE. YOU'RE A GODDAMNED GIFT, THAT'S WHAT YOU ARE.
...
ARE *YOU* A MONSTER?
HA! THAT'S THE PROBLEM, AIN'T IT? IF I WAS, I WOULDN'T KNOW.
IT'S TIME TO GO.
YOUR CROW TALKS.
SHE DOES. TOO MUCH, IF YOU ASK ME.
THAT SEEM STRANGE TO YOU?
I GUESS NOT. NOT ANYMORE.
WHERE ARE WE GOING?
GOING TO MEET OUR DESTINIES.
WHAT FUN WOULD THAT BE?
HOW COME NOBODY EVER GIVES ME A STRAIGHT ANSWER?
LOTS?
ASK ME HOW I GOT THAT BINDER IN THE FIRST PLACE.
HOW'D YOU GET IT?
I *STOLE* IT! FROM THE BIG MAN HIMSELF! NOW ASK ME WHY.
WHY?
...WHOLE LOTTA REASONS, I GUESS.
CAN WE JUST BE QUIET FOR A WHILE?
YEAH... OKAY.

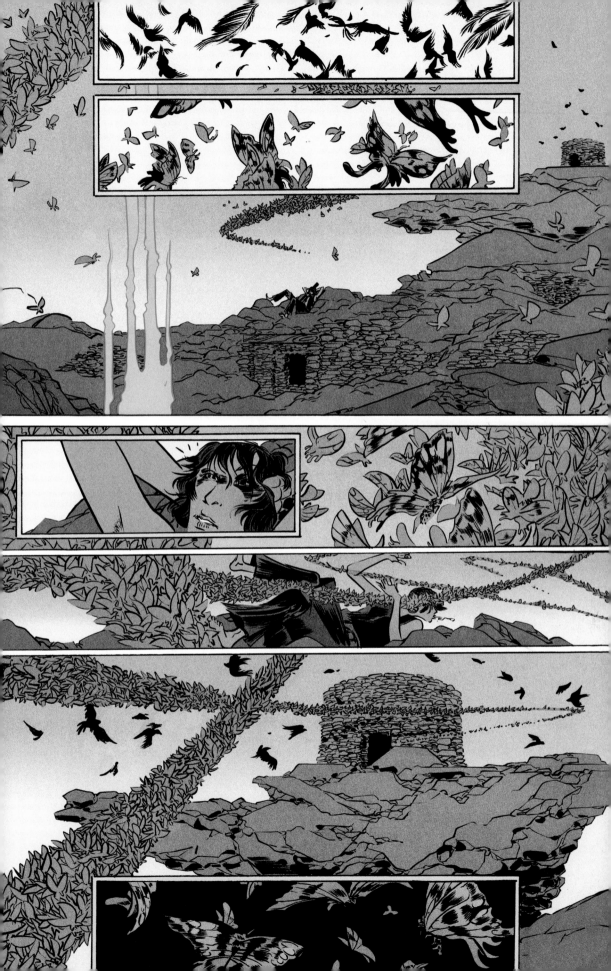

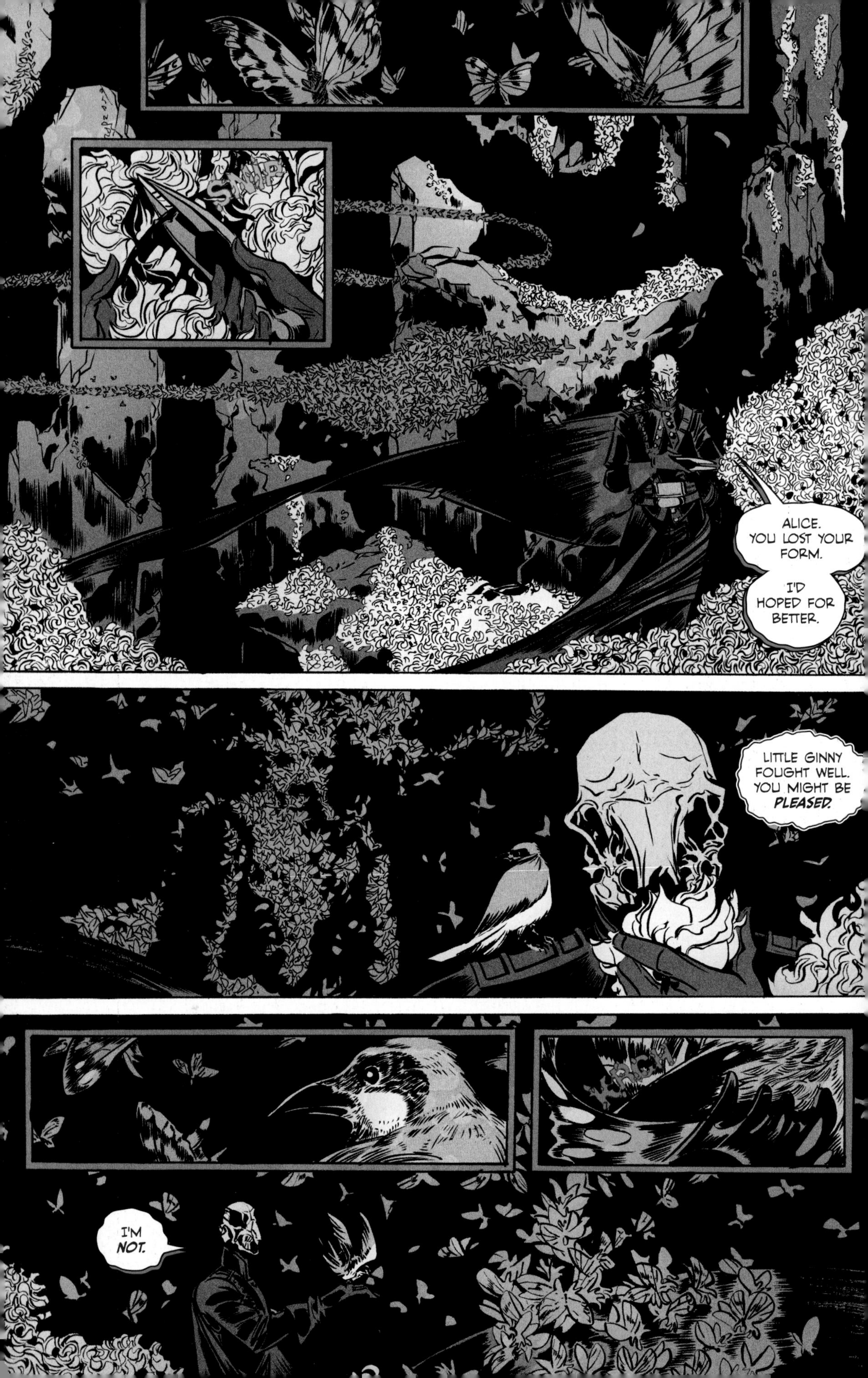
ALICE. YOU LOST YOUR FORM.
I'D HOPED FOR BETTER.
LITTLE GINNY FOUGHT WELL. YOU MIGHT BE *PLEASED.*
I'M *NOT.*

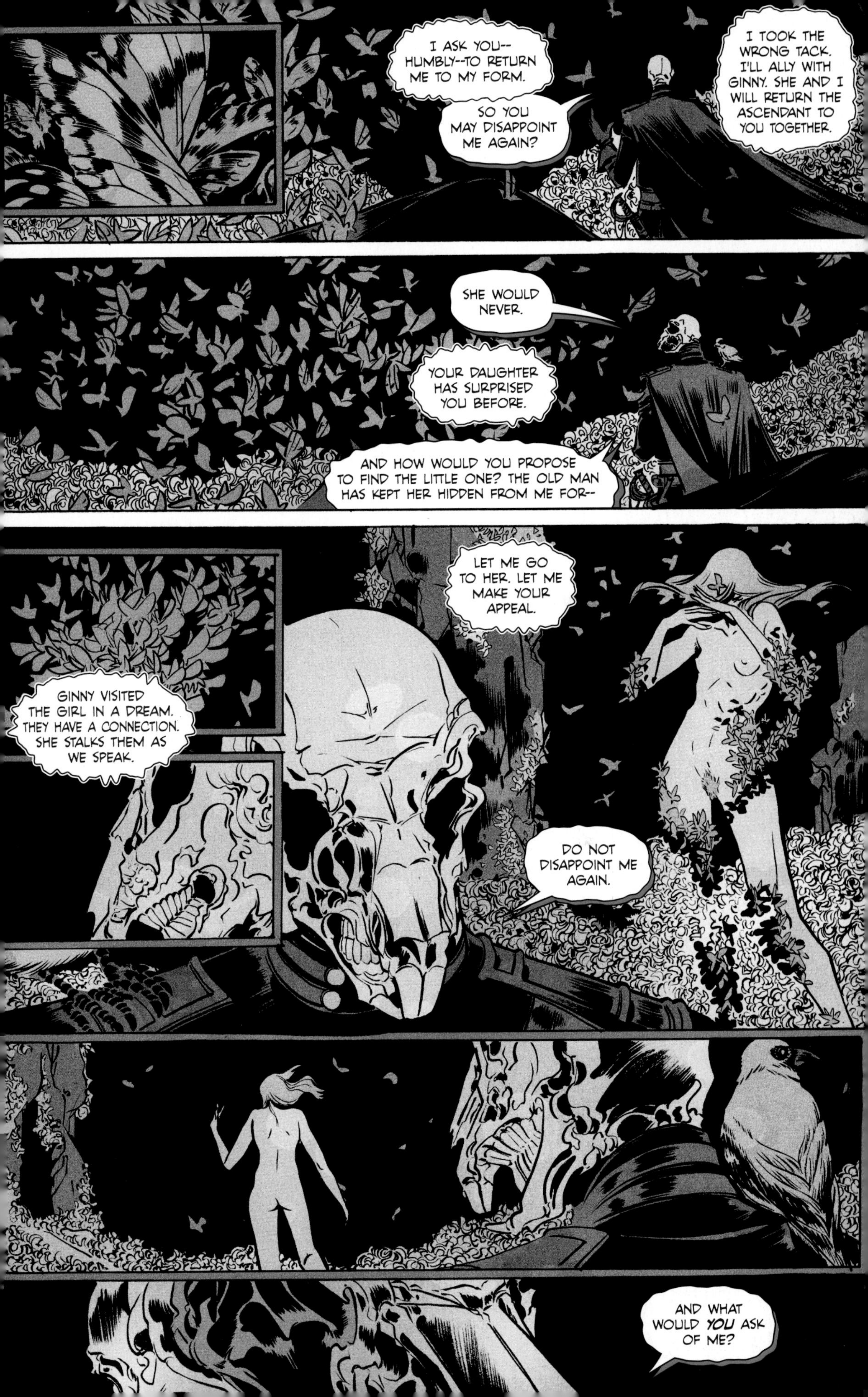
I ASK YOU--HUMBLY--TO RETURN ME TO MY FORM.
SO YOU MAY DISAPPOINT ME AGAIN?
I TOOK THE WRONG TACK. I'LL ALLY WITH GINNY. SHE AND I WILL RETURN THE ASCENDANT TO YOU TOGETHER.
SHE WOULD NEVER.
YOUR DAUGHTER HAS SURPRISED YOU BEFORE.
AND HOW WOULD YOU PROPOSE TO FIND THE LITTLE ONE? THE OLD MAN HAS KEPT HER HIDDEN FROM ME FOR--
GINNY VISITED THE GIRL IN A DREAM. THEY HAVE A CONNECTION. SHE STALKS THEM AS WE SPEAK.
LET ME GO TO HER. LET ME MAKE YOUR APPEAL.
DO NOT DISAPPOINT ME AGAIN.
AND WHAT WOULD *YOU* ASK OF ME?

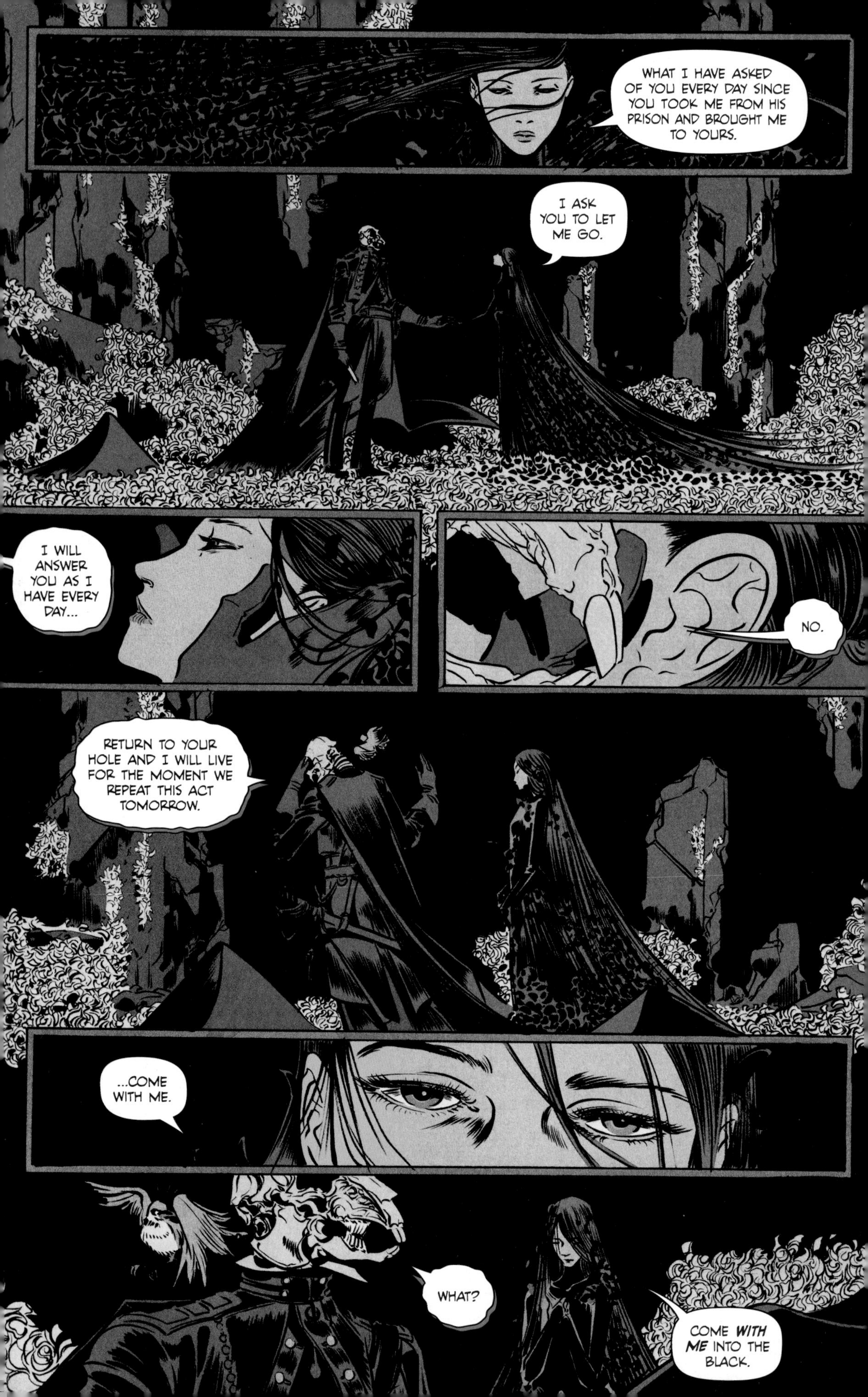
WHAT I HAVE ASKED OF YOU EVERY DAY SINCE YOU TOOK ME FROM HIS PRISON AND BROUGHT ME TO YOURS.
I ASK YOU TO LET ME GO.
I WILL ANSWER YOU AS I HAVE EVERY DAY...
NO.
RETURN TO YOUR HOLE AND I WILL LIVE FOR THE MOMENT WE REPEAT THIS ACT TOMORROW.
...COME WITH ME.
WHAT?
COME WITH ME INTO THE BLACK.

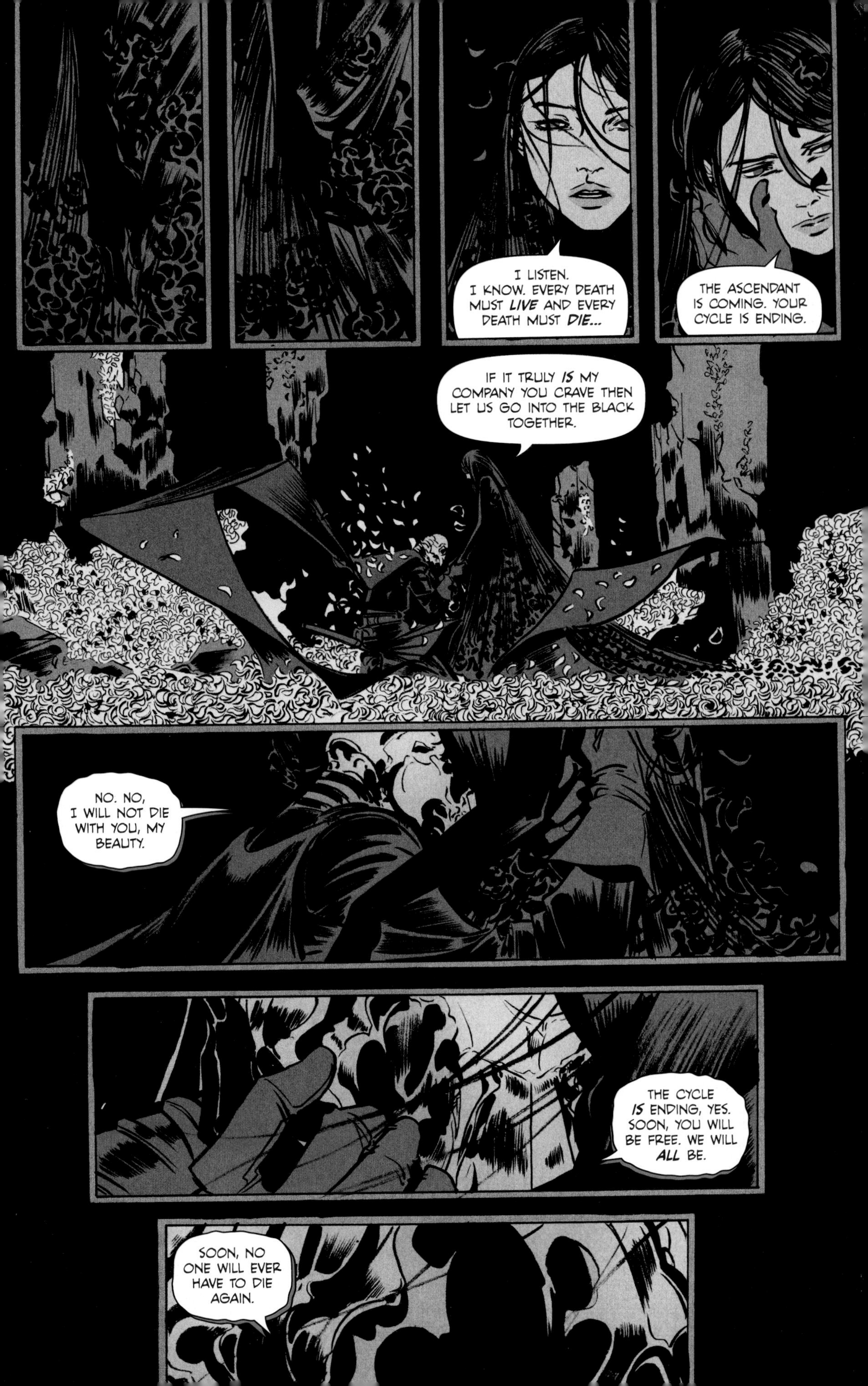
I LISTEN. I KNOW. EVERY DEATH MUST LIVE AND EVERY DEATH MUST DIE...
THE ASCENDANT IS COMING. YOUR CYCLE IS ENDING.
IF IT TRULY IS MY COMPANY YOU CRAVE THEN LET US GO INTO THE BLACK TOGETHER.
NO. NO, I WILL NOT DIE WITH YOU, MY BEAUTY.
THE CYCLE IS ENDING, YES. SOON, YOU WILL BE FREE. WE WILL ALL BE.
SOON, NO ONE WILL EVER HAVE TO DIE AGAIN.

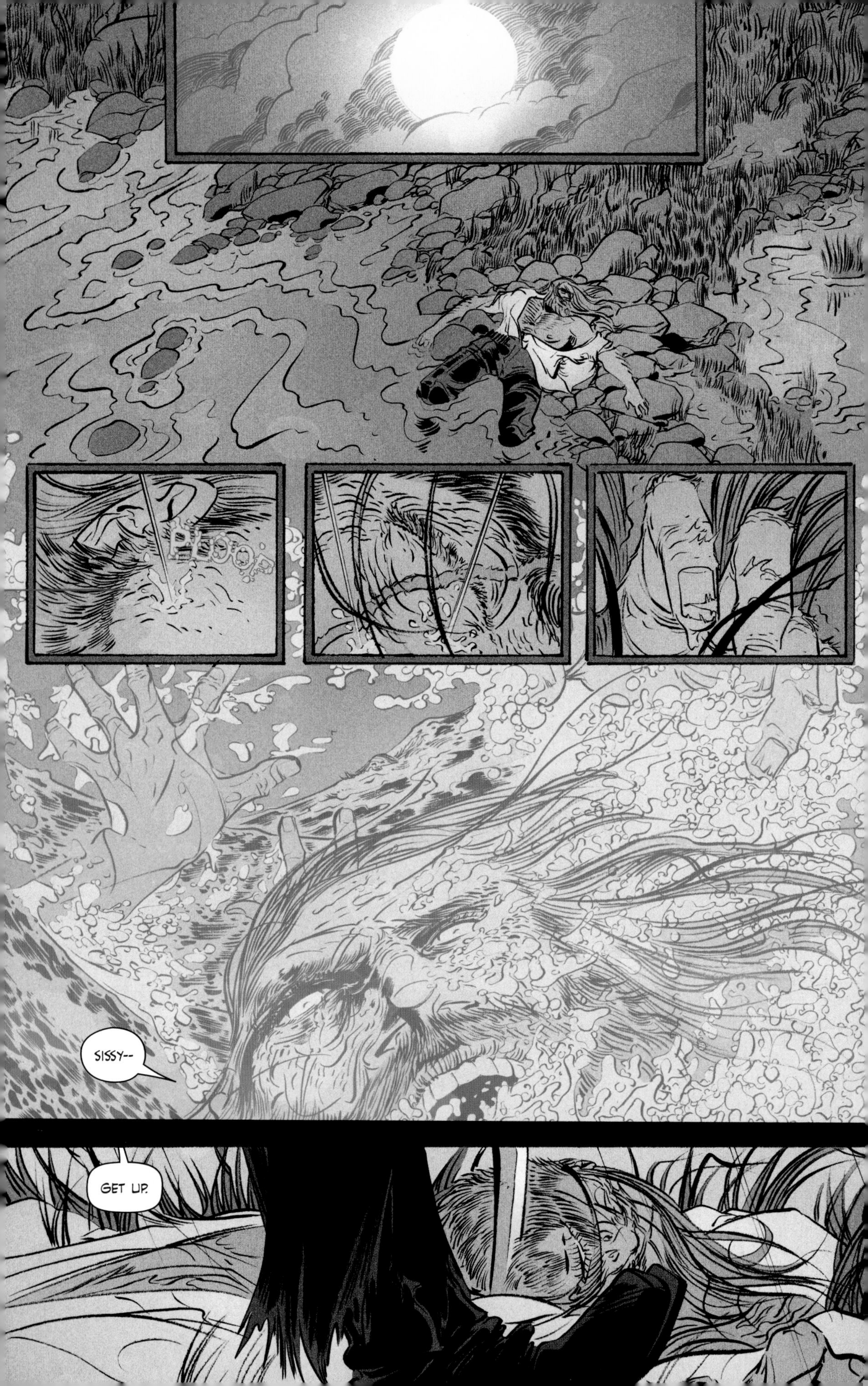
PLOOP
SISSY--
GET UP.

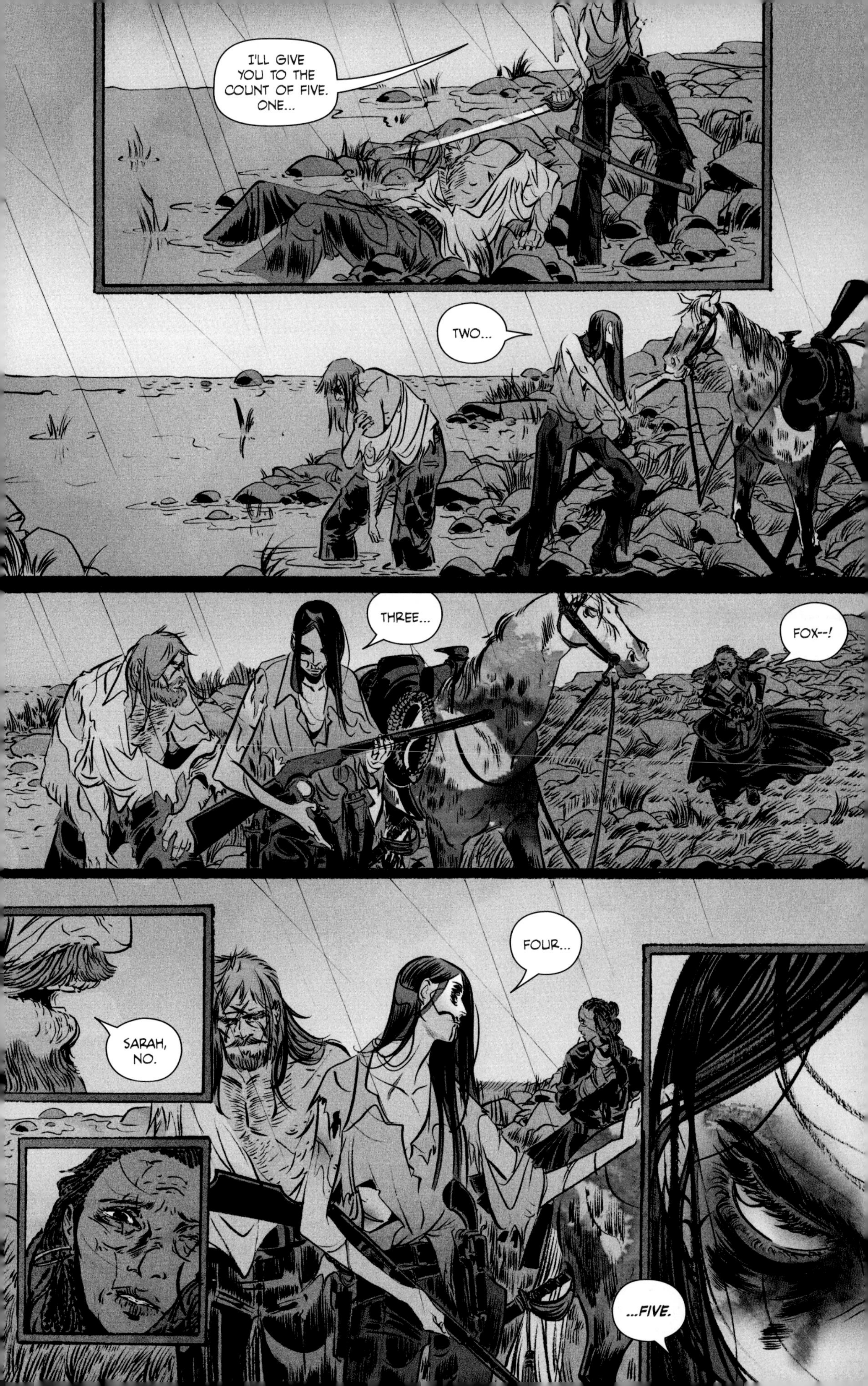
I'LL GIVE YOU TO THE COUNT OF FIVE. ONE...
TWO...
THREE...
FOX--!
SARAH, NO.
FOUR...
...FIVE.

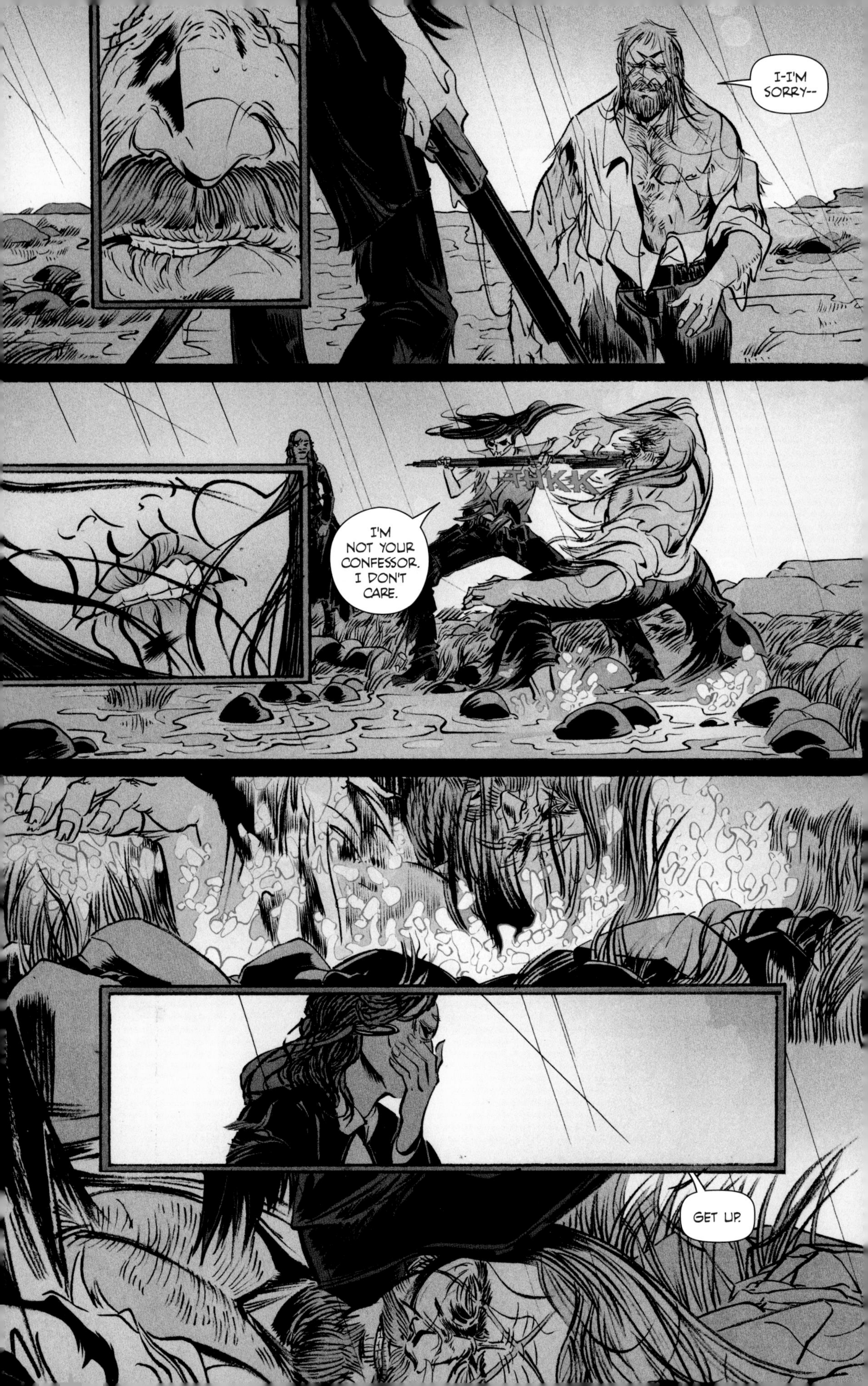
I-I'M SORRY--
THKK
I'M NOT YOUR CONFESSOR. I DON'T CARE.
GET UP.

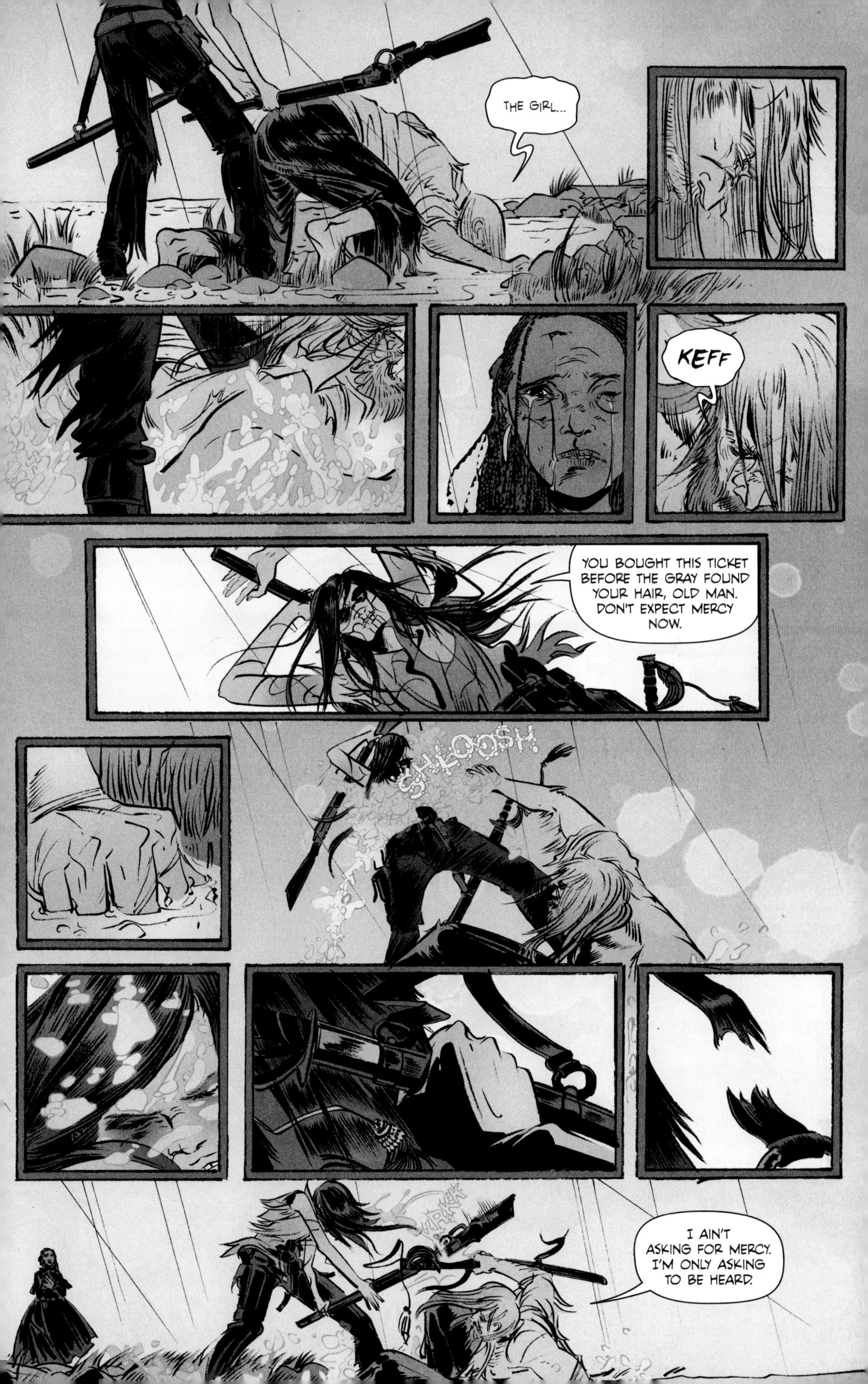
THE GIRL...
KEFF
YOU BOUGHT THIS TICKET BEFORE THE GRAY FOUND YOUR HAIR, OLD MAN. DON'T EXPECT MERCY NOW.
SHLOOSH
I AIN'T ASKING FOR MERCY. I'M ONLY ASKING TO BE HEARD.

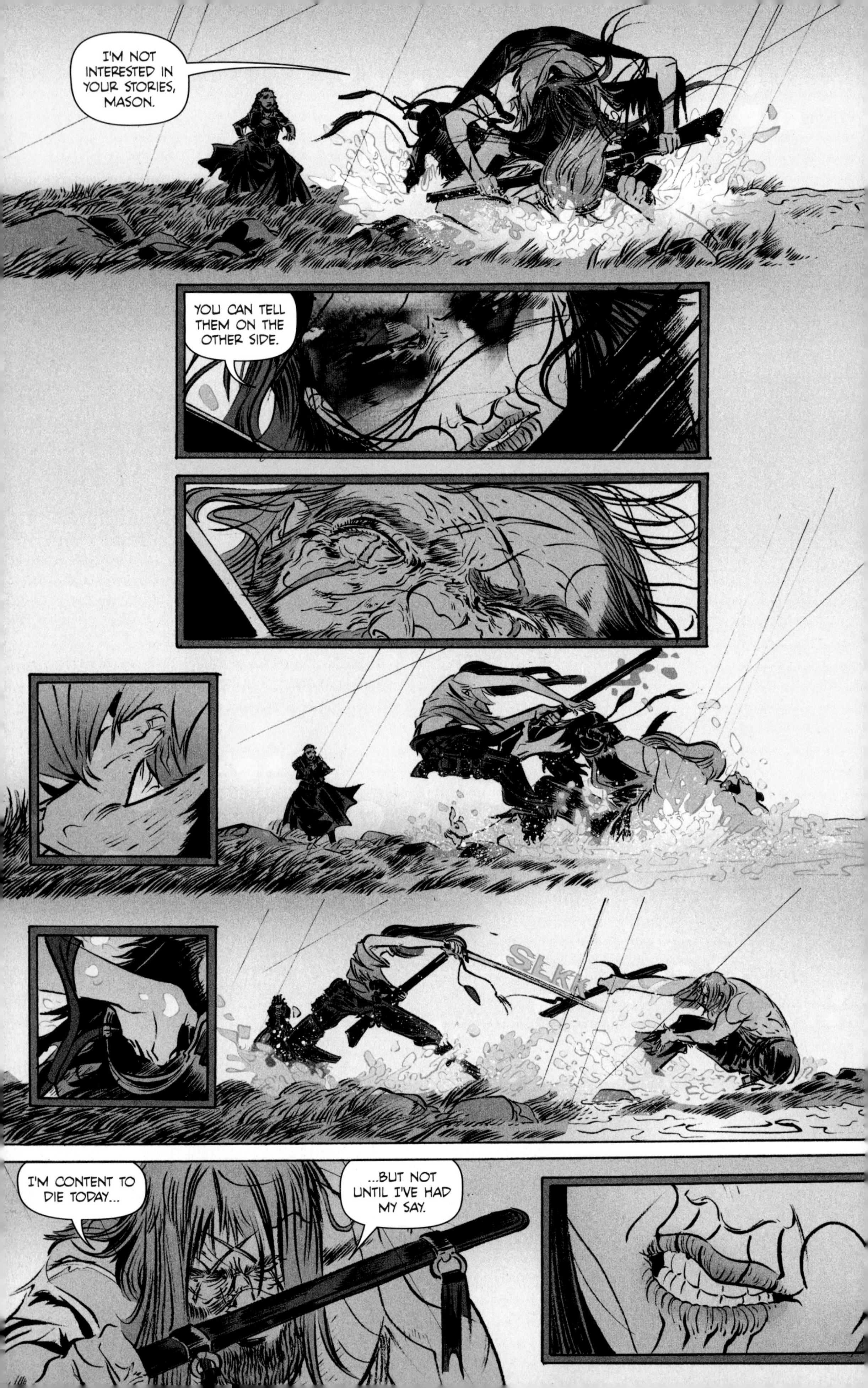
I'M NOT INTERESTED IN YOUR STORIES, MASON.
YOU CAN TELL THEM ON THE OTHER SIDE.
SLKK
I'M CONTENT TO DIE TODAY...
...BUT NOT UNTIL I'VE HAD MY SAY.

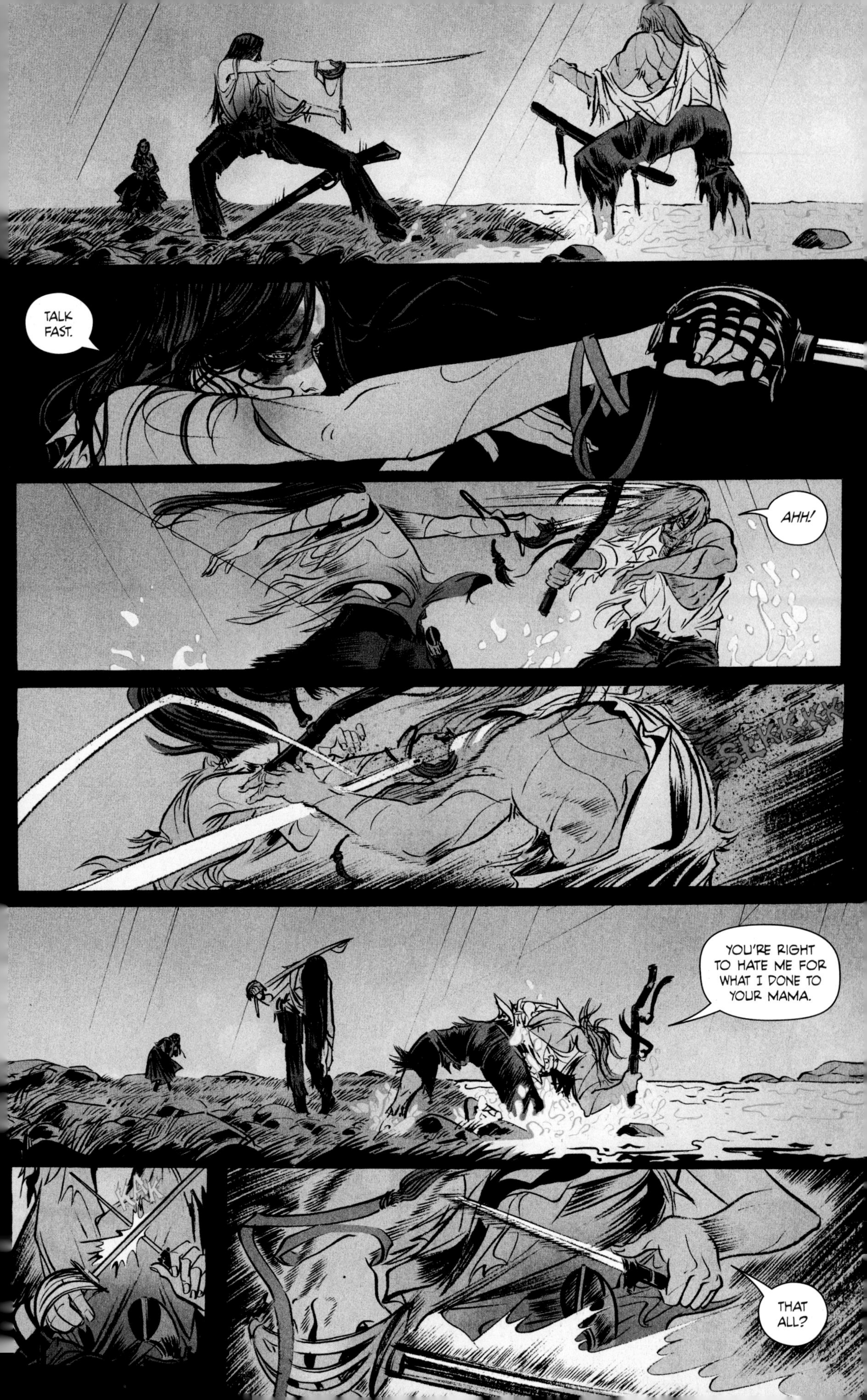
TALK FAST.
AHH!
SLKKKKK
YOU'RE RIGHT TO HATE ME FOR WHAT I DONE TO YOUR MAMA.
KAK
THAT ALL?

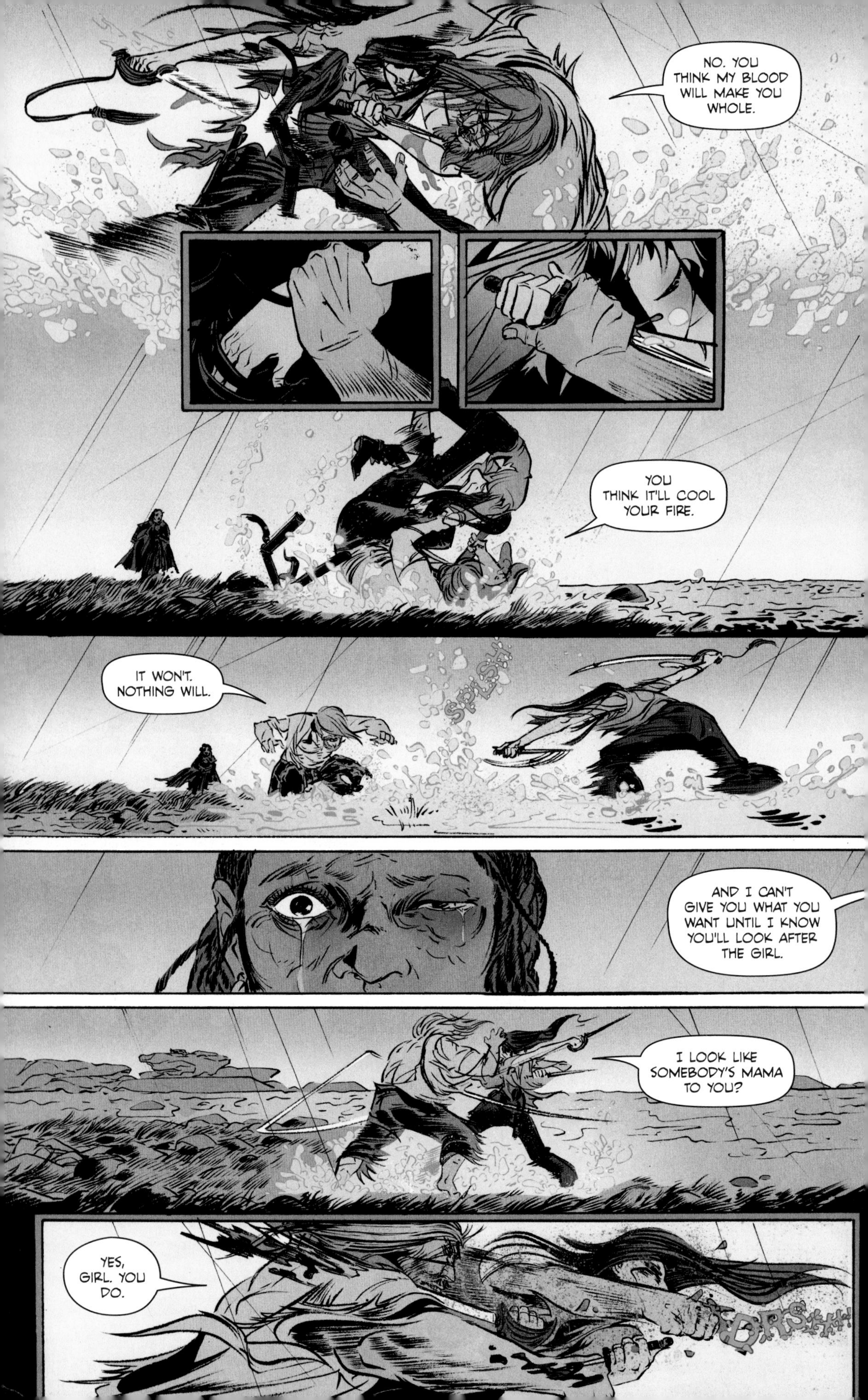
NO. YOU THINK MY BLOOD WILL MAKE YOU WHOLE.
YOU THINK IT'LL COOL YOUR FIRE.
IT WON'T. NOTHING WILL.
SPLSH
AND I CAN'T GIVE YOU WHAT YOU WANT UNTIL I KNOW YOU'LL LOOK AFTER THE GIRL.
I LOOK LIKE SOMEBODY'S MAMA TO YOU?
YES, GIRL. YOU DO.
DRSHH!

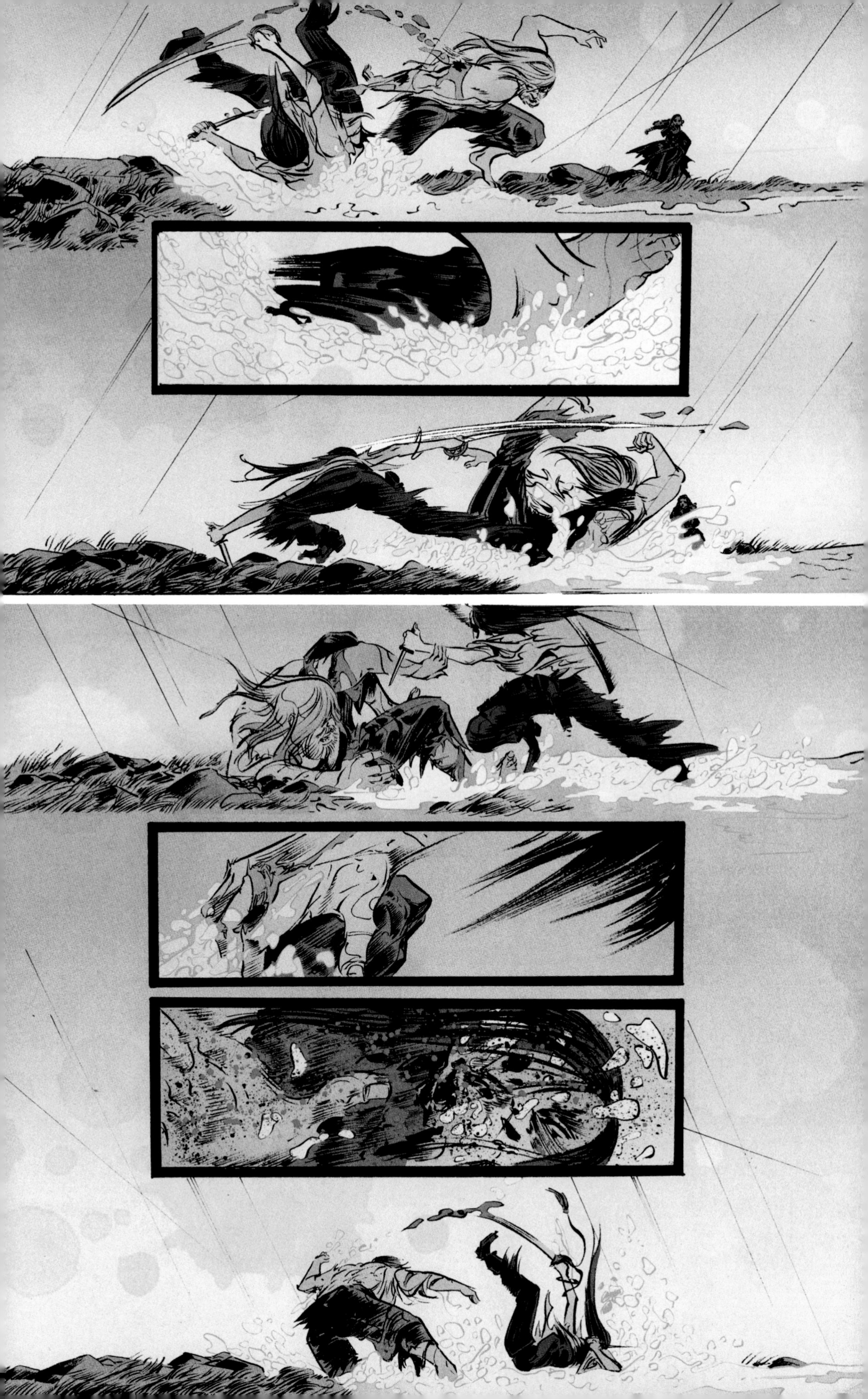

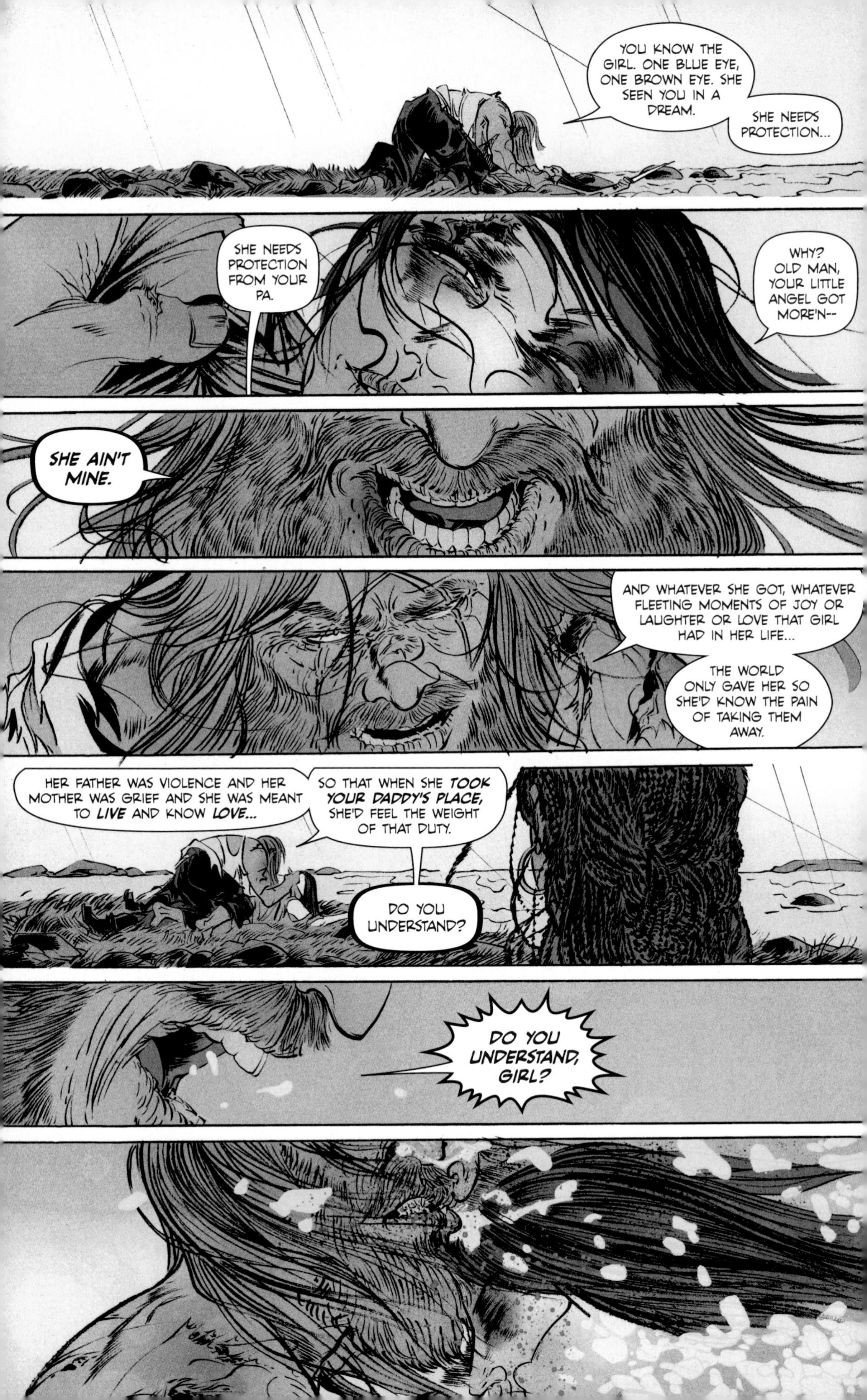
YOU KNOW THE GIRL. ONE BLUE EYE, ONE BROWN EYE. SHE SEEN YOU IN A DREAM.
SHE NEEDS PROTECTION...
SHE NEEDS PROTECTION FROM YOUR PA.
WHY? OLD MAN, YOUR LITTLE ANGEL GOT MORE'N--
SHE AIN'T MINE.
AND WHATEVER SHE GOT, WHATEVER FLEETING MOMENTS OF JOY OR LAUGHTER OR LOVE THAT GIRL HAD IN HER LIFE...
THE WORLD ONLY GAVE HER SO SHE'D KNOW THE PAIN OF TAKING THEM AWAY.
HER FATHER WAS VIOLENCE AND HER MOTHER WAS GRIEF AND SHE WAS MEANT TO LIVE AND KNOW LOVE...
SO THAT WHEN SHE TOOK YOUR DADDY'S PLACE, SHE'D FEEL THE WEIGHT OF THAT DUTY.
DO YOU UNDERSTAND?
DO YOU UNDERSTAND, GIRL?

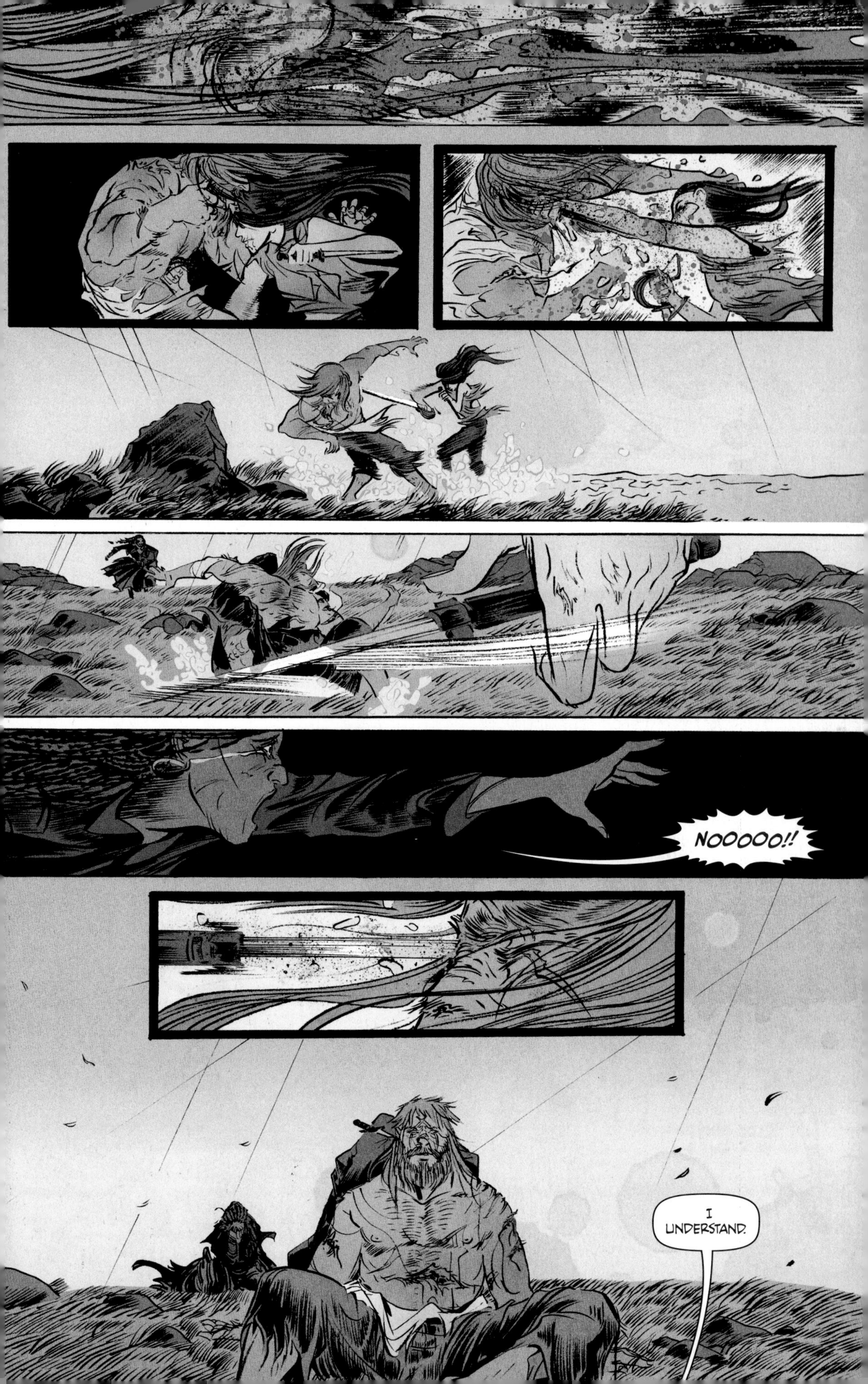
NOOOOO!!
I UNDERSTAND.

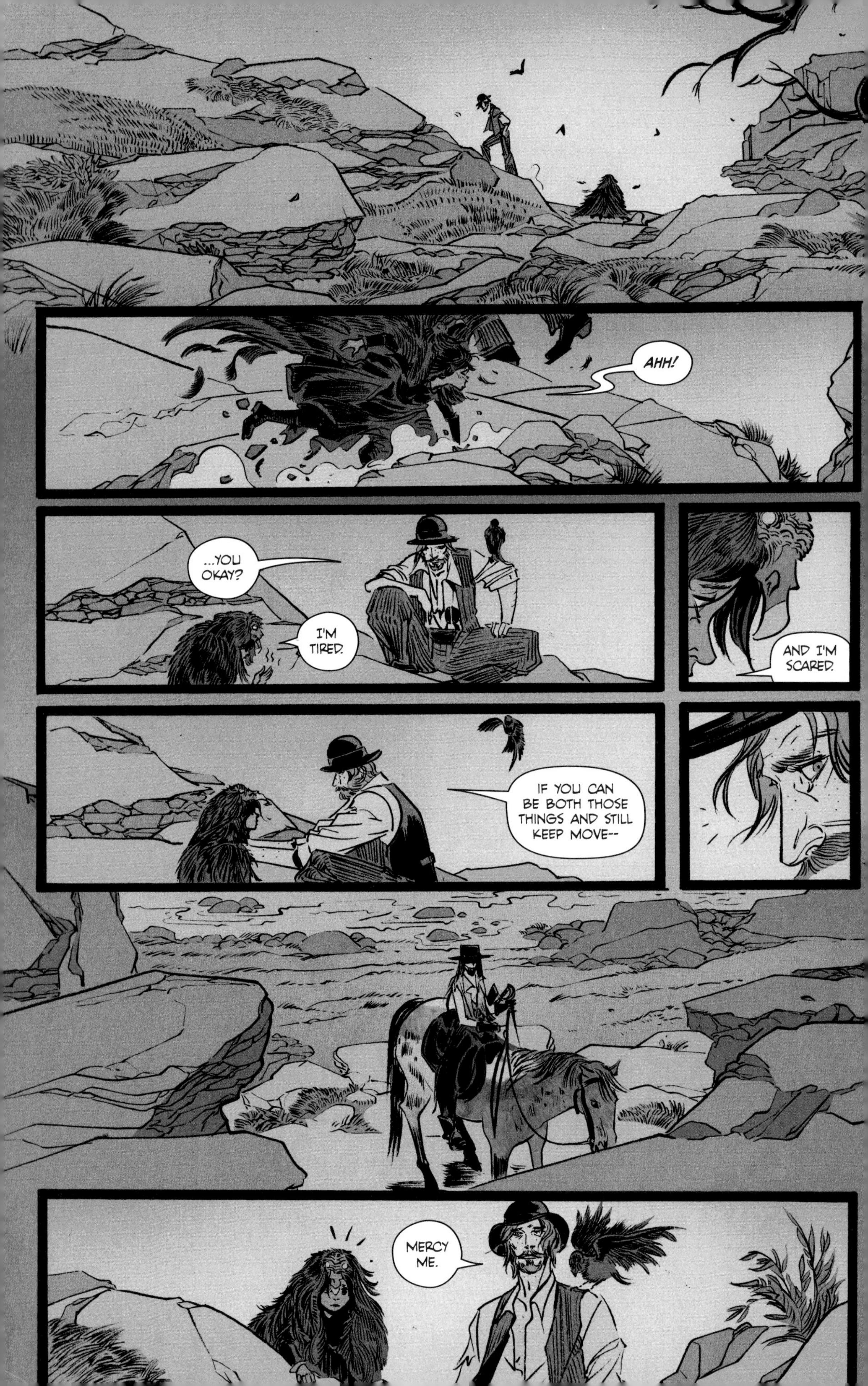
AHH!
...YOU OKAY?
I'M TIRED.
AND I'M SCARED.
IF YOU CAN BE BOTH THOSE THINGS AND STILL KEEP MOVE--
MERCY ME.

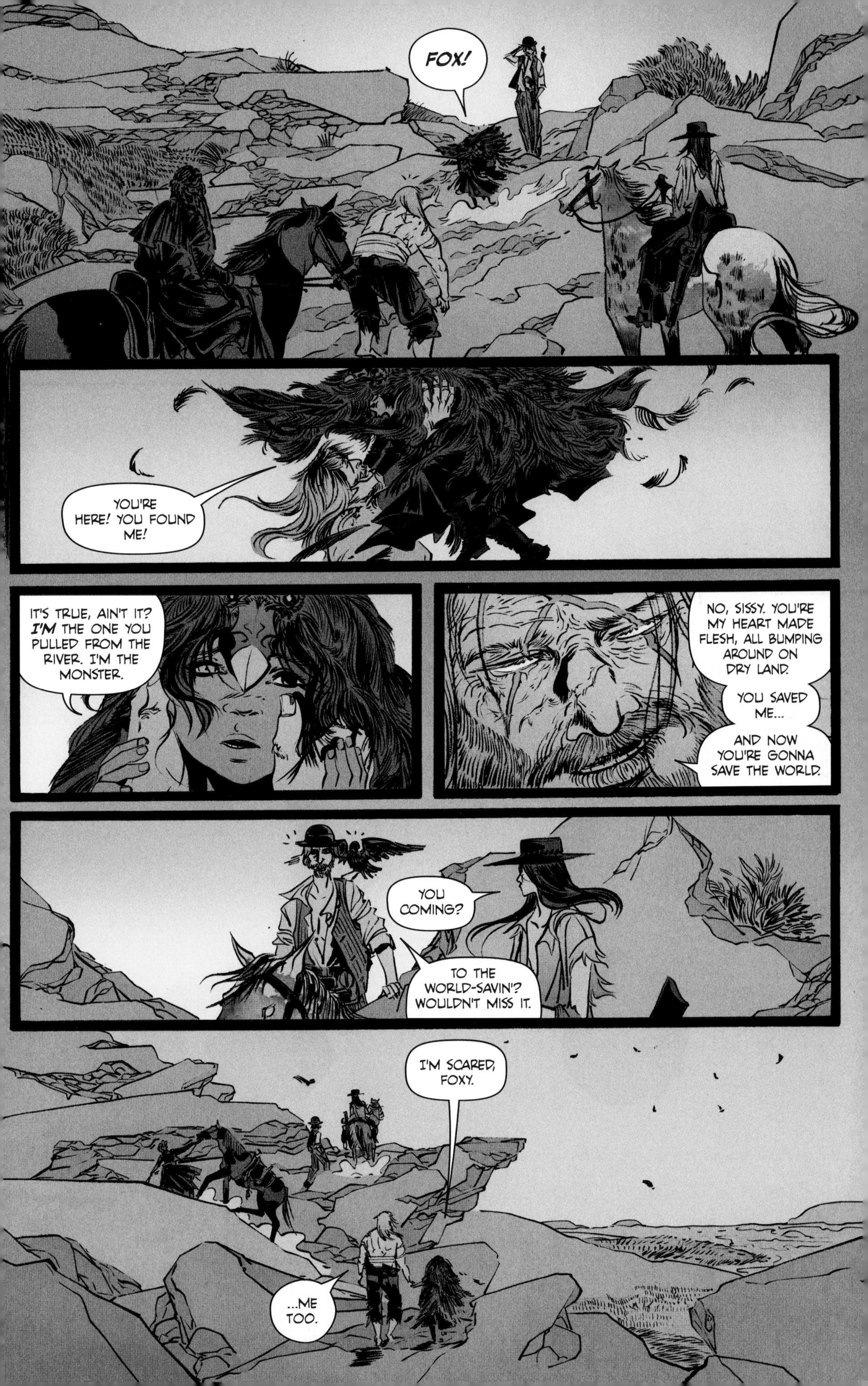
FOX!
YOU'RE HERE! YOU FOUND ME!
IT'S TRUE, AIN'T IT? I'M THE ONE YOU PULLED FROM THE RIVER. I'M THE MONSTER.
NO, SISSY. YOU'RE MY HEART MADE FLESH, ALL BUMPING AROUND ON DRY LAND.
YOU SAVED ME...
AND NOW YOU'RE GONNA SAVE THE WORLD.
YOU COMING?
TO THE WORLD-SAVIN'? WOULDN'T MISS IT.
I'M SCARED, FOXY.
...ME TOO.

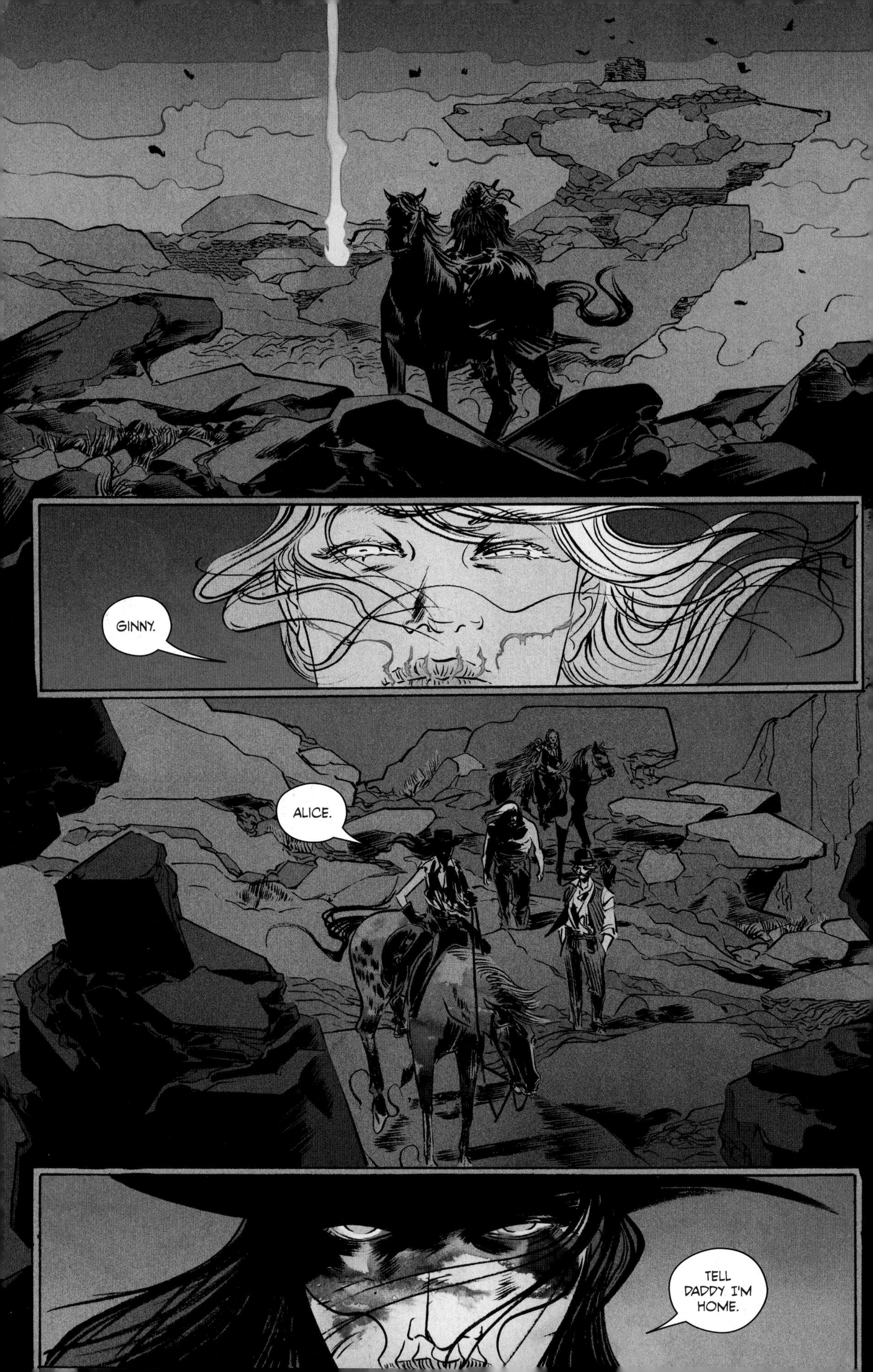
GINNY.
ALICE.
TELL DADDY I'M HOME.

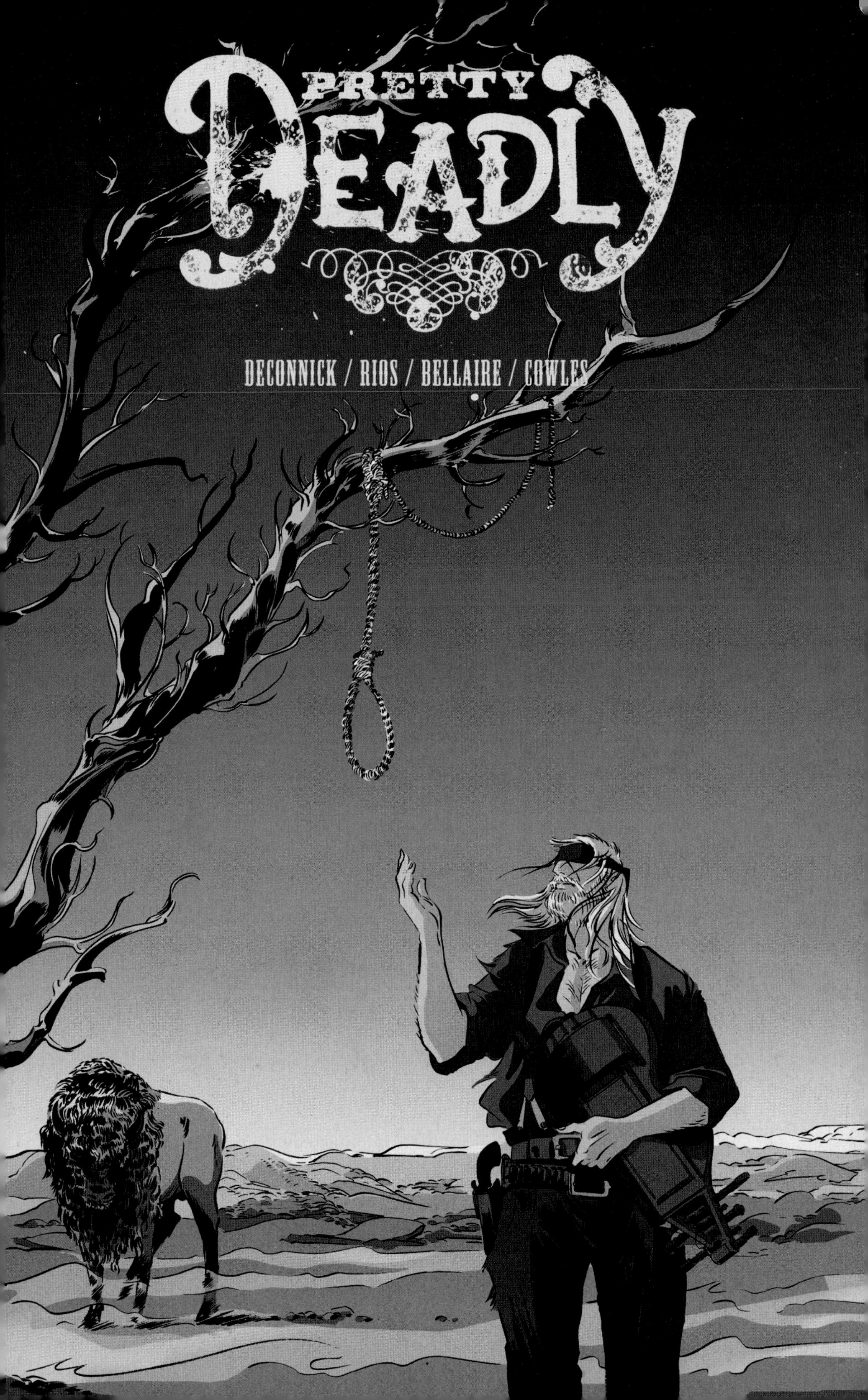
PRETTY
DEADLY
DECONNICK / RIOS / BELLAIRE / COWLES

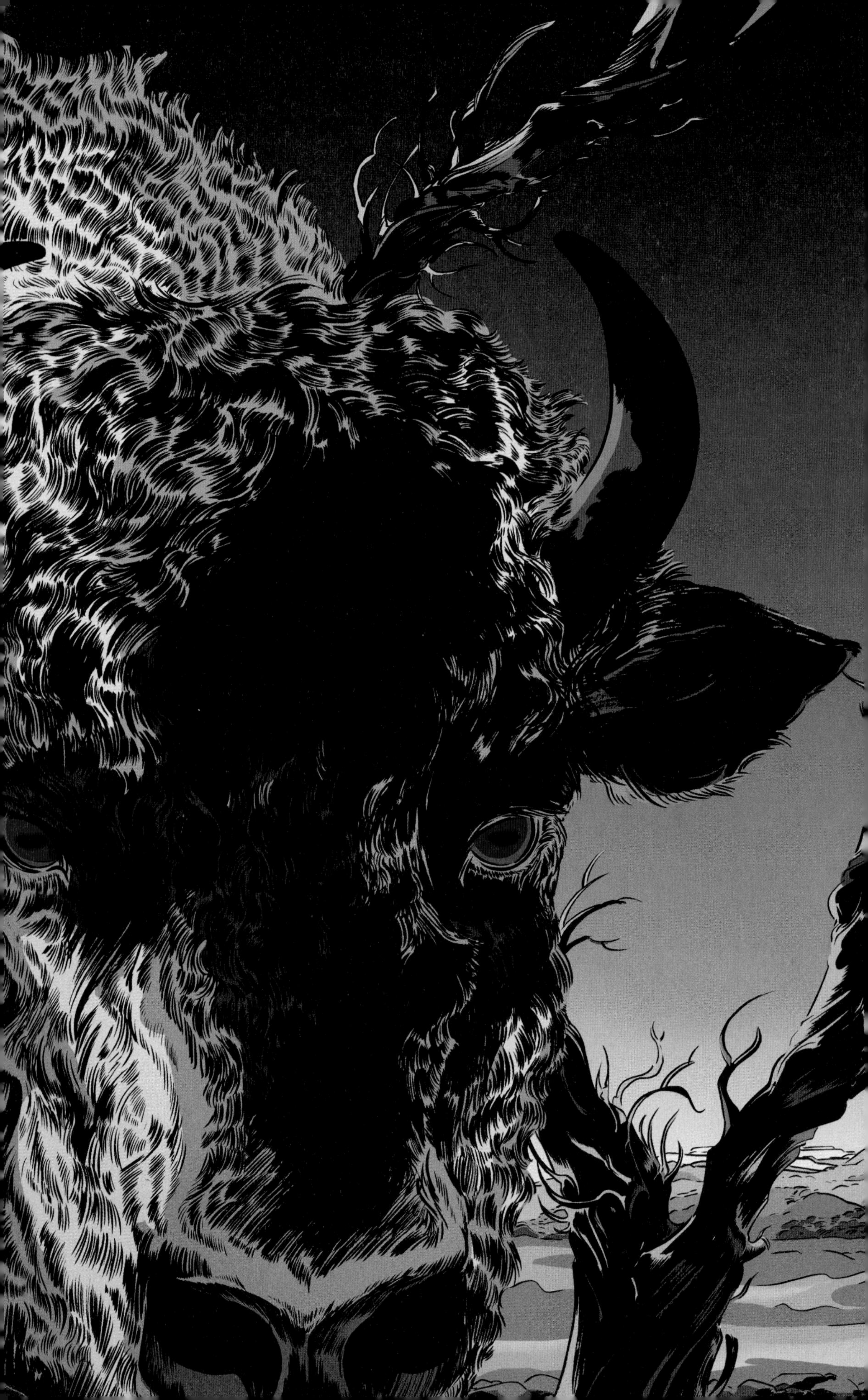

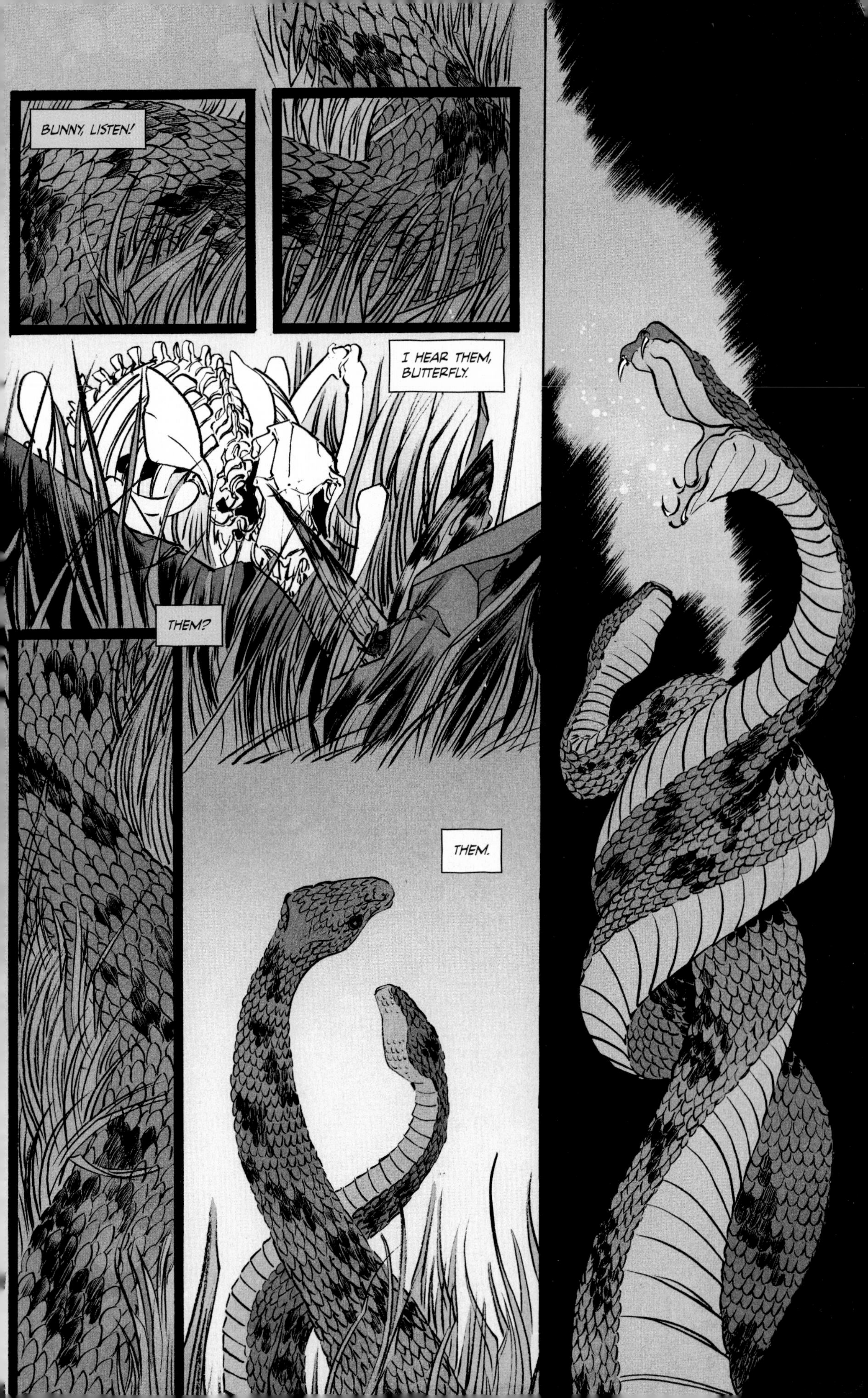
BUNNY, LISTEN!
I HEAR THEM, BUTTERFLY.
THEM?
THEM.

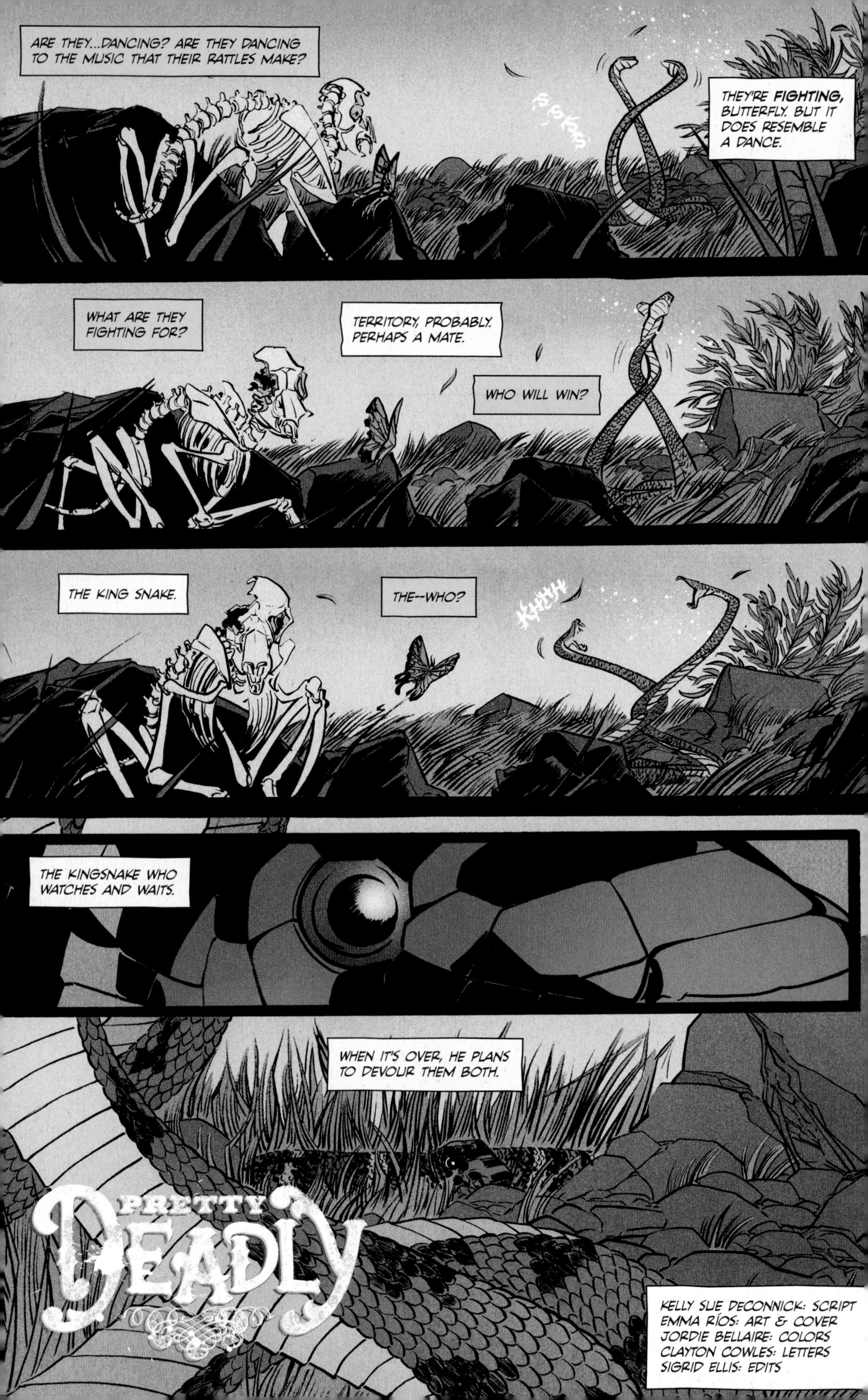
ARE THEY...DANCING? ARE THEY DANCING TO THE MUSIC THAT THEIR RATTLES MAKE?
RSSSS
THEY'RE **FIGHTING,** BUTTERFLY. BUT IT DOES RESEMBLE A DANCE.
WHAT ARE THEY FIGHTING FOR?
TERRITORY, PROBABLY. PERHAPS A MATE.
WHO WILL WIN?
THE KING SNAKE.
THE--WHO?
KHHHH
THE KINGSNAKE WHO WATCHES AND WAITS.
WHEN IT'S OVER, HE PLANS TO DEVOUR THEM BOTH.
PRETTY DEADLY
KELLY SUE DECONNICK: SCRIPT
EMMA RÍOS: ART & COVER
JORDIE BELLAIRE: COLORS
CLAYTON COWLES: LETTERS
SIGRID ELLIS: EDITS

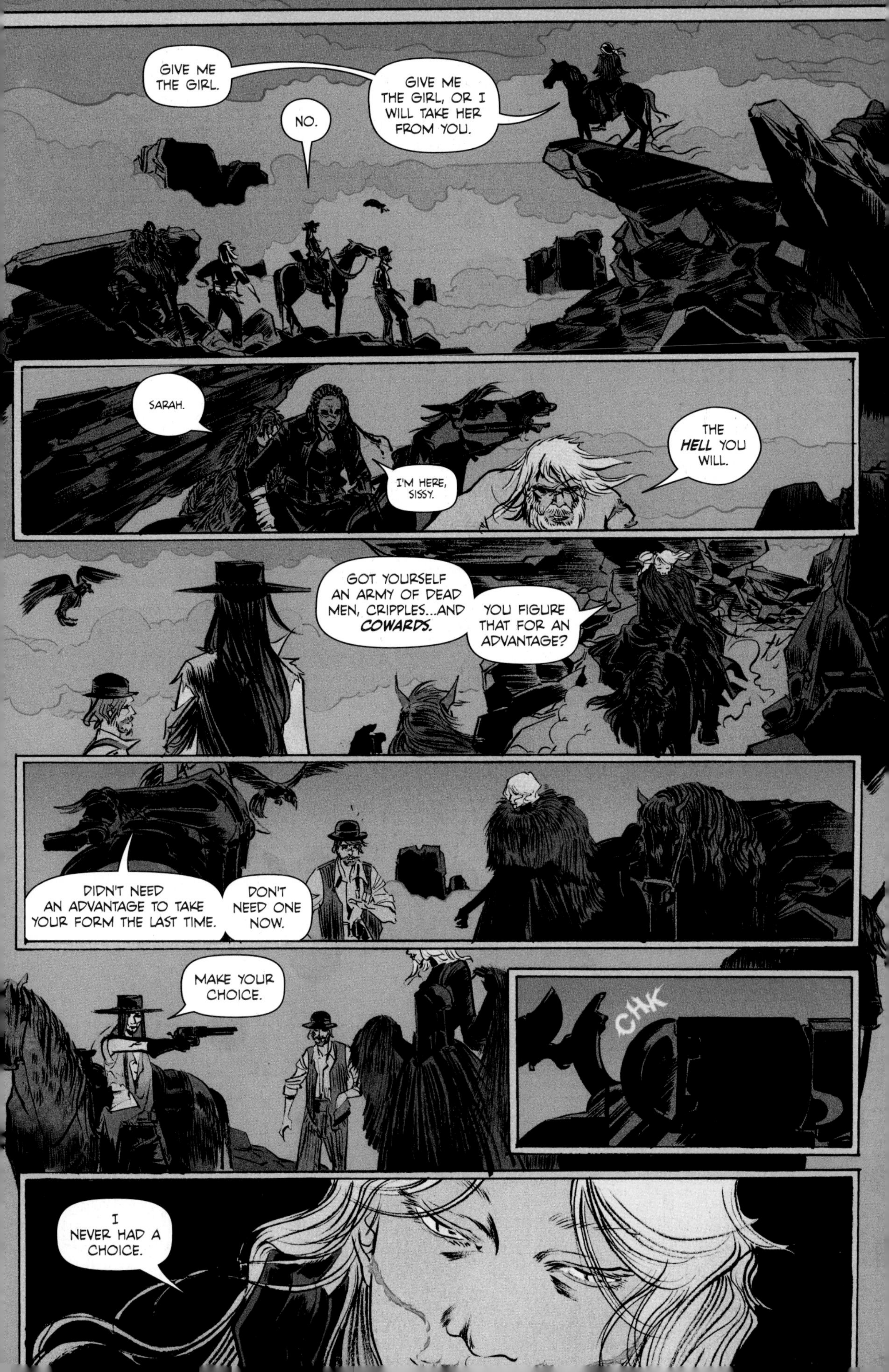
GIVE ME THE GIRL.
NO.
GIVE ME THE GIRL, OR I WILL TAKE HER FROM YOU.
SARAH.
I'M HERE, SISSY.
THE HELL YOU WILL.
GOT YOURSELF AN ARMY OF DEAD MEN, CRIPPLES...AND COWARDS.
YOU FIGURE THAT FOR AN ADVANTAGE?
DIDN'T NEED AN ADVANTAGE TO TAKE YOUR FORM THE LAST TIME.
DON'T NEED ONE NOW.
MAKE YOUR CHOICE.
CHK
I NEVER HAD A CHOICE.

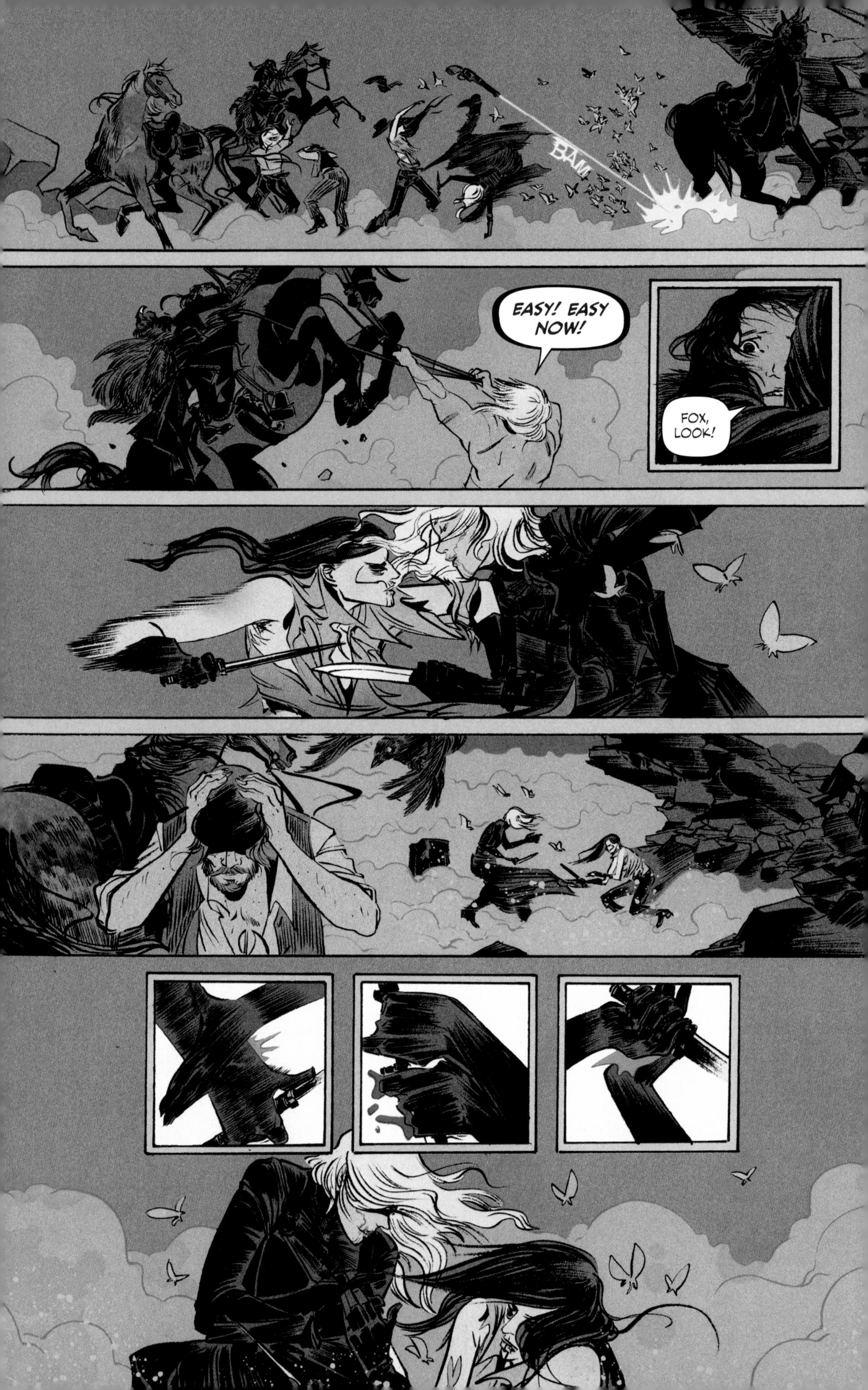
BAM
EASY! EASY NOW!
FOX, LOOK!

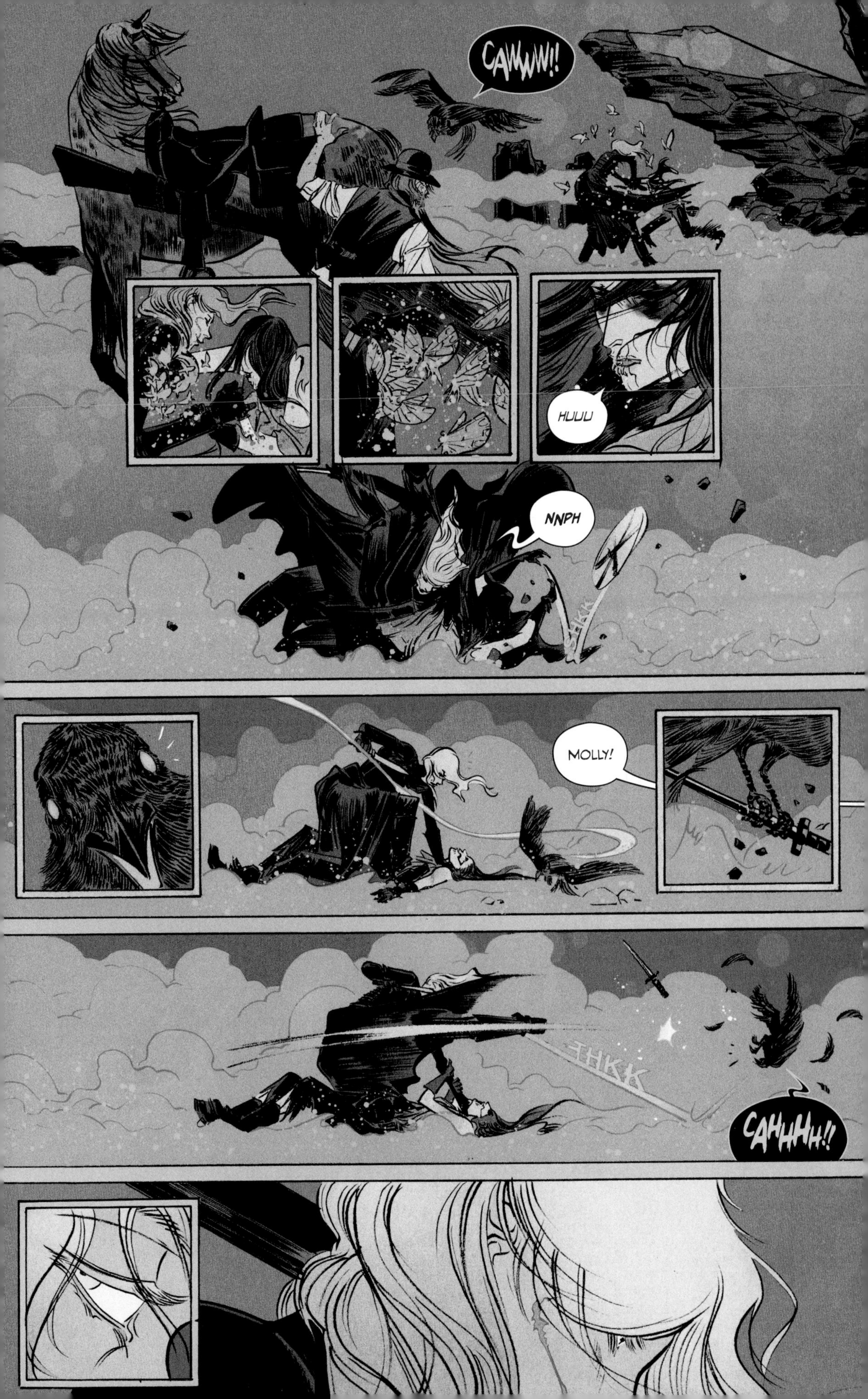
CAWWW!!
HUUU
NNPH
SHKK
MOLLY!
THKK
CAHHHH!!

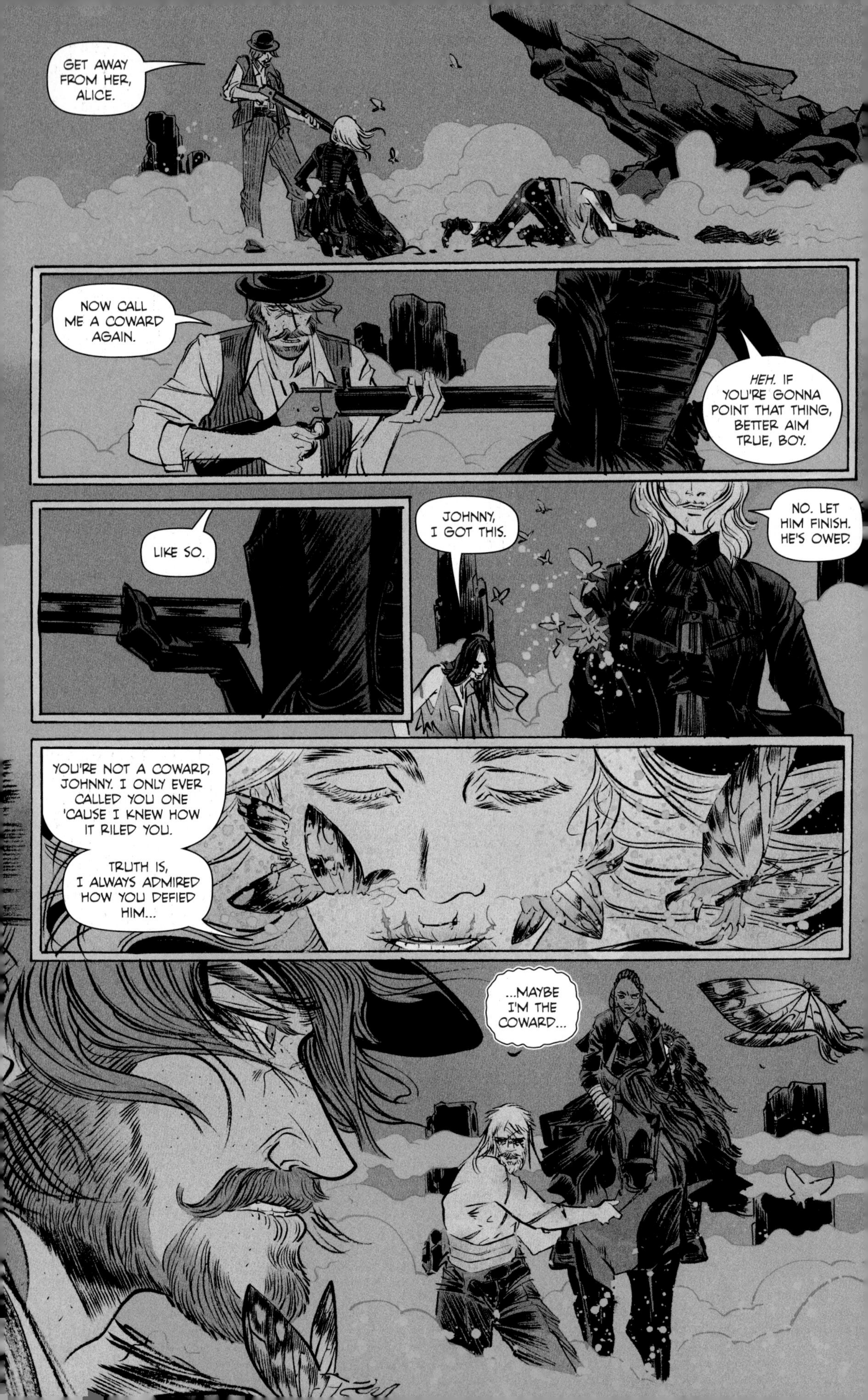
GET AWAY FROM HER, ALICE.
NOW CALL ME A COWARD AGAIN.
HEH. IF YOU'RE GONNA POINT THAT THING, BETTER AIM TRUE, BOY.
LIKE SO.
JOHNNY, I GOT THIS.
NO. LET HIM FINISH. HE'S OWED.
YOU'RE NOT A COWARD, JOHNNY. I ONLY EVER CALLED YOU ONE 'CAUSE I KNEW HOW IT RILED YOU.
TRUTH IS, I ALWAYS ADMIRED HOW YOU DEFIED HIM...
...MAYBE I'M THE COWARD...

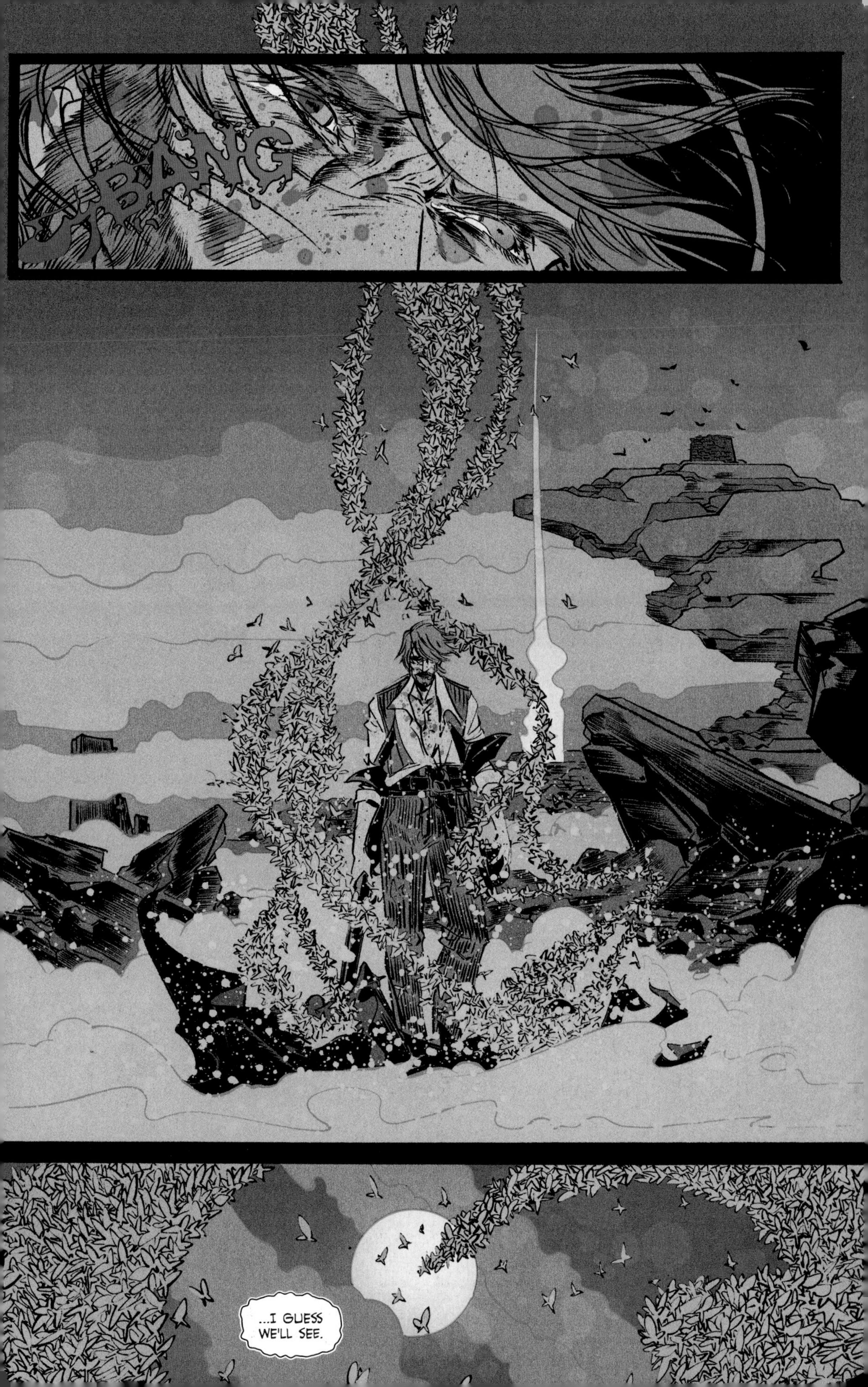
BANG
...I GUESS WE'LL SEE.

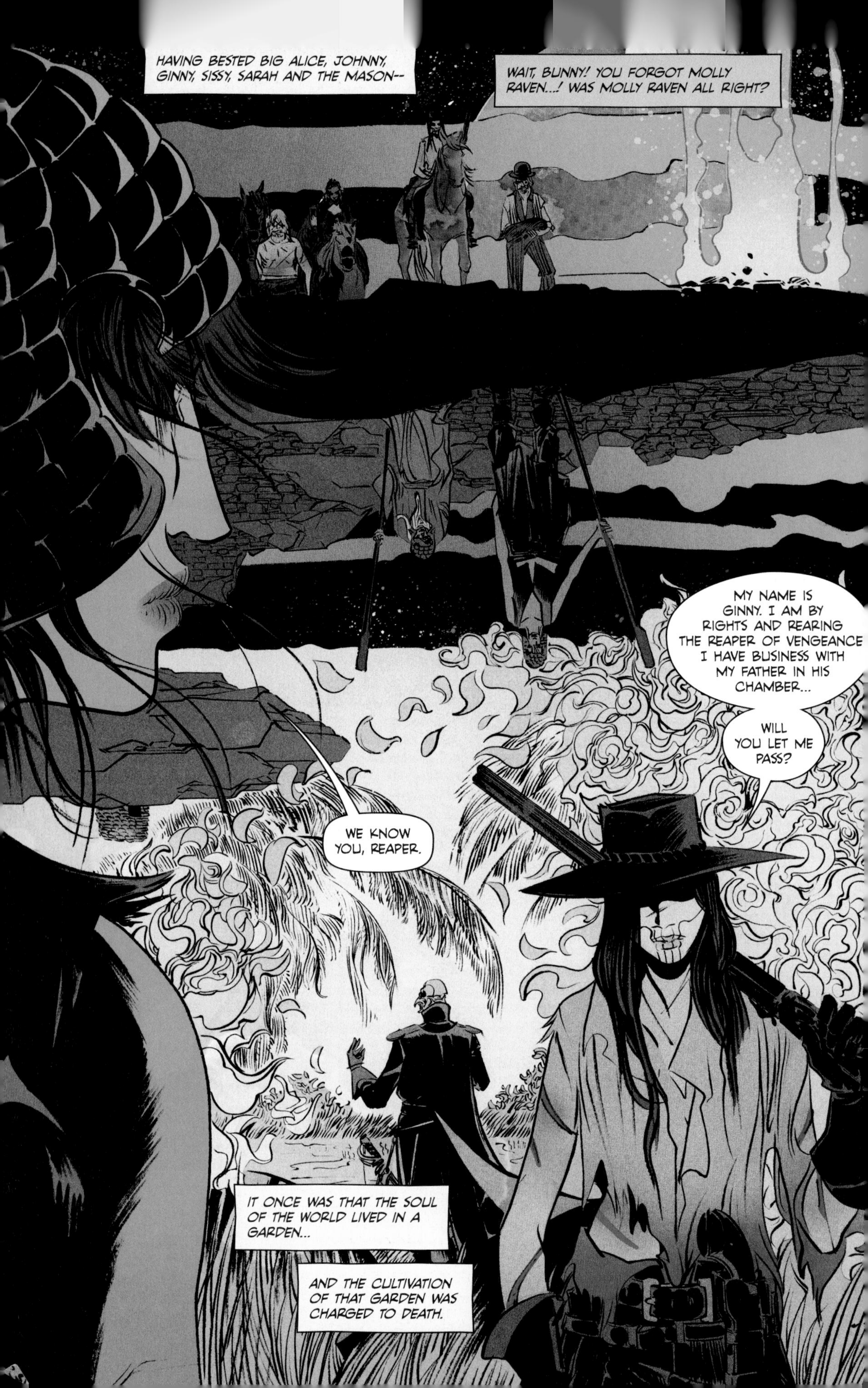
HAVING BESTED BIG ALICE, JOHNNY, GINNY, SISSY, SARAH AND THE MASON--
WAIT, BUNNY! YOU FORGOT MOLLY RAVEN...! WAS MOLLY RAVEN ALL RIGHT?
MY NAME IS GINNY. I AM BY RIGHTS AND REARING THE REAPER OF VENGEANCE I HAVE BUSINESS WITH MY FATHER IN HIS CHAMBER...
WILL YOU LET ME PASS?
WE KNOW YOU, REAPER.
IT ONCE WAS THAT THE SOUL OF THE WORLD LIVED IN A GARDEN...
AND THE CULTIVATION OF THAT GARDEN WAS CHARGED TO DEATH.

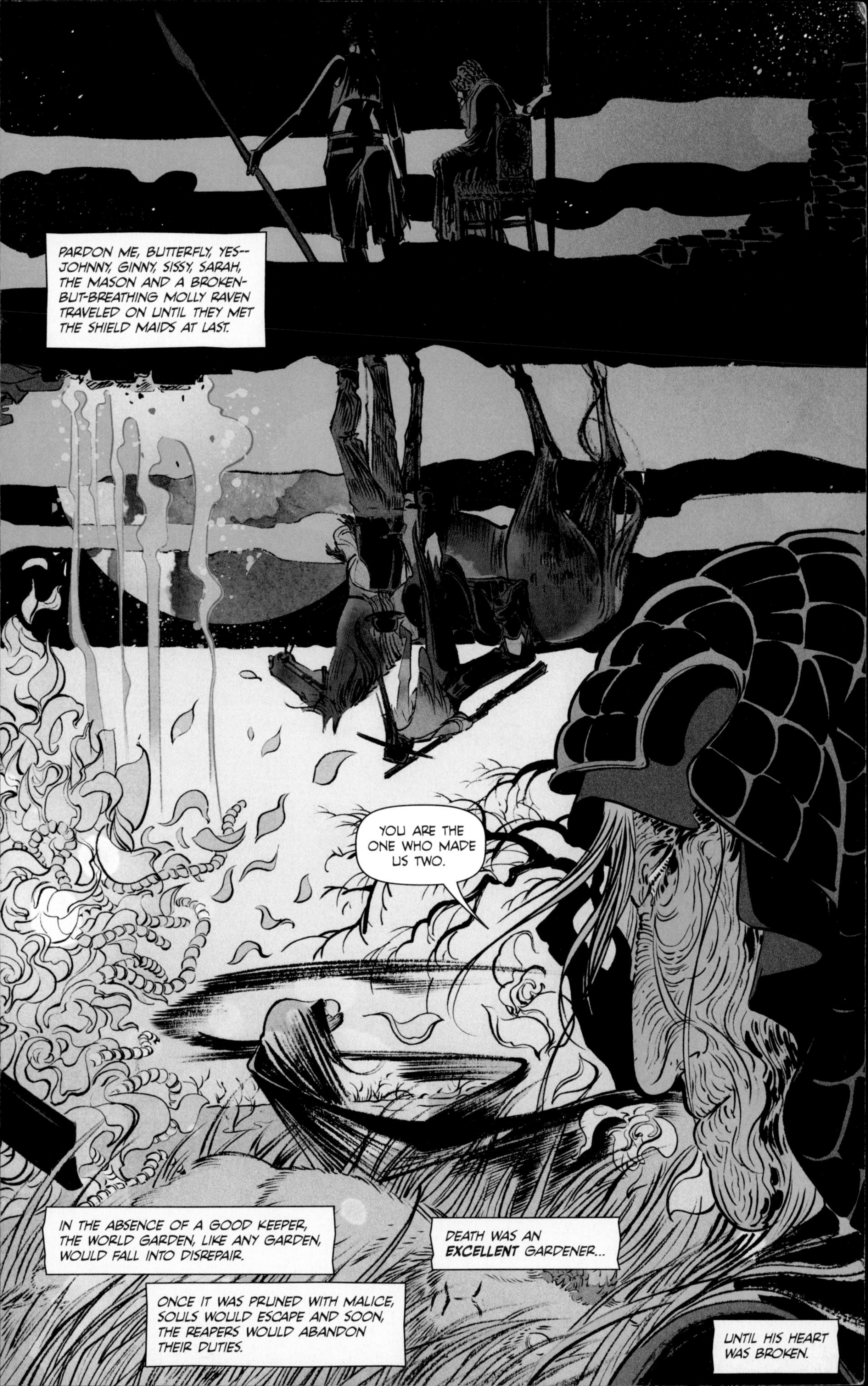
PARDON ME, BUTTERFLY, YES--JOHNNY, GINNY, SISSY, SARAH, THE MASON AND A BROKEN-BUT-BREATHING MOLLY RAVEN TRAVELED ON UNTIL THEY MET THE SHIELD MAIDS AT LAST.
YOU ARE THE ONE WHO MADE US TWO.
IN THE ABSENCE OF A GOOD KEEPER, THE WORLD GARDEN, LIKE ANY GARDEN, WOULD FALL INTO DISREPAIR.
DEATH WAS AN **EXCELLENT** GARDENER...
ONCE IT WAS PRUNED WITH MALICE, SOULS WOULD ESCAPE AND SOON, THE REAPERS WOULD ABANDON THEIR DUTIES.
UNTIL HIS HEART WAS BROKEN.

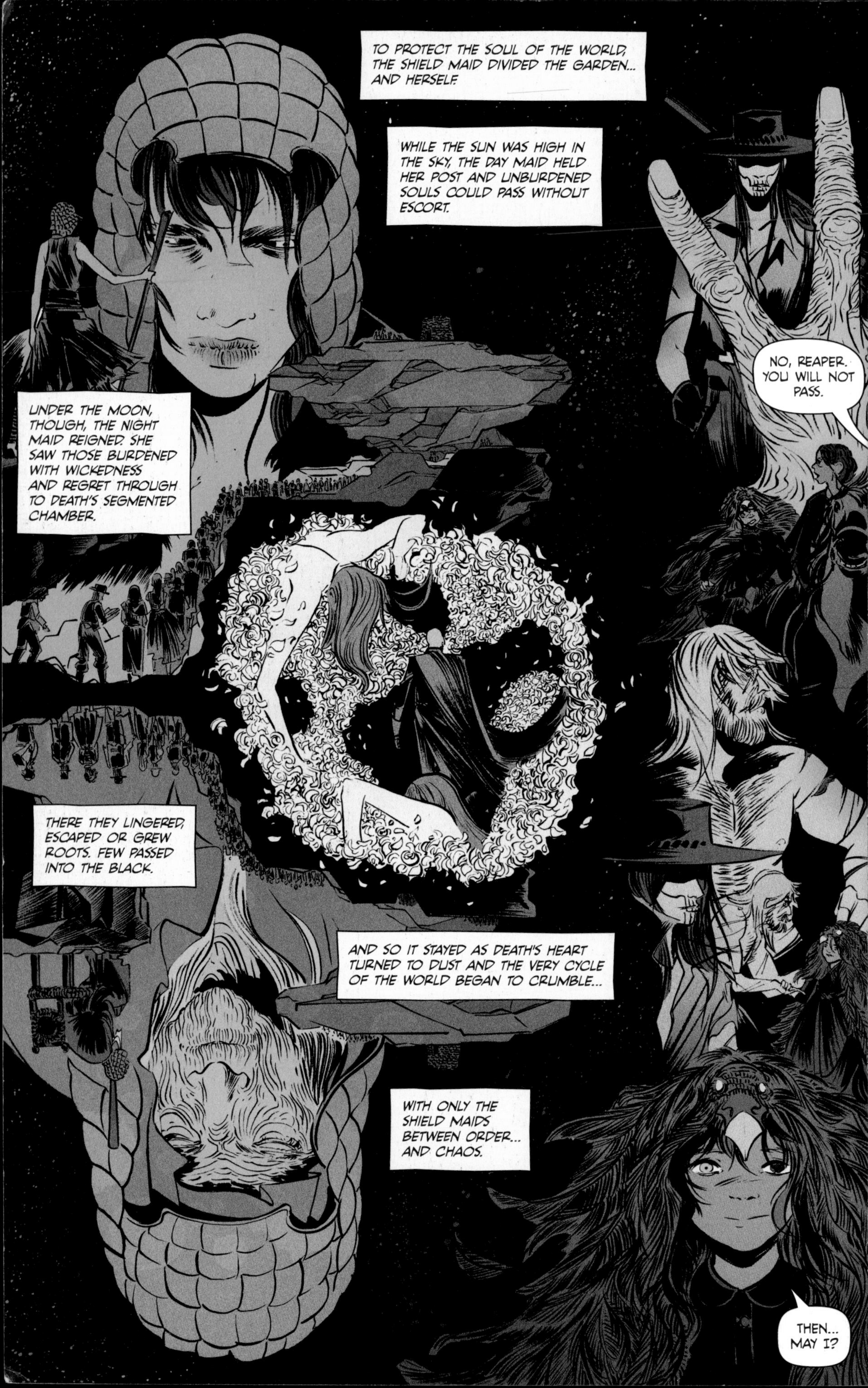
TO PROTECT THE SOUL OF THE WORLD, THE SHIELD MAID DIVIDED THE GARDEN... AND HERSELF.
WHILE THE SUN WAS HIGH IN THE SKY, THE DAY MAID HELD HER POST AND UNBURDENED SOULS COULD PASS WITHOUT ESCORT.
NO, REAPER. YOU WILL NOT PASS.
UNDER THE MOON, THOUGH, THE NIGHT MAID REIGNED. SHE SAW THOSE BURDENED WITH WICKEDNESS AND REGRET THROUGH TO DEATH'S SEGMENTED CHAMBER.
THERE THEY LINGERED, ESCAPED OR GREW ROOTS. FEW PASSED INTO THE BLACK.
AND SO IT STAYED AS DEATH'S HEART TURNED TO DUST AND THE VERY CYCLE OF THE WORLD BEGAN TO CRUMBLE...
WITH ONLY THE SHIELD MAIDS BETWEEN ORDER... AND CHAOS.
THEN... MAY I?

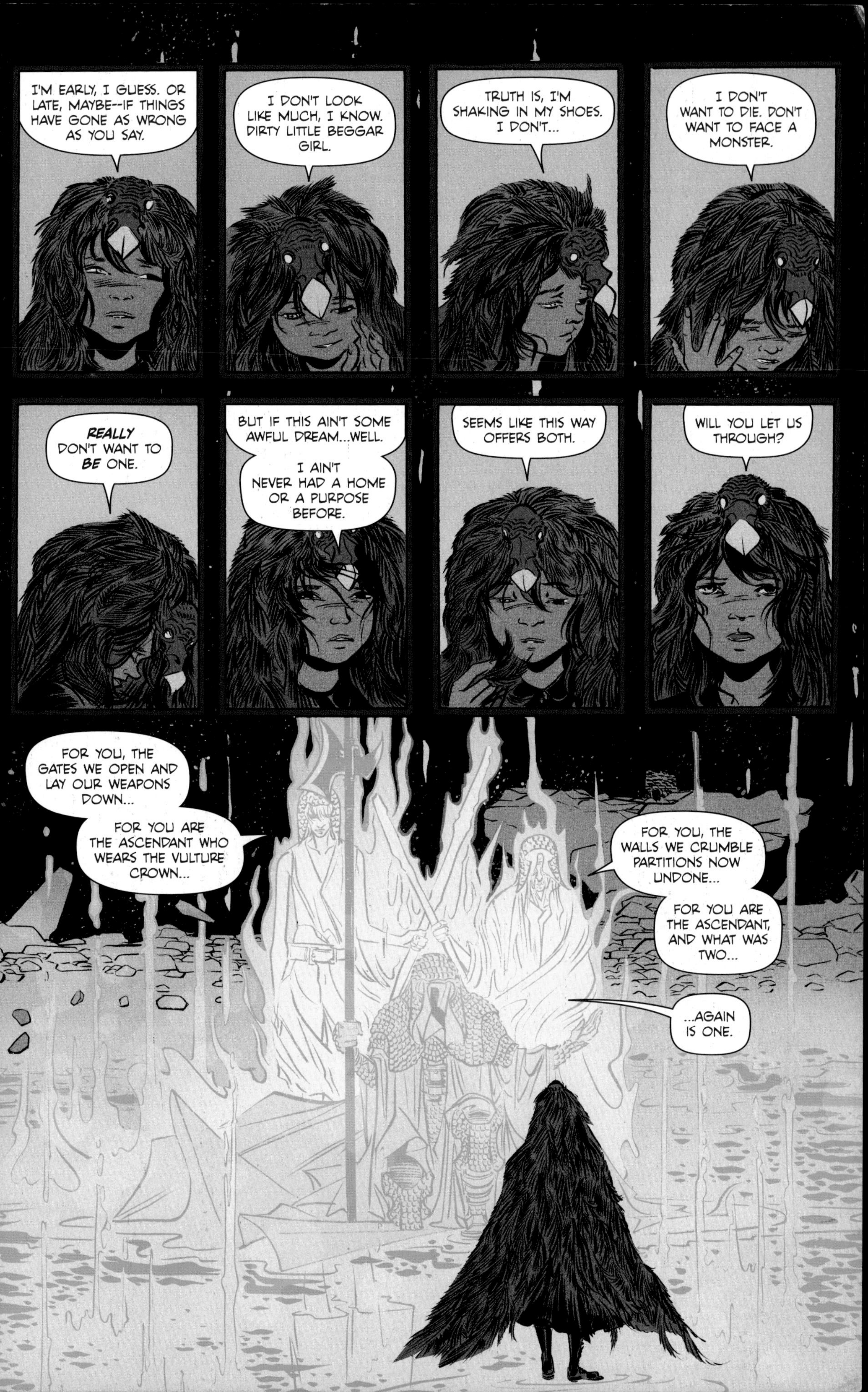
I'M EARLY, I GUESS. OR LATE, MAYBE--IF THINGS HAVE GONE AS WRONG AS YOU SAY.
I DON'T LOOK LIKE MUCH, I KNOW. DIRTY LITTLE BEGGAR GIRL.
TRUTH IS, I'M SHAKING IN MY SHOES. I DON'T...
I DON'T WANT TO DIE. DON'T WANT TO FACE A MONSTER.
REALLY DON'T WANT TO *BE* ONE.
BUT IF THIS AIN'T SOME AWFUL DREAM...WELL.
I AIN'T NEVER HAD A HOME OR A PURPOSE BEFORE.
SEEMS LIKE THIS WAY OFFERS BOTH.
WILL YOU LET US THROUGH?
FOR YOU, THE GATES WE OPEN AND LAY OUR WEAPONS DOWN...
FOR YOU ARE THE ASCENDANT WHO WEARS THE VULTURE CROWN...
FOR YOU, THE WALLS WE CRUMBLE PARTITIONS NOW UNDONE...
FOR YOU ARE THE ASCENDANT, AND WHAT WAS TWO...
...AGAIN IS ONE.

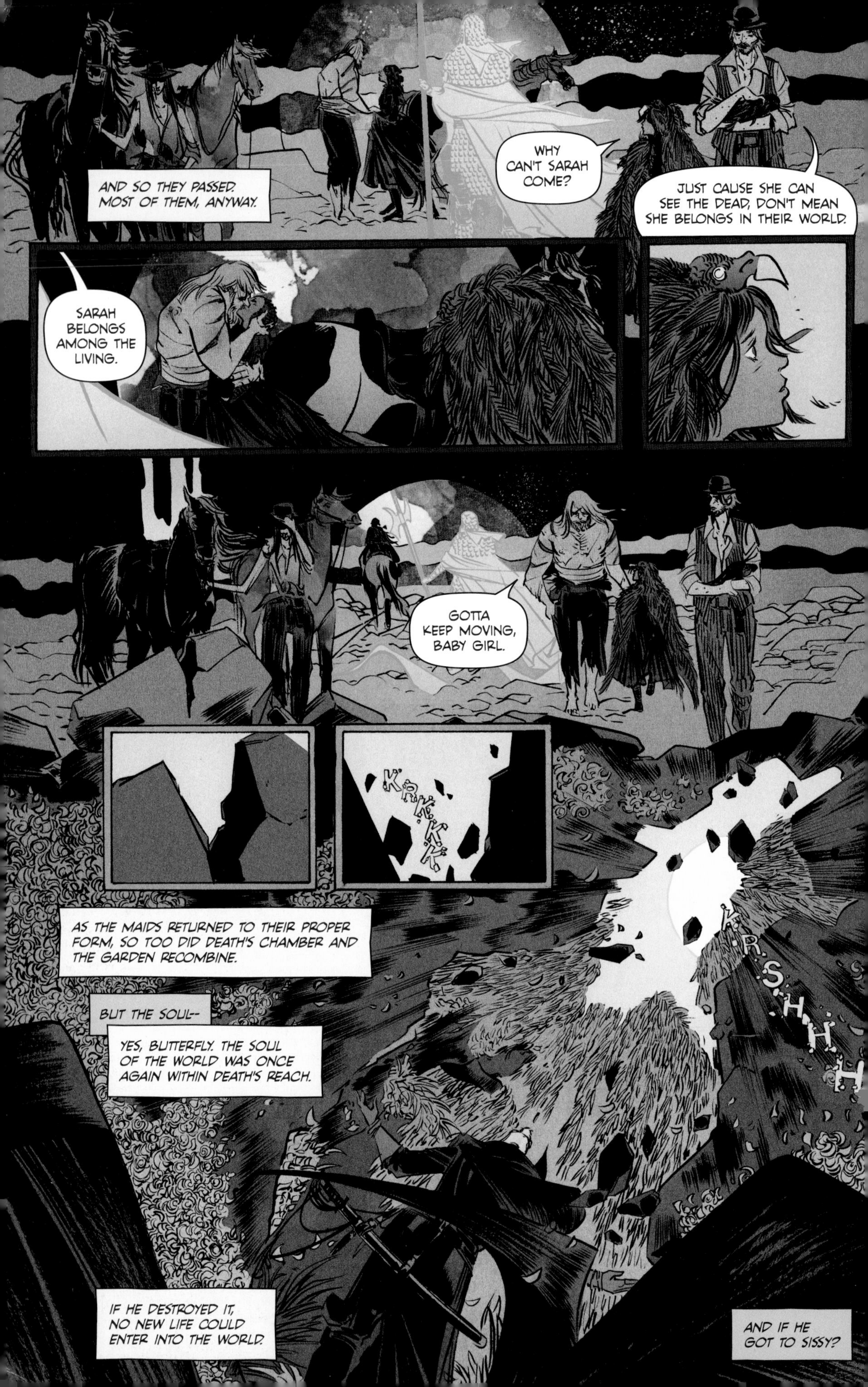
AND SO THEY PASSED. MOST OF THEM, ANYWAY.
WHY CAN'T SARAH COME?
JUST CAUSE SHE CAN SEE THE DEAD, DON'T MEAN SHE BELONGS IN THEIR WORLD.
SARAH BELONGS AMONG THE LIVING.
GOTTA KEEP MOVING, BABY GIRL.
KRKKKK
AS THE MAIDS RETURNED TO THEIR PROPER FORM, SO TOO DID DEATH'S CHAMBER AND THE GARDEN RECOMBINE.
KRSHHHH
BUT THE SOUL--
YES, BUTTERFLY. THE SOUL OF THE WORLD WAS ONCE AGAIN WITHIN DEATH'S REACH.
IF HE DESTROYED IT, NO NEW LIFE COULD ENTER INTO THE WORLD.
AND IF HE GOT TO SISSY?

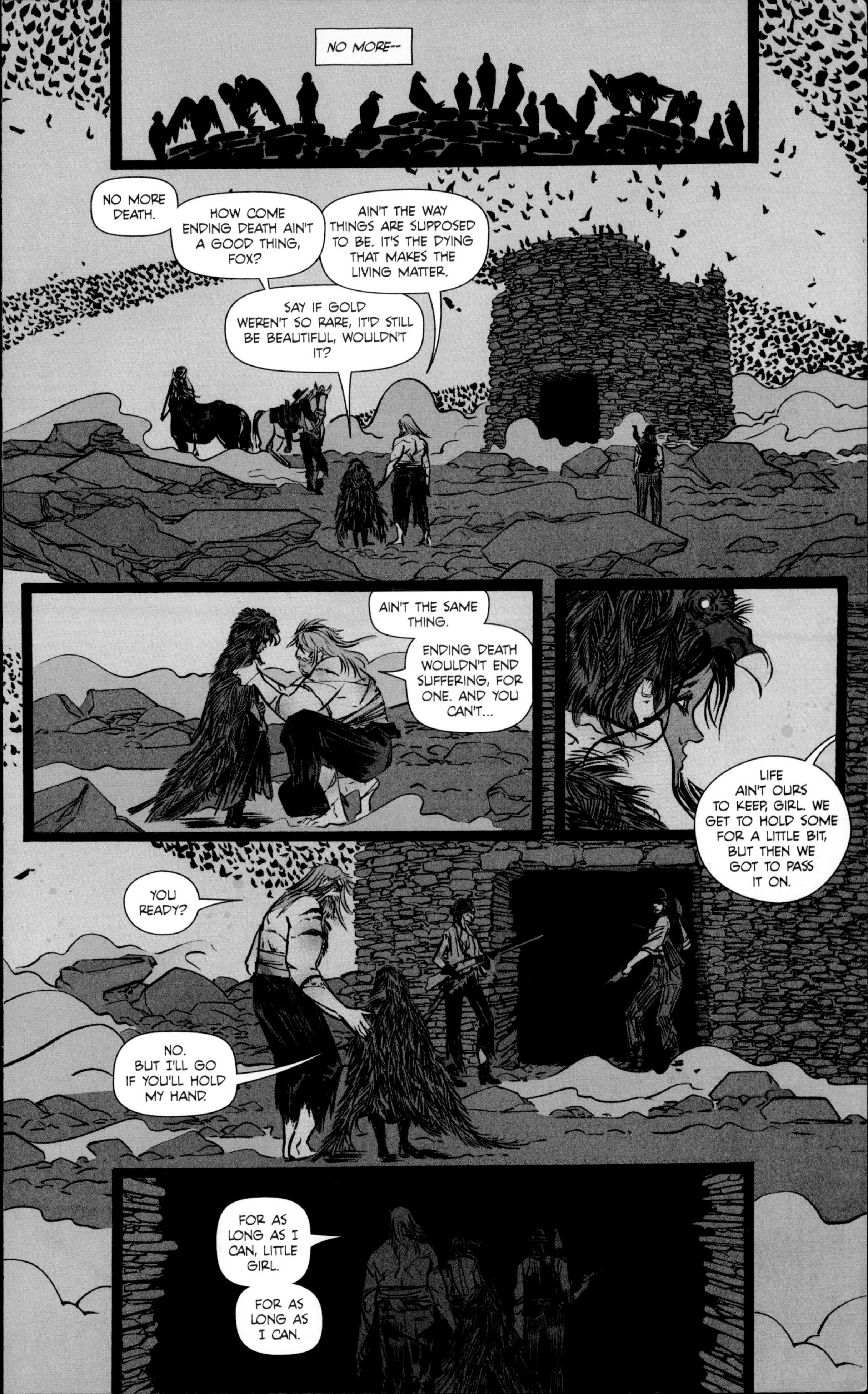
NO MORE--
NO MORE DEATH.
HOW COME ENDING DEATH AIN'T A GOOD THING, FOX?
AIN'T THE WAY THINGS ARE SUPPOSED TO BE. IT'S THE DYING THAT MAKES THE LIVING MATTER.
SAY IF GOLD WEREN'T SO RARE, IT'D STILL BE BEAUTIFUL, WOULDN'T IT?
AIN'T THE SAME THING.
ENDING DEATH WOULDN'T END SUFFERING, FOR ONE. AND YOU CAN'T...
LIFE AIN'T OURS TO KEEP, GIRL. WE GET TO HOLD SOME FOR A LITTLE BIT, BUT THEN WE GOT TO PASS IT ON.
YOU READY?
NO. BUT I'LL GO IF YOU'LL HOLD MY HAND.
FOR AS LONG AS I CAN, LITTLE GIRL.
FOR AS LONG AS I CAN.

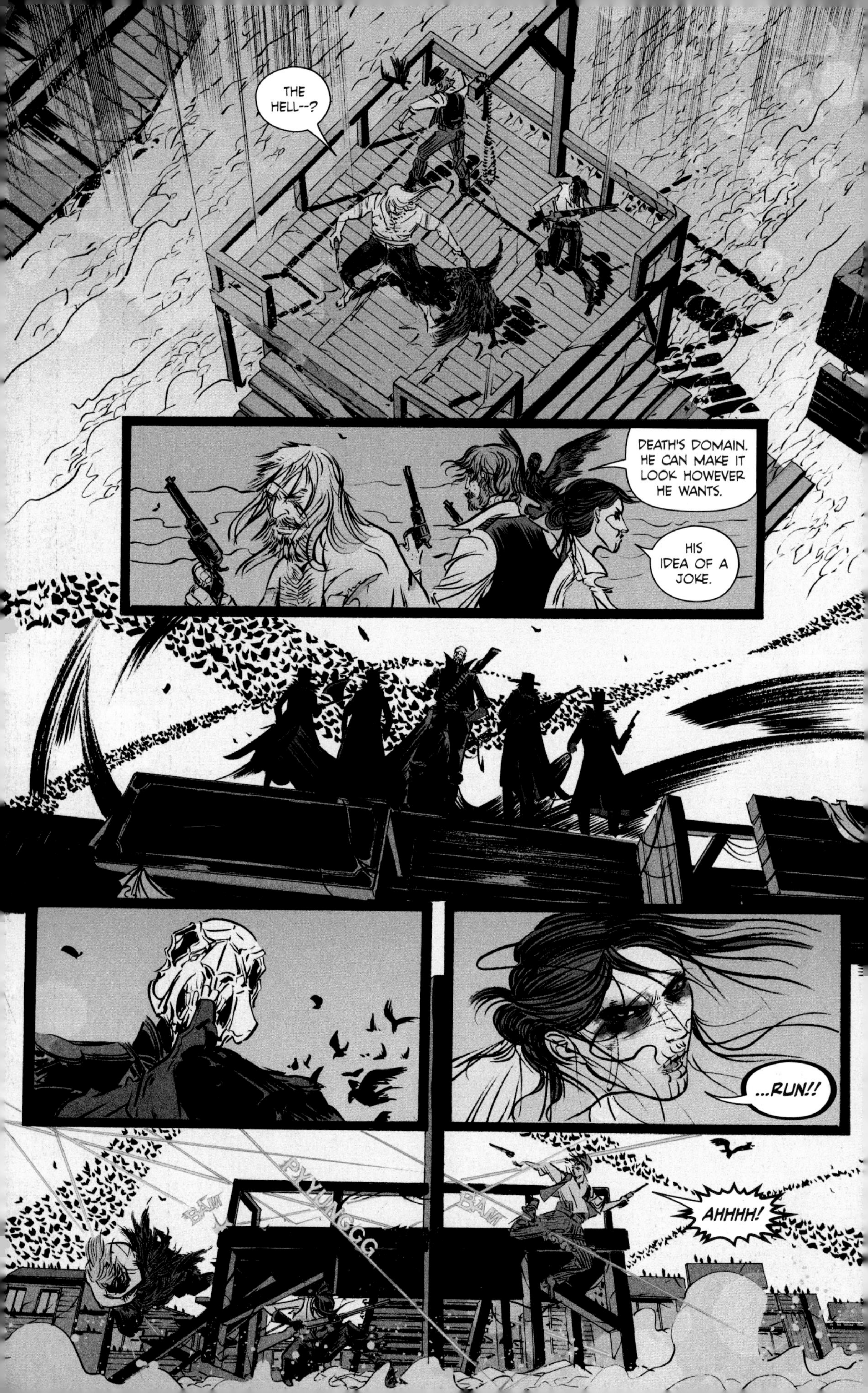
THE HELL--?
DEATH'S DOMAIN. HE CAN MAKE IT LOOK HOWEVER HE WANTS.
HIS IDEA OF A JOKE.
...RUN!!
BAM
PYYUNGGG
BAM
AHHHH!

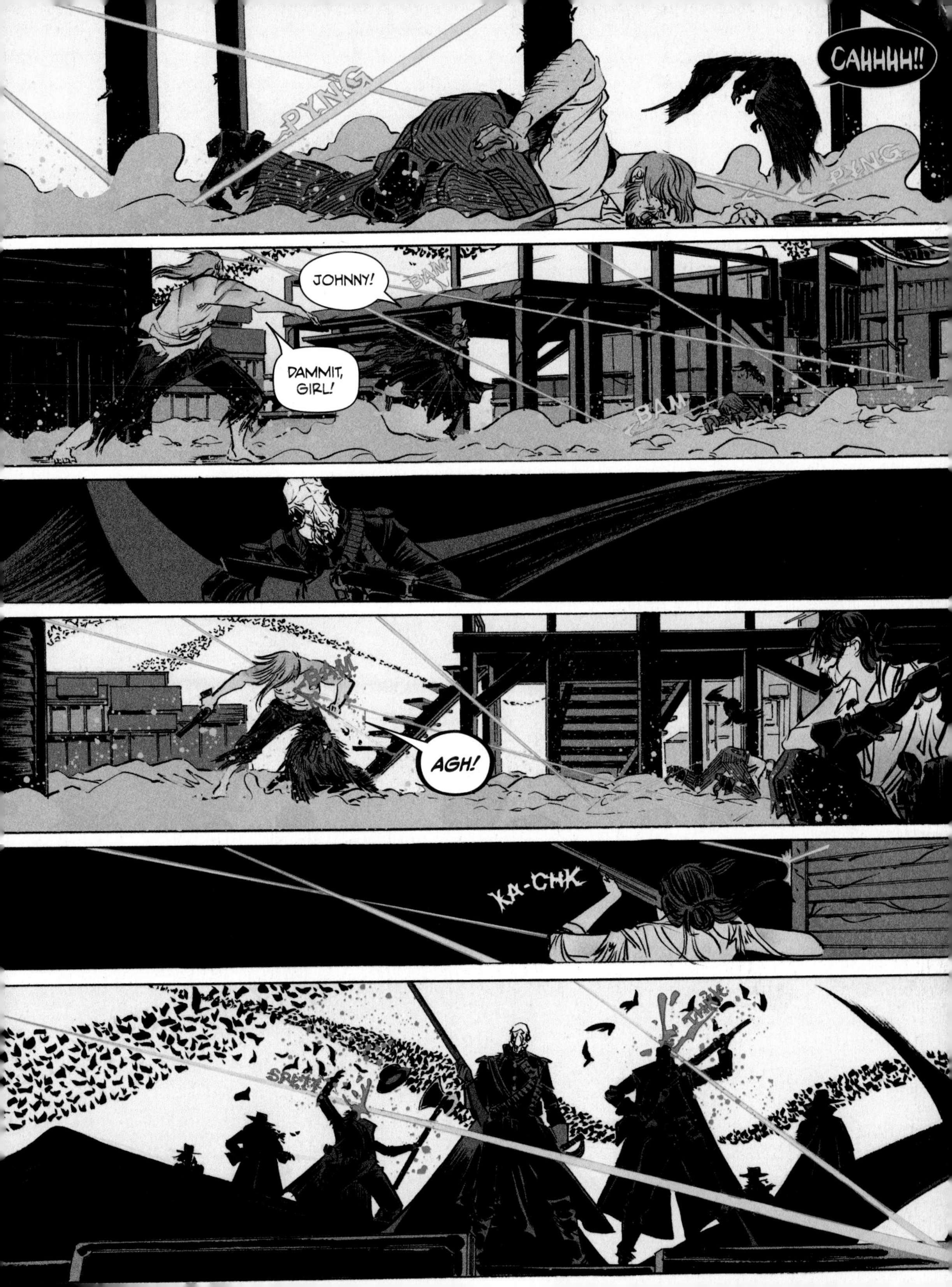
CAHHHH!!
PYNG
PYNG
JOHNNY!
BAM
DAMMIT, GIRL!
BAM
BAM
AGH!
KA-CHK

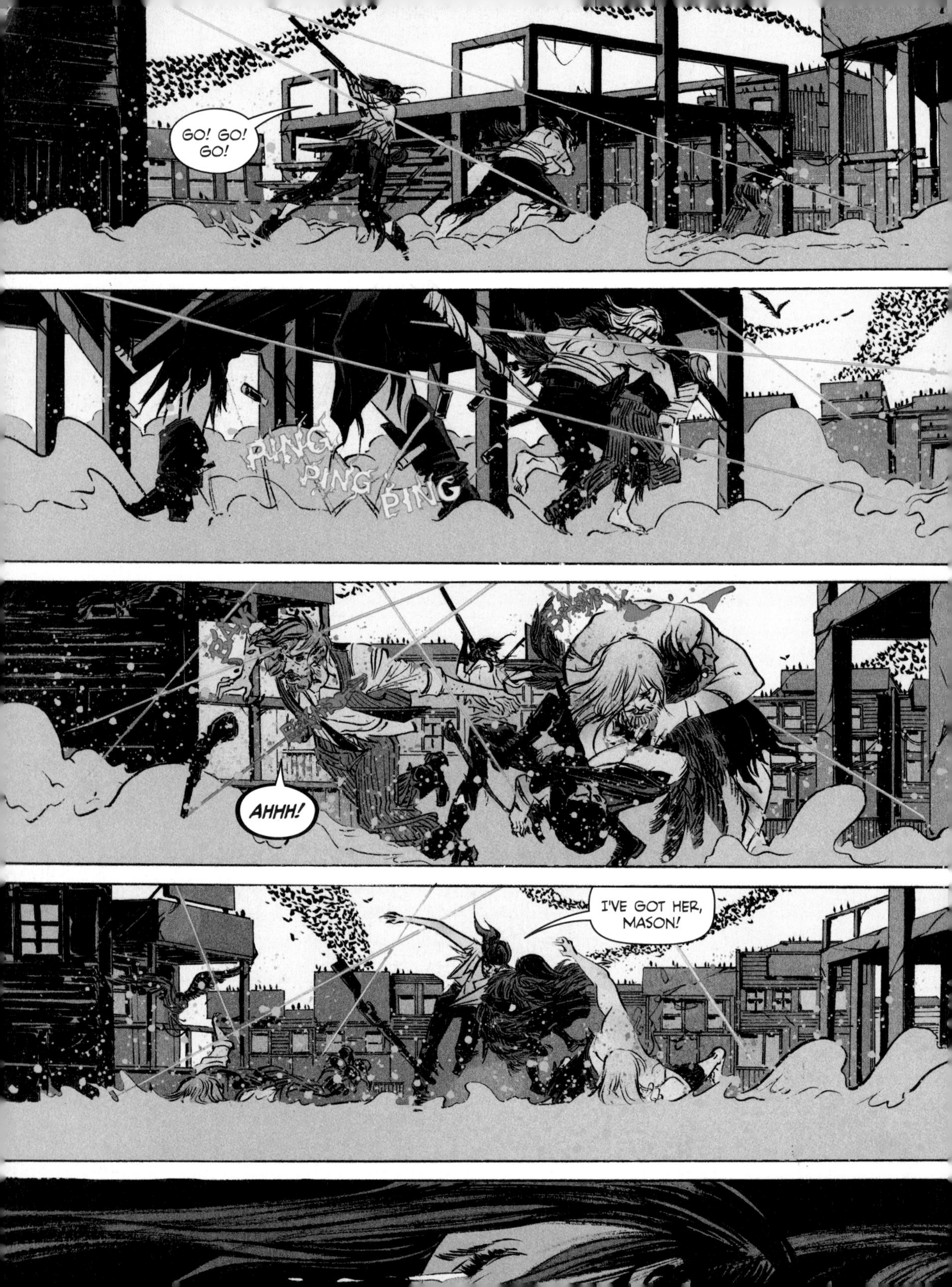
GO! GO! GO!
PING PING PING
AHHH!
I'VE GOT HER, MASON!

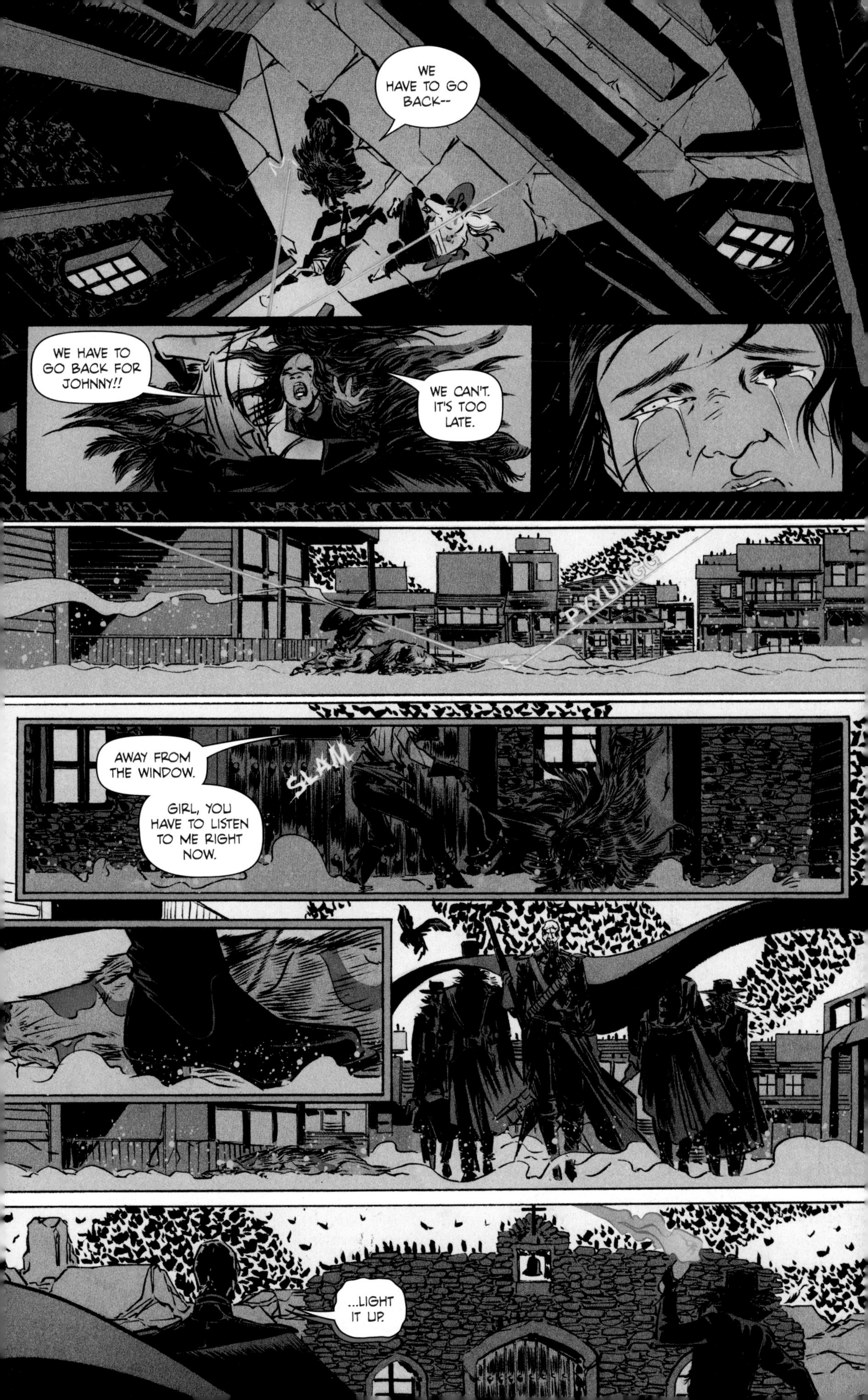
WE HAVE TO GO BACK--
WE HAVE TO GO BACK FOR JOHNNY!!
WE CAN'T. IT'S TOO LATE.
PYYUNGG
AWAY FROM THE WINDOW.
SLAM
GIRL, YOU HAVE TO LISTEN TO ME RIGHT NOW.
...LIGHT IT UP.

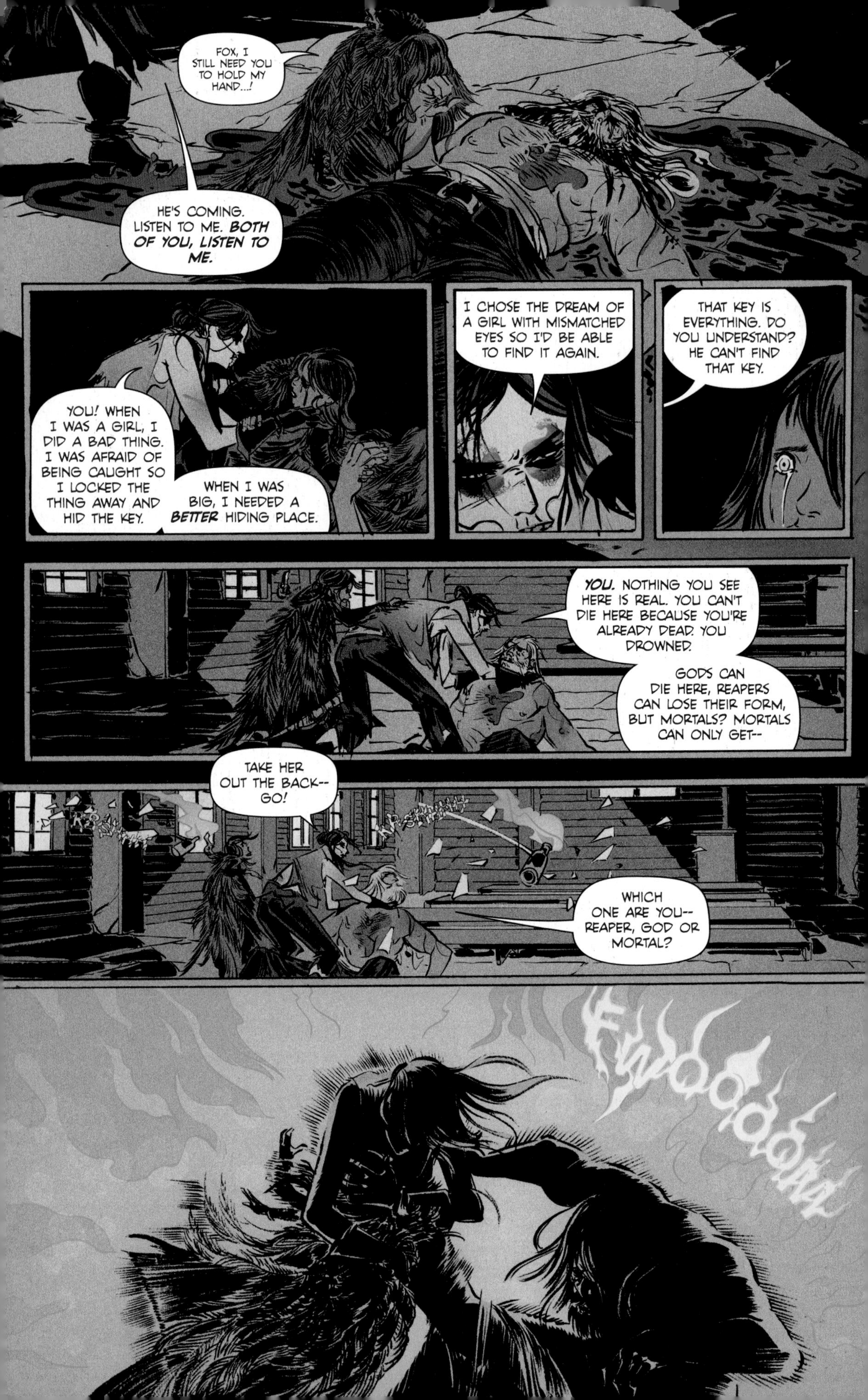
FOX, I STILL NEED YOU TO HOLD MY HAND...!
HE'S COMING. LISTEN TO ME. BOTH OF YOU, LISTEN TO ME.
YOU! WHEN I WAS A GIRL, I DID A BAD THING. I WAS AFRAID OF BEING CAUGHT SO I LOCKED THE THING AWAY AND HID THE KEY.
WHEN I WAS BIG, I NEEDED A BETTER HIDING PLACE.
I CHOSE THE DREAM OF A GIRL WITH MISMATCHED EYES SO I'D BE ABLE TO FIND IT AGAIN.
THAT KEY IS EVERYTHING. DO YOU UNDERSTAND? HE CAN'T FIND THAT KEY.
YOU. NOTHING YOU SEE HERE IS REAL. YOU CAN'T DIE HERE BECAUSE YOU'RE ALREADY DEAD. YOU DROWNED.
GODS CAN DIE HERE, REAPERS CAN LOSE THEIR FORM, BUT MORTALS? MORTALS CAN ONLY GET--
TAKE HER OUT THE BACK-- GO!
WHICH ONE ARE YOU-- REAPER, GOD OR MORTAL?

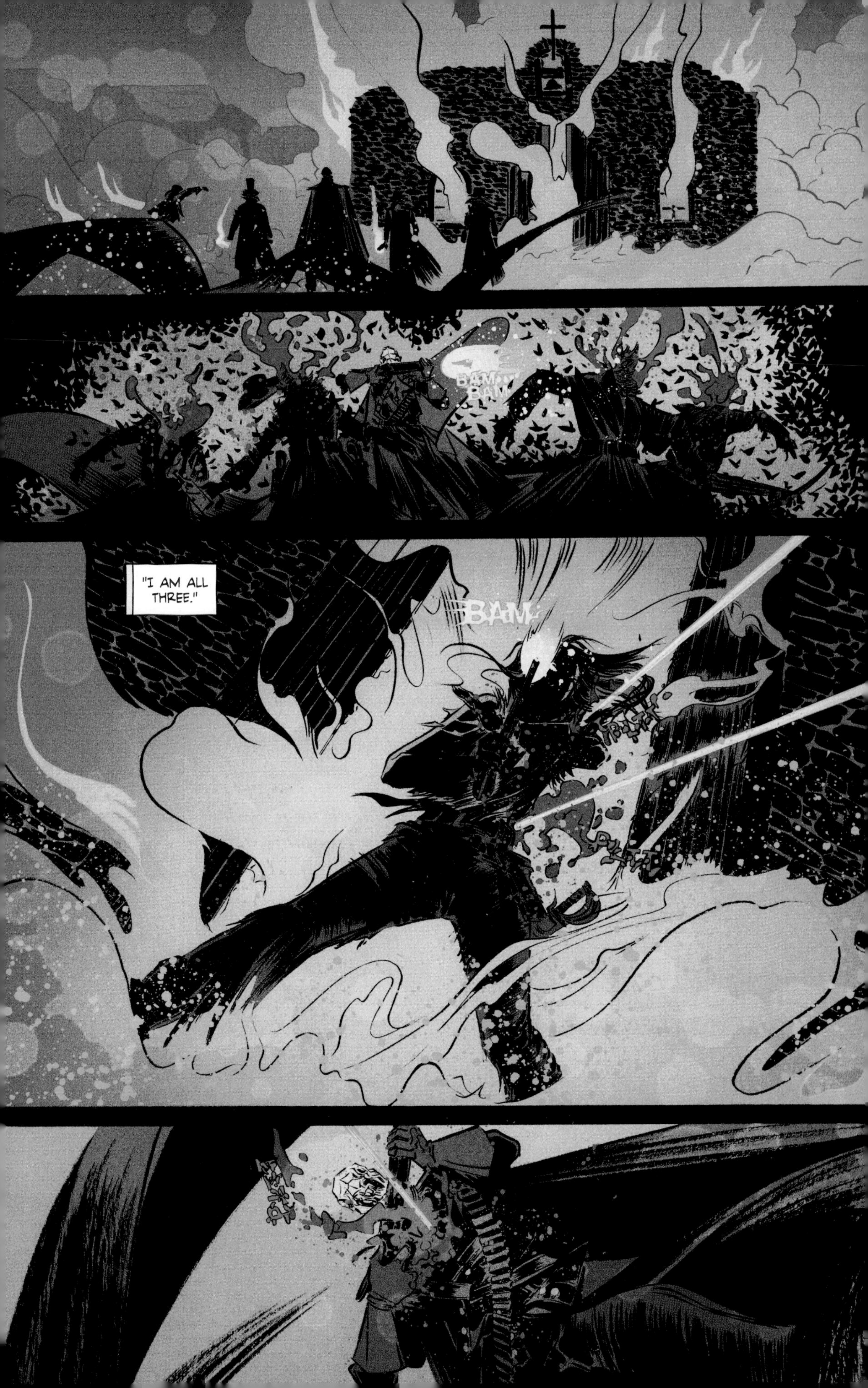
BAM BAM
"I AM ALL THREE."
BAM

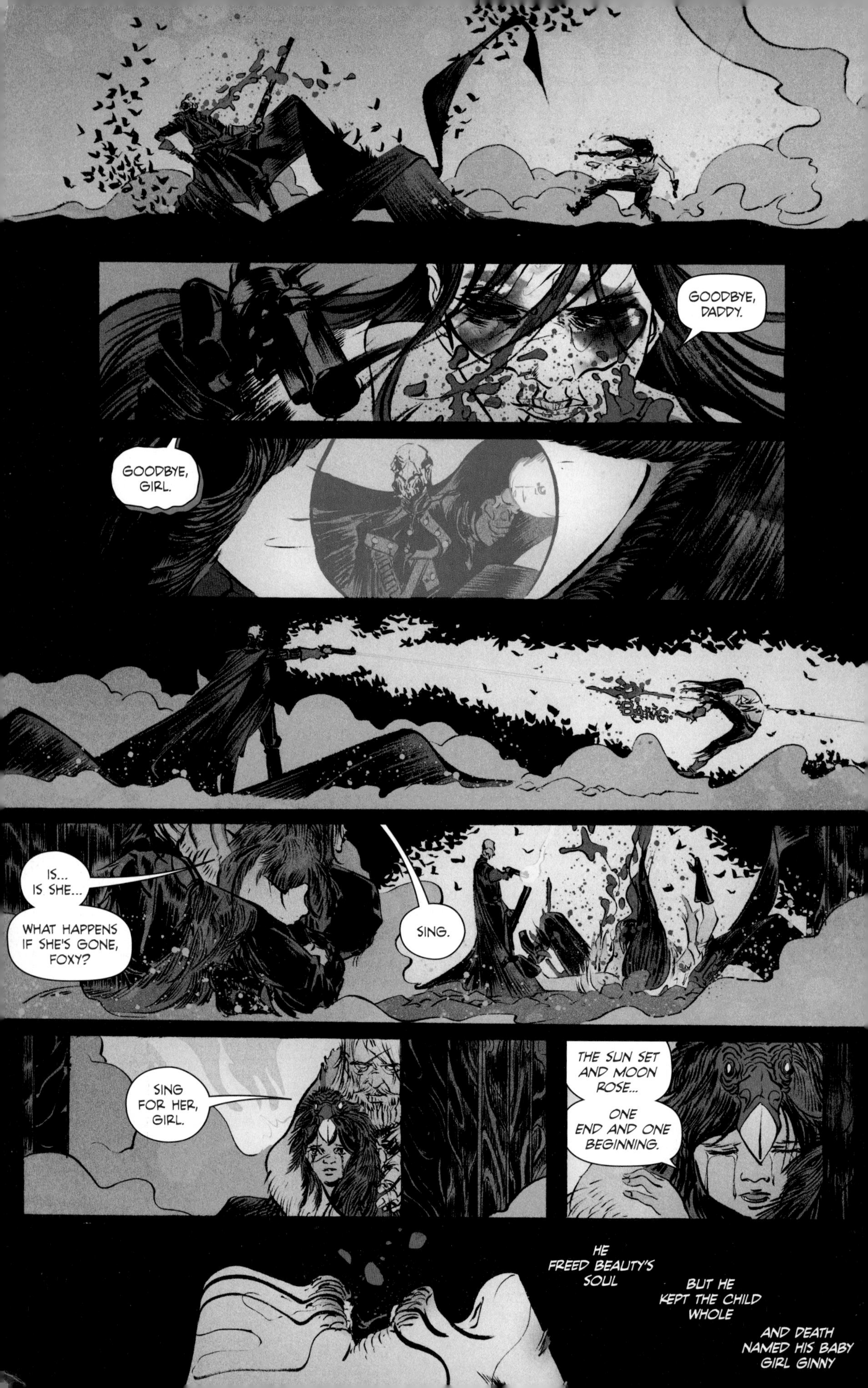
GOODBYE, DADDY.
GOODBYE, GIRL.
BANG
IS... IS SHE...
WHAT HAPPENS IF SHE'S GONE, FOXY?
SING.
SING FOR HER, GIRL.
THE SUN SET AND MOON ROSE...
ONE END AND ONE BEGINNING.
HE FREED BEAUTY'S SOUL
BUT HE KEPT THE CHILD WHOLE
AND DEATH NAMED HIS BABY GIRL GINNY

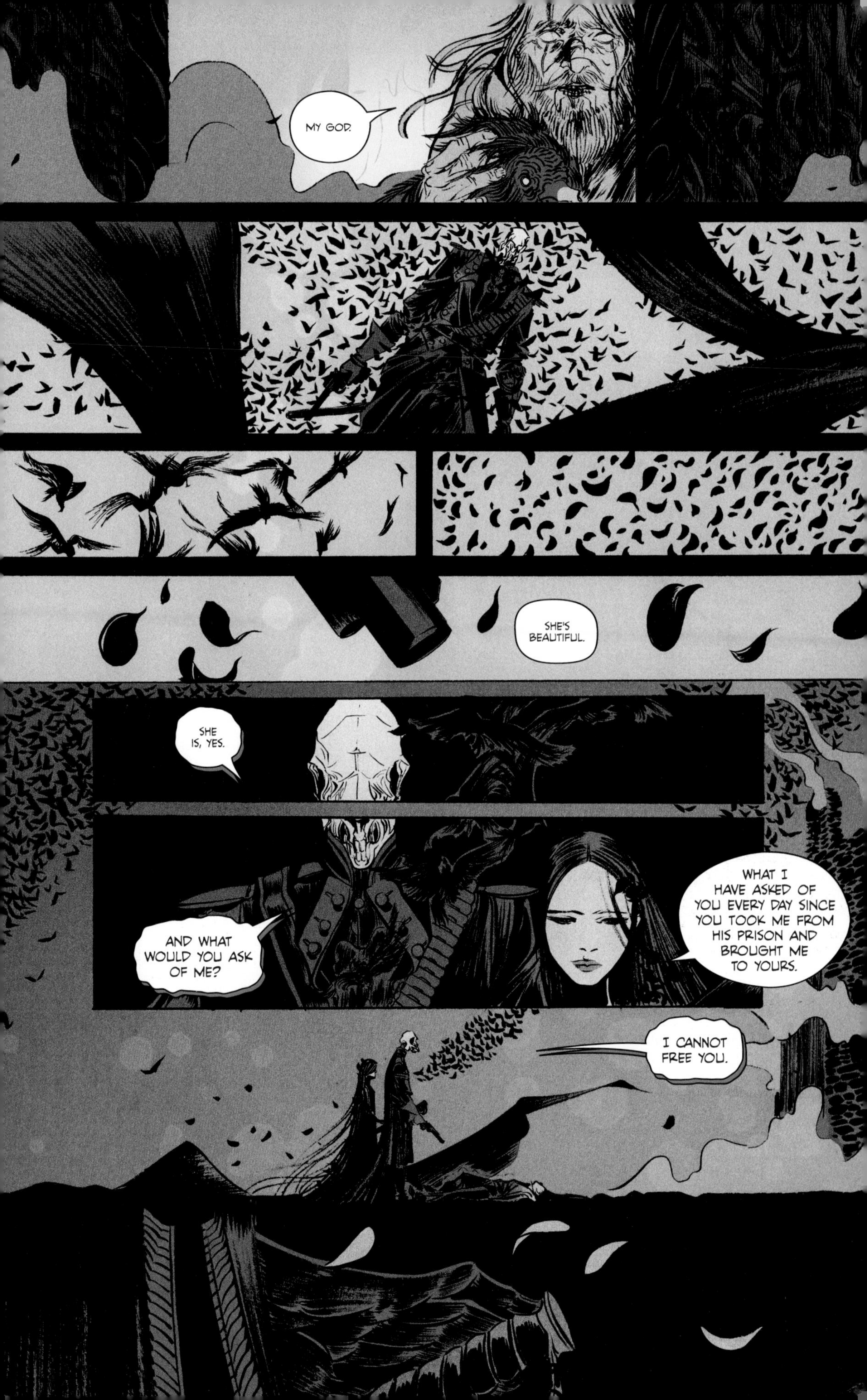
MY GOD.
SHE'S BEAUTIFUL.
SHE IS, YES.
AND WHAT WOULD YOU ASK OF ME?
WHAT I HAVE ASKED OF YOU EVERY DAY SINCE YOU TOOK ME FROM HIS PRISON AND BROUGHT ME TO YOURS.
I CANNOT FREE YOU.

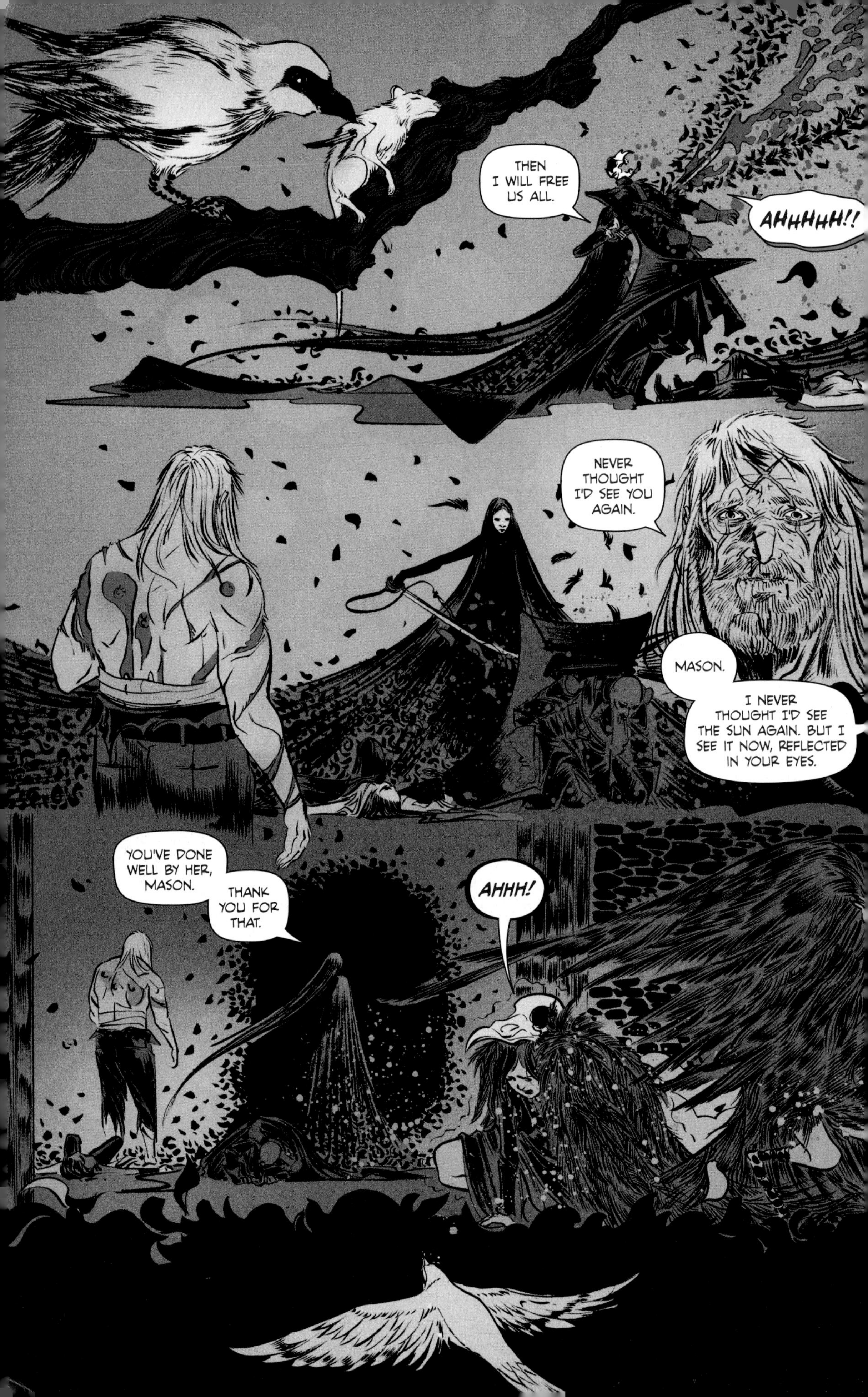
THEN I WILL FREE US ALL.
AHHHHH!!
NEVER THOUGHT I'D SEE YOU AGAIN.
MASON.
I NEVER THOUGHT I'D SEE THE SUN AGAIN. BUT I SEE IT NOW, REFLECTED IN YOUR EYES.
YOU'VE DONE WELL BY HER, MASON.
THANK YOU FOR THAT.
AHHH!

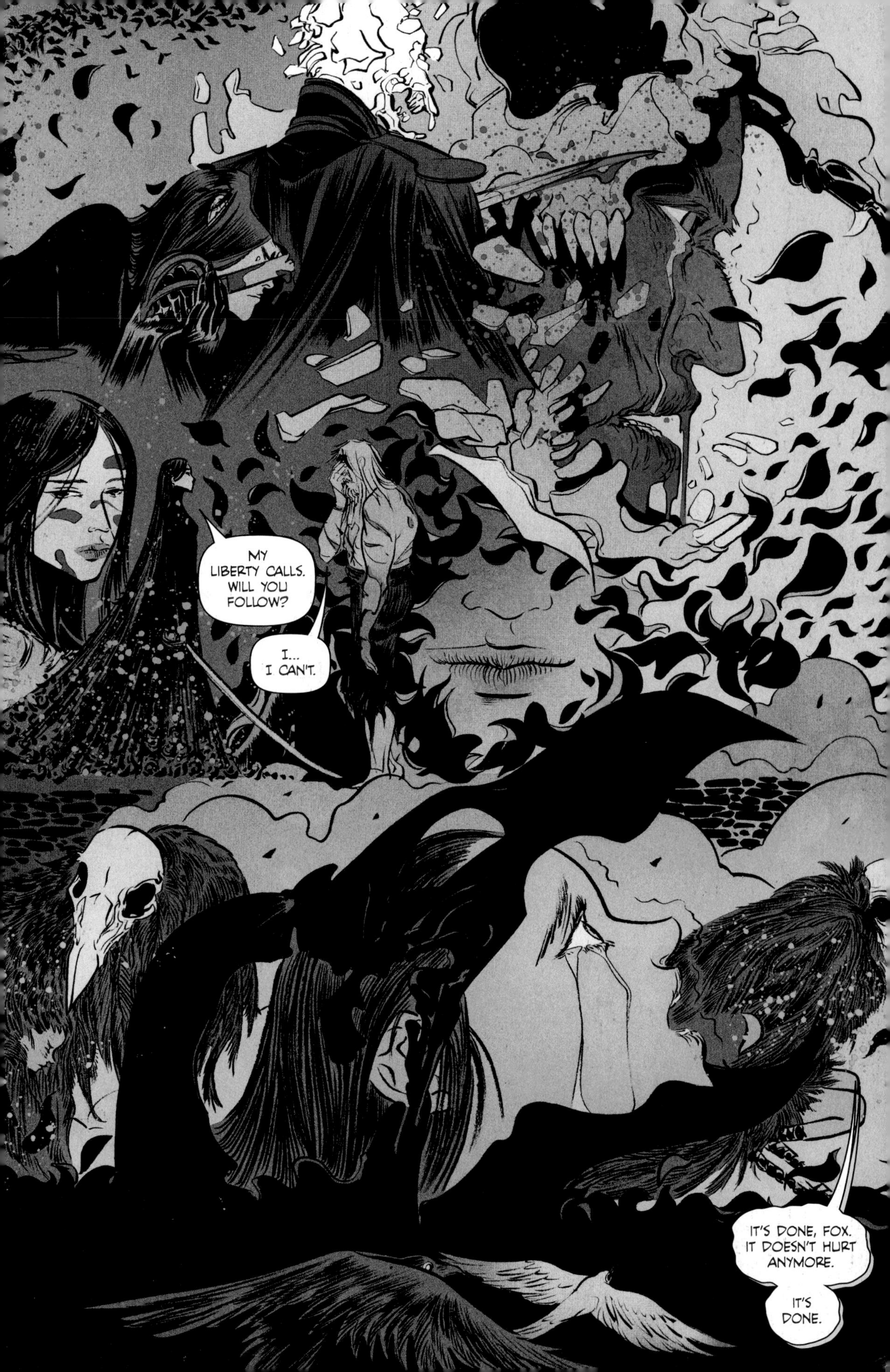
MY LIBERTY CALLS. WILL YOU FOLLOW?
I... I CAN'T.
IT'S DONE, FOX. IT DOESN'T HURT ANYMORE.
IT'S DONE.

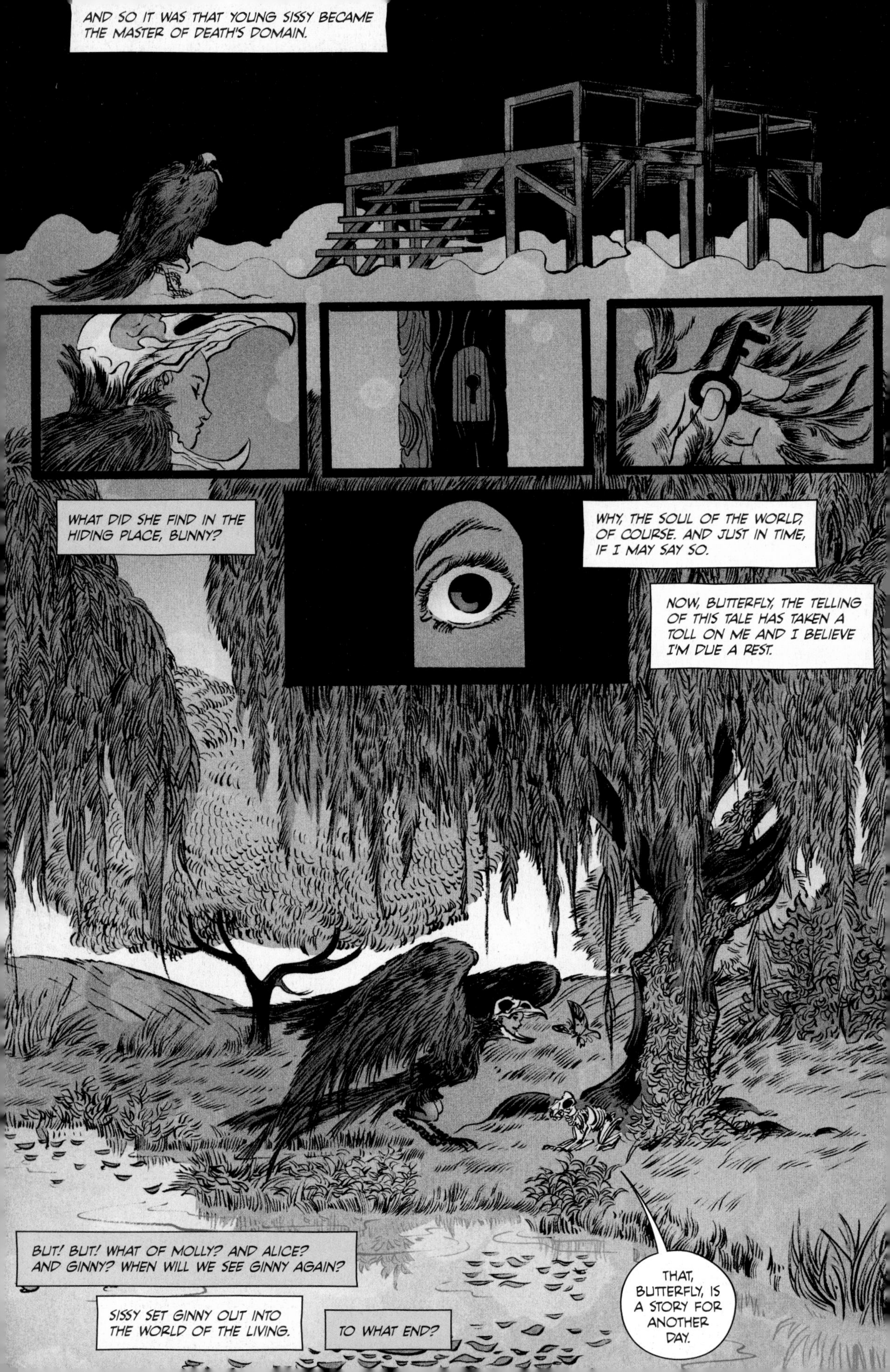
AND SO IT WAS THAT YOUNG SISSY BECAME THE MASTER OF DEATH'S DOMAIN.
WHAT DID SHE FIND IN THE HIDING PLACE, BUNNY?
WHY, THE SOUL OF THE WORLD, OF COURSE. AND JUST IN TIME, IF I MAY SAY SO.
NOW, BUTTERFLY, THE TELLING OF THIS TALE HAS TAKEN A TOLL ON ME AND I BELIEVE I'M DUE A REST.
BUT! BUT! WHAT OF MOLLY? AND ALICE? AND GINNY? WHEN WILL WE SEE GINNY AGAIN?
SISSY SET GINNY OUT INTO THE WORLD OF THE LIVING.
TO WHAT END?
THAT, BUTTERFLY, IS A STORY FOR ANOTHER DAY.

DEATHFACE GINNY
WILL RETURN IN
PRETTY DEADLY: VOLUME 2

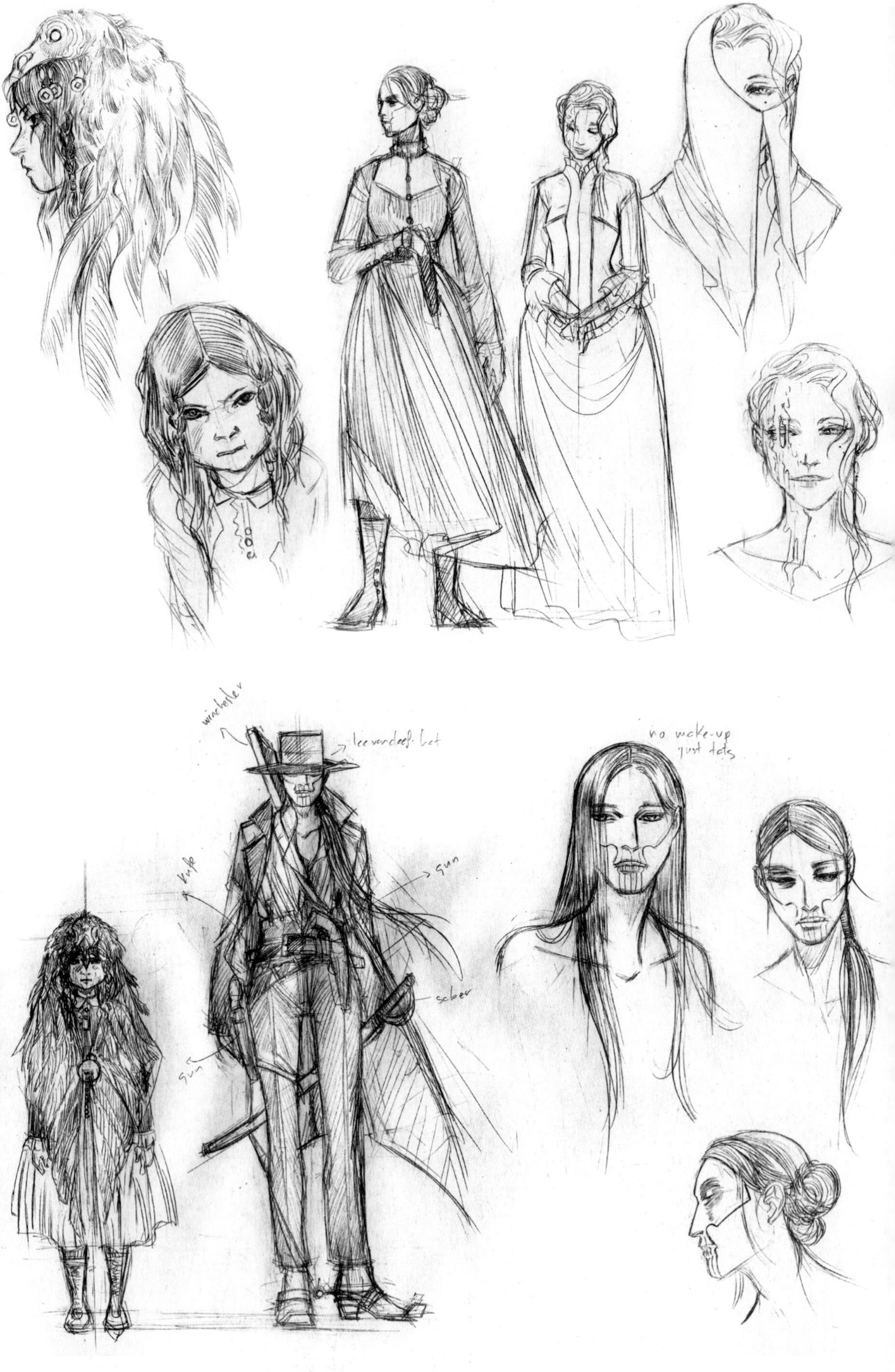

winchester
lee van cleef hat
knife
gun
saber
gun
no make-up
just tats